HOW EAST NEW YORK BECAME A GHETTO

WALTER THABIT

HOW EAST NEW YORK BECAME A GHETTO

With a foreword by Frances Fox Piven

New York University Press • *New York and London*

NEW YORK UNIVERSITY PRESS
New York and London

© 2003 by New York University

Library of Congress Cataloging-in-Publication Data
Thabit, Walter.
How East New York became a ghetto / Walter Thabit ; with a
foreword by Frances Fox Piven.
p. cm.
Includes bibliographical references and index.
ISBN 0-8147-8266-3 (cloth : alk. paper)
1. Minorities—New York (State)—New York—Social conditions—
20th century. 2. African Americans—New York (State)—New York—
Social conditions—20th century. 3. Ethnic neighborhoods—New
York (State)—New York—History—20th century. 4. Inner cities—
New York (State)—New York—History—20th century. 5. Urban
policy—New York (State)—New York—History—20th century.
6. Brooklyn (New York, N.Y.)—Social conditions—20th century.
7. Brooklyn (New York, N.Y.)—Ethnic relations. 8. New York (N.Y.)—
Social conditions—20th century. 9. New York (N.Y.)—Ethnic relations.
I. Title.
F129.B7T47 2003
305.8'009747'23—dc21   2003002709

To Lillie Martin, for forty years the quintessential East New York activist and a friend.

Contents

Foreword

Frances Fox Piven

Walter Thabit eloquently tells the story of East New York, a neighborhood in eastern Brooklyn, complementing his close observation of events in the neighborhood with astute analyses of the bearing of larger forces on this big city slum. Events in East New York reveal in microcosm the turbulent national forces that have determined the fate of inner city ghettos across the country over the past forty years.

Since the mid-nineteenth century, East New York had been a neighborhood of working-class immigrants, of successive waves of Germans, Italians, Jews, and East Europeans. Life was hard for these people, at least until the prosperity spurred by World War II and the boom decades that followed. For these immigrants, their neighborhoods were a kind of protected haven where they could speak their own languages, shop at stores that catered to their ethnic tastes, and form associations that offered some protection from a harsh economy and a hostile society.

Then, after World War II, new waves of immigrants began to arrive. These were internal migrants, impoverished African Americans forced off the plantations of the South by mechanization and, in New York City, equally impoverished Puerto Ricans displaced from agriculture on the island. This massive dislocation of people was not simply the consequence of economic change but rather the compound consequence of a series of national public policies that encouraged economic growth at the expense of the people who worked the land.

Most communities resisted these newcomers, but some did not have the economic or political clout to resist effectively. As millions of economic refugees from the American south and Puerto Rico poured into the cities, they crowded into the neighborhoods that were open to them, which as a consequence became increasingly compacted and segregated. Real estate practices and public policy exacerbated the situation in the impacted neighborhoods, as banks redlined the areas, predatory real estate operators used blockbusting tactics to force sales by frightened whites, and landlords "milked" their buildings, cutting back on services and then abandoning them. Meanwhile, urban renewal policies added to the problem by destroying much of the housing the new migrants had occupied, with the result that they were successively displaced to other impacted slums.

In East New York, the new migrants came to a neighborhood already suffering from neglected public services, especially poor schools and restrictive welfare practices. Moreover, they arrived at a time when the New York economy was deindustrializing, so there were fewer jobs for rural people without urban skills, and the jobs they did find paid poorly. Moreover, as a result of predatory real estate practices and urban renewal policies, they were subjected to an unprecedented level of residential instability, making it difficult for the new migrants to establish the neighborhood-based organizations that had offered some succor and support to earlier generations of immigrants.

These conditions contributed to the urban political explosions of the 1960s, beginning with escalating white-black conflicts over schools and neighborhoods and culminating in the riots of 1964–68. And government did respond, although Thabit is right to consider the response paltry relative to the scale of ghetto problems. Still, there were new federal programs, including the antipoverty and Model Cities programs, and a new effort by city government to respond to some of the grievances of the newcomers.

Walter Thabit's long-term engagement with the community of East New York was the result of one such response by the Lindsay administration. In 1966, the city employed Thabit's firm to work with the community to prepare the Vest Pocket and Rehabilitation plan for low-rent public and moderate-income housing. In the fall of 1967, the plan was approved; by 1971, 106 dwelling units had been rehabilitated and 1,095 more were under construction. Seven years later, the last of the planned 2,300 units was completed. The process was hardly simple or straightforward, and it is Thabit's account of the painfully arduous process of community participation, of the blundering and blindness of city, state, and federal agencies, of the technical complexities of rehabilitation, and ultimately of the moral and technical pitfalls of community participation that makes this book so illuminating.

The story of East New York reveals Walter Thabit's story as well, and that is also what this book is about. Thabit is an "advocate planner"; indeed, he is the leader of a dissenting current that emerged in the planning profession in the 1960s that called on planners to be suspicious of city governments and the real estate allies that city governments inevitably attracted. Instead, planners should regard local communities, especially poor communities, as their clients. Thabit created and led a national organization of advocates, Planners for Equal Opportunity. He has devoted his professional life to such work, and in this book we learn of the extraordinary persistence and talent that it demands.

Sometimes, the very fact of four decades of effort tempts a benign and happy conclusion, an inclination to say it was all for the best. Thabit, however, never allows himself such delusion. The completion of the Vest Pocket plan led to higher rents and persistent maintenance problems. He also revealed the "seedy side" of community participation, as some of the community leaders and local nonprofit organizations skimmed government contracts, made payoffs, and let contracts for shoddy construction.

In any case, the Vest Pocket plan was too small to reverse the larger trends that were undermining East New York. Housing continued to deteriorate, the community's residents remained mired in poverty, the schools did not improve. Yet visiting East New York after an absence of some two decades, Thabit sees real signs of improvement, in new housing construction and rehabilitation promoted by ACORN, the EBC (East Brooklyn Congregations), and others, in the hesitant revival of commercial activity, and in the creation of community services, including a large day-care facility by United Community Centers. None of this could have been done, of course, without outside sources of funding. But it was the initiative and vigor of local community groups that brought outside funding to the neighborhood of East New York. So there is reason to hope that Thabit's deep faith in the potential of local community participation is finally being redeemed.

FRANCES FOX PIVEN
Graduate Center, City University of New York; co-author of
Regulating the Poor, Poor People's Movements, and
Why Americans Still Don't Vote

Acknowledgments

For the six years it took to finish this book, I owe Frances Goldin, my significant other, my agent, and my friend, a great debt for her unswerving support, for her many readings of the chapters, for finding a publisher, and for many other contributions to my well being.

FOR OTHER HELP WITH THE MANUSCRIPT

I owe a huge debt to Frances Piven, a long-time friend and associate who suggested I not try to write about the nationwide "Forces of Community Destruction" but concentrate instead on East New York. She also read and made many useful suggestions and comments on the manuscript, to say nothing of her magnificent Foreword.

My warmest thanks to the others who reviewed the manuscript, including Perry Winston, Lisa Margonelli, Stephen Magro (my editor at New York University Press), and Stanley B. Winters, as well as to those who reviewed parts of it, including Judy Baum, Zachary Brown, Sydelle Kramer, Anne Farrar, and Mary Nelson. I am indebted to all for their comments and suggestions for improvement.

My thanks also go to the Mesa Refuge writers retreat, where I spent two weeks in April 2001. I was gratified beyond words at the enormous progress I made over those two weeks, and how they energized my later efforts. My thanks to Chester Hartman, who introduced me to the Mesa Refuge, to my writing comrades Lisa Margonelli and Jan Sells, and to Peter Barnes, who created and funded it.

THE EAST NEW YORK CROWD

The people of East New York, those I've known since the 1960s and those only recently met, were of great and varied assistance throughout the preparation of this book. They include Corinna Grant, Mel Grizer, Lillie Martin, Bill Wright, Marshall Stukes (whose recent death left me saddened), Mike Gecan, Bill Willkins and Ojeda Hall-Phillips, Priscilla Wooten, Martin Eisenberg, Marilyn Bayona, Walter Campbell, and Anthony Rajkumar. Add Zachary Brown, Dennis Taylor and Eze Van Buckley, all of Weed and Seed, and Michel Neugabauer and Maria Collyer, of the Cypress Hills LDC.

And, finally, greetings to Leo Lillard, currently in Nashville, Tennessee, a constant supporter and friend throughout the East New York experience.

OTHER ASSISTANCE

Many thanks are due Ron Shiffman, Perry Winston, and Katie Taylor, of Pratt Institute's PICCED (Center for Community and Environmental Development) and PPAC (Pratt Planning and Architectural Collaborative) for their collaboration and assistance. Perry Winston also contributed an accurate history and chronology of East New York's housing progress. A special note of appreciation is due Mannix Gordon, also of Pratt Institute, who prepared the maps under an extremely tight deadline.

Thanks also to: Ms. Hui of the Citywide Committee for Children; Dean Mauro, New York State Division of Criminal Justice Services; and Jack Ryan and Dedra Grant-Wade, of the New York City Department of Probation.

In the area of school planning and decentralization, thanks go to Norm Fruchter, Sara Arnold, Judy Baum, Dolores Schaefer, Bob Riccobono, and Catherine Ravici and to my inspiration on all matters educational, Marilyn Gittell.

My son Darius kept me computer savvy; my son Nikolai helped with the review of page proofs.

MY PLANNING STAFF

While they are scattered to the four winds, I would be remiss if I did not acknowledge the staff members most involved in the planning activities of my firm, both in the Vest Pocket and Rehabilitation Program and in the Model Cities program in East New York. In the Vest Pocket program, the principal actors included David Stoloff, Jacqueline Leavitt, Bill Chase, Jack Seto, Raymond Yin, Hugh Tunney, Warren Hillman, James Norman and Elliot Barowitz. In the Model Cities program, many of this group continued on staff, supplemented by Judith Stoloff, Bill Dawkins, Betty Woody, David Gurin, Andrea Malester, and Connie Bloomfield, as well as my gifted architectural consultants, Bernard Rothzeid and Tunney Lee.

Introduction

THE CENTRAL PART of East New York in Brooklyn, home to 100,000 people in 1965, was largely destroyed in the following decade. The destruction accompanied a racial shift in the population, from 85 percent white in 1960 to 80 percent black and Puerto Rican by 1966.[1] During that period, the racially biased policies of real estate brokers and speculators and their unrestrained exploitation of house-hungry blacks and Puerto Ricans, the redlining of the community by the banks, and the almost total neglect of the situation by the city and its agencies brought the area to the brink of collapse.

Following riots in the summer of 1966, the city finally decided to use its housing resources toward rebuilding in the riot-torn areas of the South Bronx, Bedford-Stuyvesant, and East New York. My consulting firm was given the contract to develop the housing program for East New York. Working with a community committee, we developed a Vest Pocket and Rehabilitation housing improvement program for 2,300 units of new and rehabilitated low-rent and moderate-income housing. Ten years later, despite the successful completion of the 2,300-unit construction program, nearly half of East New York had been destroyed.

The community destruction phase actually began in the early 1960s, when up to 200 real estate firms worked overtime to turn East New York from white to black. "Ripe" blocks were flooded with scare literature; brokers and speculators paraded black families up and down the streets to frighten whites into selling. Middle-income minority families bought houses at inflated prices during the early 1960s, but, as whites moved out, as stores and institutions closed, and as welfare families moved in, middle-income blacks began looking elsewhere for housing.

The East New York story is typical of ghetto communities in big cities across the country. In the St. Louis Model Cities area, for example, 31 percent of the housing stock was vacated and vandalized or demolished between 1960 and 1966, creating a ghost town that stretched for blocks at a time. In Newark, massive urban renewal clearance in its Central Ward, combined with rapacious real estate tactics in adjacent wards, accelerated a transition from white middle- and working-class to almost totally black fringe neighborhoods. In Cleveland, to view a darker (more racist) side, newly emerging black ghettos were rezoned to permit bars, gambling dens, and houses of prostitution. Nevertheless, East New York remains a fair enough example of what happened to blacks and other minorities who moved into newly created ghetto communities.

The ghetto was ruled by standards and laws different from those that operated in white society. The ruthless exploitation of helpless black and other minority families, not only by private parties but by government officials and agencies as well, was typical. Deception, profiteering, negligence, criminality, and community-destroying behavior were practiced on a grand scale, unfettered by ethical, professional, or (often) legal standards. An example: top FHA (Federal Housing Authority) officials and even the prestigious firm of Dun and Bradstreet were indicted for lying about East New York homebuyer incomes, appraised values, and housing quality in the service of unscrupulous mortgage brokers who were paying them off.[2] In East New York, it was open season.

Make no mistake. Ghettos are created by the apartheid policies of white society. In July 1966, Martin Luther King embarked on a campaign to end the extreme segregation of blacks in Chicago, one of the continuing legacies of slavery. He began his campaign with a rally in Soldier Field and a march on City Hall during which he was stoned and spat upon. After meeting with Mayor Richard Daley the following day, he announced that nonviolence had not produced victories in Chicago. The unproductive rally was followed by marches into Cicero and other white Chicago suburbs, after which King said he had never met anything like the concentrated hatred and violence poured out by northern segregationists.

Blacks and other minorities channeled into the ghettos have needs just like everyone else. They want decent homes in decent neighborhoods, with quality schools and a watchful, impartial police force. But none of these things are freely available to them.

In most of its important responsibilities, the New York City government has failed to satisfy the needs of its local communities. These include the need to (1) rigidly enforce an open housing policy throughout the five boroughs, (2) maintain high standards of housing, police, fire, sanitation, schooling, and similar services, and (3) grapple effectively with the social, physical, and economic problems of the urban ghetto.

Most big cities have long been indifferent to these needs. None of the central agencies are responsible for the well-being of a local community, nor are they used to viewing them as entities. The normal tendency of a city agency is to administer and evaluate its own program as an isolated citywide function; thus, a police force is concerned primarily with the number of arrests it makes, not with the service it provides to the communities it occupies. Even if the inadequacies are exposed, a chronic shortage of funds and a rigid definition of functions inhibits attempts to develop real solutions. Failures and cynical indifference are the inevitable results.

The impacts of racial and economic segregation are manifold. Today, more than 9 million people in the United States live in concentrated urban enclaves where more than 40 percent or more of the residents are poor.[3] These are communities where jobs have moved to the suburbs, the streets are unsafe, and good child care is beyond most working families' means, if it exists at all. In 1997, 5.4 million households with 12.3 million individuals paid more than half their income for rent.[4] These households represented 5 percent of the nation's population and a disturbing one-sixth of all U.S. renters.

For many people, safe, decent housing is an unattainable luxury. Despite a booming economy, 750,000 people currently live on the streets. Five million women struggle alone to provide financial support and child care for their children. Most of these unfortunates struggle for survival in the nation's ghettos.

This book provides a case study of the ghettoization of East New York and its impacts. It shows what really did happen when a pleasant working-class community was destroyed. For many people, including those who lived there or whose families lived there, the process by which their community was destroyed remains a mystery. Coverage in the major media has always been spotty, except when murder or riots get front-page coverage.[5] To the extent that the destruction is noted in the major media, the blame is generally laid at the feet of the blacks and Puerto Ricans who moved into the community.

This book describes the etiology of ghetto formation. It began with steps to prevent blacks from living in most communities occupied by whites and forced them instead to live in East New York and other communities slated by real estate forces for minority occupancy. It continued with an endless series of real estate swindles, speculations, and foreclosures, followed by an almost universal halt to normal maintenance and repair. This produced a shocking reduction in housing quality within two or three short years.

Once they moved into East New York, minorities were confronted with the lack of services. While families with thousands of children were moving into the community, the New York City Board of Education was not moved to provide the additional school seats needed. A report by my office on school needs in 1969 recommended the immediate construction of four elementary and four intermediate schools. Yet, between 1966 and 1974, the Board of Education was unable (or unwilling?) to build a single school in East New York.

It is my hope that this book will open our eyes to what racial segregation has done to those who inhabit the urban ghettos. It is also my hope that black and Puerto Rican people (and any other ethnic or racial minorities) will learn more fully about the history of their exploitation and oppression at the hands of white society—and that they will feel strongly enough about it to renew their efforts to win the right to live anywhere in this great city and to secure the high quality of services they deserve.

There is also the distinct possibility that blacks and Puerto Ricans will not recognize themselves as victims. When interviewed, many blacks and other minorities felt they were being treated fairly by the police and their government. They saw their problems as their own fault or nobody's fault, according to responses. If they didn't get further ahead, there was something lacking in the home, or perhaps in the school. If there was a lot of crime around, it was not the government's fault or anyone's fault. There just weren't any jobs, so young people got into trouble.

The following pages show that it really was someone's fault and that the perpetrators were usually white. This is not to say that blacks have not committed their fair share of crimes or done their share of exploiting their own people or of profiteering at the expense of their community. But it is to say that much of this misbehavior stems from the social and economic straitjacket into which the black and Puerto Rican community has been crammed.

Many minority crimes and cases of corruption, exploitation, and profiteering are an attempt by those committing them to find a place in the sun. They are perhaps misguided, and that is something that has to be addressed. To make great strides forward, blacks and Puerto Ricans will have to rally and organize their community in ways they have not yet always been able to manage.

Some progress has been made. Local community organizations have been and are useful instruments for changing the ways things are done. They have a direct stake in the outcome, a detailed knowledge of conditions, experience with the way things are, the spirit and determination to succeed, and the intelligence and imagination to develop new approaches and solutions. Not being part of the centralized governmental bureaucracy, they can develop logical solutions without worrying about agency prerogatives or bureaucratic limits. They can also freely pressure government and public-spirited business to make the needed changes, though getting government to see the light is often the main stumbling block.

Local community activity has already been the inspiration for the construction of more than 1,200 Nehemiah homes and another 1,300 units of new and rehabilitated housing in East New York during the past two decades. Advances in education, child care, health, youth programs, and other social services are also described in the pages that follow. Much more could have been accomplished if it were not for an entrenched political cabal, which ignored community needs and served its own selfish interests. The continuing criminalization of East New York's youth (indeed, almost its entire male population) and the intense concentration of welfare recipients and other desperately poor families remain terrible burdens for the community. The tendency for most organizations to go it alone, to compete rather than cooperate, also impedes progress.

Yet, a glimmer of hope has just appeared on the horizon. As I type these words on the evening of November 6, 2001, I see that the reformer Charles Barron has won the City Council seat vacated by Priscilla Wooten, who held sway in East New York for more than thirty years. Diane Gordon, another newcomer, defeated Assemblyman Ed Griffith, another perennial, in last year's New York state election. If this emerging new leadership commits itself to community improvement, it might just be able to rally all the local organizations around the highest priority community needs and to design programs and plan campaigns to meet those needs. It is not too hard to visualize a coalition of ghetto communities firmly pressing city, state, and federal governments for the programs and services they need.

A word about the events of September 11, 2001, and how they have affected East New York. Hard though it may be for some to understand, the explosions, fire, and meltdown of the World Trade Center and everything around it had little effect on the community. The East New York ghetto is not part of the mainstream economic system; it is part of an alternate social and economic system. While many individuals grieved along with the rest of the city, while many lost jobs and haven't found new ones, the disaster had no great emotional or physical impact on the community.

This will not prevent the city from using *its* disaster-related fiscal poverty as an excuse to defer the improvement of housing, social services, the small-business climate, and the infrastructure of East New York. Worse yet, the city will likely try to force draconian budget cuts on East New York and other ghetto communities in Brooklyn and the Bronx, just as it did during the fiscal crisis of the 1970s. It is not too early to start organizing against any such outcome. East New York deserves sufficient city resources to bring itself out of the hole that has been dug in *its* ground zero over the past forty years.

I

Welcome to East New York

THIS CHAPTER INTRODUCES East New York as it appeared to my consulting firm late in 1966–67 (see map 1).[1] At the start of the 1960s, the population was 85 percent white. By the end of 1966, the population of 100,000 was close to 80 percent black and Puerto Rican. Hundreds of small businesses closed during the changeover; churches and synagogues were abandoned, then vandalized and burned before they could be put to use by the incoming population. Public services and private agencies were unprepared (and often unwilling) to address the needs of the new minority population.

What brought the community to its sorry state is a story with many threads. This chapter describes where, under what local circumstances, and to what extent the transformation from white to minority took place.

In 1966, central East New York was a major community, its 100,000 people formed into 29,500 households.[2] Some 45 percent of the population lived in female-headed households, only one member of which was an adult. Racially and ethnically, there were close to 48,000 blacks, 30,000 Puerto Ricans, and 22,000 whites. Of the 29,500 households, about 6,000 (equal numbers of blacks and Puerto Ricans) with an average of five persons per household were on welfare, with another 5,500 households with an average of three persons per household (80 percent black and 20 percent Puerto Rican) were eligible for welfare but not on it. Many eligible households that applied were illegally denied welfare benefits.[3] It is also intriguing that a female-headed household with fewer than three children was normally not on welfare, while a mother with three or more children usually was.[4] However it was sliced, 40 percent of East New York households were living in poverty.

Not everyone in East New York was poor. In addition to the 11,500 households on welfare or eligible for it, there were approximately 8,000 homeowners, with an average household size of three persons. Fewer than 40 percent of the homeowners were white, three-quarters

East New York
Community District 5
with central ENY sections

QUEENS

JAMAICA BAY

CYPRESS HILLS

NORTHEASTERN TIER

INDUSTRIAL QUADRANT

EAST SECTOR

TENEMENT AREA

1-4 FAMILY AREA

NEW LOTS TO LINDEN

TENEMENT AREA SOUTH

SPRING CREEK

STARRETT CITY

Jamaica Av
Eldert Ln
Atlantic Av
Vermont Av
Highland Blvd
Bushwick Av
Broadway
Atlantic Av
Fulton St
Liberty Av
Conduit Aves
Mother Av
Fountain Av
Euclid Av
78th St
Sapphire St
Pitkin Blvd
Van Siclen Av
Barbey St
Pennsylvania Av
Sutter Av
Dumont Av
Van Sinderen Av
Livonia Av
New Lots Av
Linden Blvd
Crescent St
Fountain Av
Stanley Av
Flatlands Av
Schenck Av
Shore Pkwy
Louisiana Av

N

M. GORDON PICCED MAP 2002

MAP I

of whom were Italian; 45 percent were black, and the remaining 15 percent were Puerto Rican. The rest of the population, some 10,000 renter households, were equally split between white middle- and working-class tenants, 75 percent Italian, 25 percent Jewish, with equal numbers of working-class blacks and Puerto Ricans.

There were large numbers of children and teenagers in the community, resulting in less adult and especially parental control. The average age in East New York was under eighteen years compared with twenty-five to thirty-five years in most stable New York City communities. Of roughly 55,000 persons under eighteen years of age, 25,000 were enrolled in public schools and 7,000 in private schools; 18,000 were in the preschool ages or out of school. Leaving aside the prekindergarten age group, my firm's analysis indicated that some 9,000 school-age children and teenagers were not attending school.

One out of every seven youths between the ages of seven and twenty was arrested during 1965. In 1966, seven crimes were reported for every 100 persons in the area.

In East New York's tenement area alone (see description later in this chapter), with only 16,000 people, there were more than 1,000 juvenile delinquents in 1965.[5] Some 400 fires and more than 1,100 crimes (about a quarter of those that actually occurred) were reported in this area. In East New York as a whole, there were 1,400 fires in 1965, 400 of them in vacant buildings. Young people used vacant buildings as clubhouses, and dope addicts set up housekeeping in them; fires started to keep the occupants warm often got out of control. Such fires were dangerous to adjoining buildings as well as to squatters in the vacant buildings, and caused more than one fatality during the course of the study. Violence, shootings, knifings, and gang terror were common.

HOW EAST NEW YORK GOT ITS NAME

The first major event in East New York's history was its settlement by the Dutch in 1690.[6] Called the New Lotts of Flatbush, the area was developed into ten farms owned by the different families such as the Schencks and the Van Sinderins, for whom many East New York streets are named. The New Lots Reformed Church, now a landmark, was first established in the seventeenth century and rebuilt in 1824.

A second major event was the appearance of Colonel John R. Pitkin. Arriving in New Lotts in 1835, with money and ambition accrued as a Connecticut merchant, he beheld a farming district little different from the Dutch settlement it had been 150 years earlier. What he envisioned for the area, however, was consummately urban. On the land then given to potatoes and wheat, dairy cows and swine, a land known as "the Market Garden of the United States," he wanted to build factories, shops, homes, and schools.[7] To make clear what he had in mind, he named his new settlement East New York.

He bought 135 acres of land from farmers in the area, built a shoe factory on one parcel, and divided the rest into lots that sold for ten to twenty-five dollars each. He named the first new thoroughfare Broadway. The financial panic of 1837 ended Pitkin's dream of metropolitan grandeur, reducing him to serving as the auctioneer of his own assets. But he was not without a legacy. Broadway came to bear his name: Pitkin Avenue. The shoe factory and the workers who built cottages around it spearheaded the area's shift from agriculture to industry. The designation "East New York" supplanted New Lotts on maps and in official records.

Through the remaining decades of the nineteenth century, East New York grew gradually through the talents and hard work of German immigrants as brushmakers, gold-beaters,[8] and tailors. With the installation of five electrified subway and trolley lines between 1880 and 1922, a genuine boom began. Many new-law tenements were built.[9] From Manhattan's Lower East Side and the older Brooklyn district of Bushwick streamed Italians and Jews, Russians and Poles, filling the new tenements and locating inexpensive home sites between the Jamaica Avenue El on the north and the Livonia Avenue trestle to the south. The immigrants bottled milk, brewed beer, stitched clothes, and cast dies. Manning factory assembly lines, they made products ranging from starch to fireworks, toys to torpedoes.

In 1906, the Williamsburg Bridge opened—the "Jewish Passover" to Brooklyn. Jews emigrated to Williamsburg, and some found their way to East New York. Other East European immigrants, Poles and Lithuanians, joined the influx. Italians, in much smaller numbers, acquired truck farms from the remaining Dutch. Some Italians became marshland squatters and later went into the private refuse-disposal business.[10]

By the Great Depression of the 1930s, East New York was completely built up north of New Lots. It was a stable, lower middle-class community, heavily Italian Catholic and Jewish, with a large enclave of Polish Catholics centering around St. John Cantious Church. There were also a number of well-to-do Dutch families that still owned substantial property and had strong attachments to the community. Churches, synagogues, and schools were all built during the pre-depression period, but little was constructed during the depths of the depression.

THE INDUSTRIAL QUADRANT

The transition from white to black and Puerto Rican started in the north-west quadrant, in Colonel Pitkin's part of town (see map 1).[11] More than half the area was in industrial or commercial use; the housing was con-centrated in only a few blocks. The older housing stock was made up in good part of nineteenth century old-law frame dwellings, as well as two-family frame dwellings that had been converted to multiple dwell-ing use. By the early 1950s, the housing stock had markedly deterio-rated. Houses stood next to vacant buildings, garbage-strewn lots, junkyards, and automotive body works, creating an oppressive atmos-phere. Industry and commerce appeared to thrive, however. Many com-panies were planning to expand, including several that had recently acquired additional properties. The area also contained the smallest number of public or semipublic facilities such as schools in East New York, and only one community improvement group was identified.

As might be expected, after World War II, many tenement dwellers from this northwest quadrant sought to improve their standard of liv-ing. As the suburban boom took hold and the postwar housing short-age eased, there were successive shifts of the white population from poorer to better housing. Industrial-quadrant families began moving into single- and two-family homes east of Pennsylvania Avenue. They were replaced initially by whites and a few blacks and Puerto Ricans who settled in the community. All seemed normal, as retired couples living in the tenement area to the south held on to their houses in the face of rising housing costs elsewhere.

As whites continued their exodus, more blacks and Puerto Ricans moved in. In a gradual progression, over a period of fifteen years, the industrial quadrant became the first section to change completely in ethnic composition. By early 1966, the area had become 90 percent black and Puerto Rican.[12] The shift caused little concern in the adjoining white community, largely because the area was a mixture of housing and industry and somewhat isolated from the main residential community.

THE TENEMENT AREA

The tenement area, the focus of the city's Vest Pocket Housing and Rehabilitation Program, for which my consulting firm did the planning, lay just south of the industrial quadrant. It was heavily built up, with four-story tenements, both old-law and early new-law, with mostly small apartments. The area contained a substantial number of two- to four-family houses, as well. Building maintenance had been neglected since the beginning of World War II; landlords continued their neglect after the war's end, complaining bitterly about New York City's rent control laws all the while.

As with residents of the industrial quadrant, dissatisfied younger families began to move out of the tenements, not only to housing east of Pennsylvania Avenue but also to residences south of Linden Boulevard, to Canarsie, to Queens, and even to Long Island. In many of these areas, a home could be had for less than a thousand dollars down. A major new rental housing development, Warbasse Houses, was built in Canarsie and proved very attractive to older Jews and other religious and ethnic groups. This was followed in the early 1970s by Starrett City in the Flatlands.

Population pressures on East New York were intense. To the north, the Bedford-Stuyvesant ghetto had been developing rapidly during and since World War II; Brownsville had already become a completely devastated black ghetto. Concurrently, the New York City Housing Authority began displacing several thousand additional Brownsville families for a series of massive public housing projects, adding greatly to the pressures on adjoining areas.

These thousands of families and other thousands spilling out of the expanding Brooklyn ghettos joined in the desperate search for housing. They scoured the streets of East New York looking for apartments. With few whites interested in renting, landlords began renting to blacks and Puerto Ricans at the higher rents permitted when apartments became vacant. Some even harassed their old white tenants, getting them to move so that they could rent to blacks at higher rates. As whites moved away, more blacks and Puerto Ricans moved in. The growing white departure yielded new vacancies, swiftly taken by friends and relatives of the blacks and Hispanics already there. Further, welfare and social agencies were also busy seeking housing for their clients, adding to the social and economic pressures.

By 1963, most young, white families had left the tenements; only elderly people and a few others were left. The streets were already undergoing a transformation. Practically every block showed at least one boarded up or burned-out building; some showed as many as three or four. Sanitation services were neglected; the streets began to fill with garbage and broken glass. Move-ins and move-outs were common, especially among welfare clientele, lending an aura of instability to the area. Black and Puerto Rican children and youths dominated the landscape; growing lawlessness, vandalism, and violence made the streets unsafe. The Jewish community panicked; many moved south of Linden Boulevard, leaving behind abandoned synagogues and community centers. Jewish and other ethnic shopkeepers, frightened by vandalism and crime, isolated from their old customers, also moved out of the area. Many others were wrenched loose by real estate speculation, robbery, and racial tension.

The first of two riots in the summer of 1966 helped complete the tenement area's transition to more than 90 percent black and Puerto Rican. The unrest was traced to turf conflicts between black and Puerto Rican youths. Hundreds of black, Puerto Rican, and white households immediately fled the area, touching off a wave of vandalism and crime that lasted well into the winter months of 1967.

TENEMENT AREA SOUTH

South of the tenement area, there was an almost complete changeover from white to black and Puerto Rican between 1960 and 1966, but with far less destruction. About half the structures in this area were one- to four-family dwellings, many of which were bought by minority families after 1960, largely due to sales promoted by "blockbusting" speculators. A substantial percentage of the new owners rented rooms to welfare families, thereby raising the population densities above their

1960 levels. The rest of the housing was in four-story walk-up brick tenements, which had also lost most of their white tenancy.

Most of the area required only minor maintenance, though one out of every four or five blockfronts could have used moderate rehabilitation. There were relatively few vacant buildings as well; one or two were noted on a few blocks bordering the tenement area. South of New Lots Avenue, one or two vacant buildings per blockfront were also found.

The Jewish and Italian residents who remained were unhappy about the minority in-migration and were worried by the increase in fires and crime. Sanitation was poor; some streets close to the tenement area were littered with broken glass. Block associations and the East New York Owners and Tenants League worked hard to maintain the area, but many owners became pessimistic about their investment. There were few public facilities, few churches, and some infrequently used synagogues.

THE NORTHEASTERN TIER

This area experienced the lowest rate of population turnover in East New York, at least until 1967. While the tier's population had aged, my firm estimated that the ethnic composition remained predominantly white and the household size relatively stable. Aside from the heavily commercial Atlantic Avenue frontage, the area was residential. Dwellings were predominantly frame structures housing one to four families. While a good many buildings had been well maintained, their owners continuing to paint and otherwise keep up their property, many buildings had deteriorated through their owners' neglect.

Recent events had also taken their toll. Vacant buildings were liberally scattered throughout the area, but rarely more than one to a block. Yet, the depressing effect of these vacant and vandalized buildings, taken together with the few vacant lots overgrown with weeds and a general air of neglect, contributed to the pessimistic outlook of many residents.

One new public school was under construction, and another had been approved. There were other public facilities, including several substantial churches, parochial schools, and related facilities. The Russian Orthodox Church was a community landmark, and St. John Cantius

Church (located just south of the Northeastern Tier boundary) was a major institution. St. John's Lutheran Church, a very old community institution, was also located there. Rising crime rates and antipathy toward the minority families living in pockets of deteriorated housing had dulled the sense of satisfaction occasioned by the new schools. At community planning meetings, many businessmen were thinking of closing their stores. The area seemed susceptible to considerable deterioration and change over the coming years.

THE ONE- TO FOUR-FAMILY AREA

In a sector of almost fifty square blocks, running from Pennsylvania Avenue east for half a mile, there was a large number of one- to four-family homes, many of which had been purchased by minority-group families as a result of blockbusting (see chapter 3 for more detail). The minority groups replaced a largely Jewish population, which moved south of Linden Boulevard or to the suburbs in the early 1960s. In 1967, my firm estimated the racial composition at 50 percent black, 30 percent Puerto Rican, and 20 percent white.

A number of white homeowners held out east of Pennsylvania and north of New Lots, but no new white families moved in; the blockbusting brokers saw to that. Most homeowners had to accept welfare tenants in their two- to four-family houses to keep the units occupied so that they could keep up with mortgage payments. According to owners, exploitative real estate practices, including onerous mortgage terms and shady home improvement schemes, operated here with devastating effect.

Nevertheless, the area was in better shape than might be expected, considering its proximity to the tenement area. This was at least partly a result of its lower densities and its amenities such as Linton Park, the Thomas Jefferson High School field, and the New Lots Branch Library. There was little mixed use, and only a few apartment buildings. The housing was more solidly constructed, the row-house facades often faced with smooth, light tan brick that resisted wear and discoloration. There were some vacant buildings, but these were scattered. Newly organized block and community organizations were active.

The second riot of 1966 was a battle that pit black and Puerto Rican youths against Italian youths. The Italians held their ground. Less than a year later, in mid-June 1967, a youth was stabbed in a racial incident in Linton Park, where black youths taunted white youths, not far from the scene of the previous year's riots. For nearly a week, groups of Italians, Puerto Ricans, and blacks skirmished with guns, bricks, pipes, chains, and Molotov cocktails. On the night of July 21, an eleven-year-old black, Eric Dean, was struck and killed by a sniper. Once word of his slaying spread, looting and insurrection erupted across thirty-three square blocks. Where seventy-five police officers normally patrolled (were supposed to patrol would be more accurate), 1,000 were dispatched, and thousands more around the city were held at their posts in reserve.[13] The Italian community south of Livonia Avenue was abandoned and turned black almost instantly.

THE EAST SECTOR

Another seven-by-fifteen square blocks to the east, both Jews and Italians had begun moving out. The area was heavily residential, with small stores along the avenues. Two- to four-family homes predominated; about half were of masonry construction. Frame houses in the Italian section were shingled with various materials or faced with stone or brick. As late as 1966, the area was still more than 50 percent white, but by the end of 1967 the area had become 70 percent black and Puerto Rican. The riots produced a modified form of the vandalism and building abandonment that characterized much of the tenement area.

More vacant buildings were found in this sector, an average of two to a block. Housing conditions were also worse in the northern parts, where most of the buildings were of wood frame construction.

About 5 percent of the units were vacant; the small stores along Pitkin, Blake, New Lots, and other avenues were closed; several synagogues and community centers had been abandoned. There were no parks or playgrounds.

NEW LOTS TO LINDEN

This area was predominantly white, especially in the eastern portion. Jewish families seemed to be concentrated at the western end, Italians at the eastern end. Some inroads had been made by blacks through blockbusting, particularly in the vicinity of the New Lots Reformed Church, in the center of the area. The area had successfully resisted the invasion of poor and welfare clients, however. South of Linden, the population was solidly white and racist.

After World War II, this area had flourished for a time. New homes were built south of New Lots Avenue. Jews and Italians made additional investments in community centers and parochial schools. Second- and third-generation Poles and Lithuanians were ready for assimilation and started heading for Long Island and New Jersey. Similarly, the Dutch began moving to the suburbs, giving up their ancient ties to the community. Jews and Italians took over Dutch-owned business and property.

After 1960, more new construction took place south of New Lots Avenue. The new housing was predominantly single-family, though there were sizable groups of two- to four-family houses. Most of the housing was in fair to good condition, except for areas in which the blockbusting had succeeded. There was still a good deal of vacant land scattered throughout the sector.

Aside from some spotty commercial uses and an attractive YM-YWHA along Linden Boulevard, the area was totally residential in character. While blockbusting was effective in parts of the area, it appeared unlikely in the area containing new housing; no racial ghetto was expected to develop there in the near future. Stiff resistance to blockbusting and to nonwhite movement into parts of the area had already been experienced.

SMALL BUSINESS

Small businesses could not survive the ongoing changes. While Jewish businesses survived the black ghettoization of Harlem, this was not true in the more volatile world of East New York. A local bakery, possibly the last Jewish bakery in East New York, was robbed and broken into six times in a two-month period. The bakery owner boarded up his windows and triple-locked his doors, but the youths always found ways to break in. The "loot" was hardly worth the effort; derring-do, doughnuts, and diversion seemed to be the main rewards. The baker ultimately closed his shop.

Literally hundreds of stores were vacated in East New York during the 1960s, nor did minority merchants replace white ones. Even the Puerto Ricans, more business oriented than blacks, opened few bodegas or other stores. The fear of being robbed, vandalized, burned out, and shot had denuded the area of most commercial uses except in peripheral areas and on major commercial (nonretail) streets. The few stores in the heart of the community were mostly tiny bodegas that catered to Puerto Ricans in the immediate vicinity. Perhaps three-quarters of the money available for retail goods in the community had to be spent outside it.

CHURCHES AND SYNAGOGUES

By the end of 1966, only a few churches flourished in the community. The experience with Jewish facilities was indicative. Of a dozen synagogues and centers active in the early 1960s, most were closed and abandoned as the Jews moved out. Several attempts were made to obtain these facilities for black and Puerto Rican use; design plans were actually made by my office and by local groups for the conversion of three of them. Before funding or approvals could be obtained, they were all vandalized and burned out. One synagogue was successfully converted to a day-care center, and a couple were sold or leased to minority congregations. What could have been a major resource for the minority community, however, was largely destroyed before it could be put to use.

The Catholic churches were also in trouble. While they were able to absorb Puerto Ricans and the change to Spanish services and congregations, they were heavily in debt. White antagonism toward Puerto Ricans in the congregation made the situation difficult at best and sharply cut into attendance. On the other hand, most whites did not abandon parochial schools when Puerto Ricans were enrolled, probably because it was still a better alternative than the public schools. But, as white families gradually moved away, the parochial schools ultimately closed as well, adding to school seat shortages throughout the community.

As the Protestant churches gradually acquired mostly black parishioners, many of the old-time white clergymen became alienated from their new congregations. Many traditional Protestant churches simply closed their doors. The more established ones were taken over by the black middle class; the New Lots Reformed Church had 400 members, 85 percent of them black.[14] Unfortunately, the new congregations could not support the overhead costs of the formerly white congregations. This resulted in continuing crises related to church maintenance. Some churches were forced to close their doors.

The Russian Orthodox Church, in the Northeastern Tier, had lost most of its members and attracted few minority people. Storefront churches were plentiful, and a few prospered. The Jewish YM-YWHA on the southern periphery of East New York had achieved token integration, but its membership form committed those who joined to religious and cultural training. In 1965, it started an extension program in nearby areas of Queens to bolster its client population. In all, the minority population enjoyed only minor use of the existing facilities.

PUBLIC SERVICES AND FACILITIES

Recreation and community space in East New York was scarce. Most of the synagogues and churches were abandoned or converted to commercial uses. After the riots, public and private youth agencies tried to stabilize the situation. New organizations were formed to work with youth and to serve poor families. While the programs seemed to have some effect, only a few of those needing the services were able to get them. The area was highly volatile and unstable. Almost every week, there was a new disaster—a fatal fire, another building vacated or vandalized, a crime of violence.

The condition of public facilities and services in 1967 was almost catastrophic. Between 1960 and 1966, elementary school enrollment rose by 40 percent and junior high enrollment by 44 percent (and another 24 percent the year after that). As a result, 5,000 pupils were on short time in thirteen schools. Portables were also placed in six schoolyards, and 500 children were being bussed. Many of the schools were more than fifty years old and lacked hot-lunch facilities, gymnasiums, science labs, and other facilities.

While a decent education from elementary through high school was in short supply, day care was virtually absent. For this entire community of 100,000 people, there wasn't a single publicly sponsored day-care center in 1967. A few centers were operating in Brownsville, and, despite their long waiting lists, some twenty East New York parents had been able to enroll their children in them. Still, only one out of twenty prekindergarten-age children were being served half a day or more in prekindergarten classes.

The streets of East New York overflowed with children and teen-agers. There were so many children that the streetscape itself seemed to be in motion. The community possessed only two block-size parks, four small playgrounds with two basketball courts between them, nine play streets in the summer, and the open space in the few schoolyards that were free of portable classrooms. A few schools had no open space to begin with. While public swimming pools had been built throughout the five boroughs, there was no public swimming pool in East New York. The parks and playgrounds were poorly maintained. In Linton Park, there were stanchions but no swings; its ballfield had long since disappeared. A school was under construction on a second park; a new park was to be built on the site of the old school on completion. The Thomas Jefferson High School field was open only to organized groups and only when not in use by the school itself. The area needed centers like the Brownsville Boys Club or the St. John's Community Center in Bedford-Stuyvesant. The director of the YM-YWHA believed that East New York needed another four centers like his. At most, 1,000 children attended after-hours school activities, including tutorial programs.

The one public library was located in the southeastern corner of the community, well over half a mile from most people, nor was its collection geared to serve black and Hispanic residents. The welfare center was in a makeshift building outside the community; families with children typically waited for hours before they were served. A small child health station was the only health facility in East New York, despite the incredible needs and the number of disabled people (see chapter 15). Rates of infant mortality, venereal disease, pneumonia, influenza, and other diseases were as severe in East New York as in other ghetto areas, but the nearest hospitals—Brookdale and Kings County—were three miles away. At both hospitals, waits for hours in emergency rooms and clinics were normal.

Community leaders protested against these and other deficiencies at meeting after meeting without success: "Portable classrooms! Portable parks! Portable pools! Portable welfare centers! Everything in East New York is portable! When are you going to give us some real attention?" Existing facilities were inadequate, poorly equipped, and under-staffed or staffed with hostile and indifferent people. The Betsy Head swimming pool, promised to neighboring Brownsville in 1966, has yet to be built. A portable swimming pool lasted a single season. City promises were made only to be broken.

COMMUNITY ORGANIZATION

In 1966–67, East New York's community structure was fragmented, its leadership new and inexperienced, and its ties to the people of the local community tenuous. The change from white to minority occupancy took place so swiftly that old community organizations perished before new leadership could take over. Only two organizations with as much as seven years' standing were identified by my office's survey. One was a settlement house far from the heart of the area, and the other was CBENY (Council for a Better East New York), a coalition of whites, blacks, and Puerto Ricans desperate to bring order out of chaos. Other organizations had been spawned mainly by antipoverty programs and, like a number of block associations formed to fight blockbusting, had been in existence for only two or three years.

About fifty of CBENY's seventy member organizations were active in 1966; its many individual members had no vote. With strong white leadership from among the area's churches, the organization pursued every avenue that even hinted at a useful response.[15] It created committees on health and welfare, housing and renewal, public services, and youth and recreation programs. It engaged in a constant fight to get more police service; it considered speculation and blockbusting major problems, and believed the area was in danger of turning into a black belt. CBENY worked to get recreation programs in seventeen schools, enrolled 1,800 in adult education courses, and fought for new schools and an educational park. East New York organizations also received antipoverty funds with which they had performed a variety of services to the community over the past several years.

CBENY saw the physical and social deterioration of the area as a basic problem. Its major complaint was that city programs were scattershot, isolated, inconsistent, and not geared to solving problems. Seven human relations programs were being operated by city agencies, CBENY complained, but there was no cooperation or coordination among them. The community was not consulted by the city when it established Community Progress Centers, another government aid program residents were left out of. An Area Services program finally came, but too late. East New York did not get priority in the city's Community Renewal Program. CBENY leadership refused to wait until the whole area was lost before it got help.

CBENY's prescription for saving the community followed a typical middle-income approach. It wanted middle-income housing in the heart of the community and public housing in vest pocket projects on the periphery, making the area attractive again to middle-income groups. CBENY also wanted a basic study of the problems in East New York and an analysis of possible solutions and their feasibility. Most of all, it wanted the city to take some definitive action.

Nonetheless, catastrophic events were riding roughshod over CBENY's hopes for public intervention. By the end of 1967, East New York had already become an almost solidly black belt, blockbusting was frighteningly thorough, and the physical devastation (see chapter 4) exceeded the community's worst nightmares. By 1968, CBENY member organizations were mostly inactive, and the group's leadership had passed to blacks and Puerto Ricans.

2

The Population Wave

THE GENESIS OF the black and Puerto Rican population wave that overwhelmed local communities in most major American cities is as relevant as the description of how it was formed and guided along its designated path. The wave started with overweening racism and ill-advised government policies in the South, and with U.S. exploitation and impoverishment of the Puerto Rican people on the Island. More than 4 million southern blacks, 2 million-plus Puerto Ricans, and other Hispanics and non-white peoples poured into the big northern cities in the thirty-year period that followed World War II.

They were not pilgrims, these new migrants. It was not religious persecution that drove blacks north and induced Puerto Ricans to cross the sea. They were also unlike the Irish who migrated en masse because of potato famines. A quest for survival and a better life is part of the force that drove them to the big cities, but it is only a portion. Both blacks and Puerto Ricans have a long history of being exploited and oppressed. As described later, they were forced from their lands by business interests and unsympathetic governments. For them, moving to the big cities was not so much a liberating experience, not so much a new opportunity, as it was a further punishment at the hands of their oppressors.

BLACK MIGRATION TO THE NORTH

The largest of these movements was the black migration northward from the rural South. Over the past several decades, half the Southern black population—more than 4 million people—moved north of the Mason-Dixon line, mainly to the big cities: Washington, D.C., Baltimore, Philadelphia, Newark, New York, Boston, Chicago, Detroit, Cleveland, St. Louis, Oakland, San Francisco, and Los Angeles. Still others moved to southern cities like Atlanta, Dallas, Houston, and

Miami. More than 2 million blacks moved to the five largest American cities.

I examined a microcosm of this mass migration in the Mississippi Delta, an eighteen-county area where cotton was king.[1] Even before World War II, blacks were leaving the Delta at the rate of 3 percent a year. Almost 115,000 moved out during the 1950s. Mechanization of cotton farming, impoverishment on small farms, destructive government policies, and a repressive white power structure sharply reduced the southern black population.

By 1965, there were still 30,000 plantation workers in the Delta. They lived in plantation-owned shacks, earned less than $6 a day. Two-thirds were jobless in 1964, and those that did have jobs worked mostly part-time, earning less than $500 for the year. Their future was grim. To shore up cotton prices, the government was offering 10.5 cents a pound on cotton yield for production cutbacks of up to one-third. The result was an expected loss of 5,000 tractor and farm jobs and 7,000 cotton-chopping jobs in the eighteen-county area. Cotton planters were also switching to chemical weed controls, fearful of a $1.25-an-hour minimum wage for cotton choppers. "A minimum wage . . . would ruin you when you've been paying $3.00 for a ten-hour day," declared the mayor of Sunflower, himself a planter.

During the summer of 1965, hundreds of plantation workers went on strike against the $3.00-a-day rate, and most were evicted from their plantation shacks. Hundreds more were evicted or lost their jobs because they registered to vote. Mississippi's paltry $343-a-year welfare payments were denied to additional thousands of black families who didn't "behave." Of 297 black children registered in Sharkey and Issaquena county white schools in accordance with a desegregation order, only forty-five made it to class. Evictions, firings, cross burnings, intimidating threats, and violence dissuaded the rest.[2]

Nevertheless, the plantation blacks—encouraged by civil rights workers—were desperate enough to fight back. The hundreds who struck started their own community and called it Strike City. In January 1966, another 110 impoverished blacks moved into an abandoned Air Force barracks in Greenville. Evicted from there, they joined the group in Strike City. Attempts were made to start cooperative farms and to develop their own new town. A brick factory was actually started and a few homes were built, but the obstacles were overwhelming. Many plantation workers were unprepared to tackle the simplest problems.

The financing essential to make real progress was denied by local banks and government agencies.

Although two-thirds of the Delta population was still black in 1965, not one black person sat on a school board, a county board, a city council, a county crop-allotment committee, or a welfare board. The state had no compulsory school laws or child labor laws. Most black farmers, even those with farms of up to 100 acres, lived in dilapidated shacks; most whites lived in houses. White-populated streets were paved; black streets were dirt. White streets had water mains and sewers; black streets had ditches. In a few towns such as Fayetteville, where the black civil rights leader Charles Evers became mayor, blacks were beginning to get some of these public health necessities, but such towns were rare in the old South.

For many southern blacks, the only answer was to go north. By way of gratuitous urging, a measure was introduced into the 1967 Mississippi legislature that provided funds to "assist" displaced black farm workers to relocate "outside the south." Racism and irresponsibility—along with federal neglect—drove blacks north by the millions.

Much of this mass migration could have been avoided if the federal government had been interested in helping the lower-income groups. Cotton supports could have been tied to more jobs and higher wages; industries could have been subsidized to come South. New cities could have been built, providing the educational and training resources needed to transform the illiterate (or at least their children) into productive members of a modern society. Direct federal aid to small farmers and poor communities could have ensured that blacks as well as whites would benefit. Their inaction showed the federal government and the Congress to be as racist as the State of Mississippi.

THE PUERTO RICAN MIGRATION

Second in scale to the black migration, at least along the eastern seaboard, was the Puerto Rican migration to the U.S. mainland. Like southern blacks, Puerto Ricans were the victims of poverty and oppression. Unemployment on the island hovered around 25 percent, median income for a family of four was about $3,000, and the cost of living was 20 to 25 percent higher than that in New York City. A fifth of all families earned less than $500 a year; another quarter were on public assistance.

Inflation was pushing prices still higher; strikes and popular revolt against rising utility costs made the front pages in 1974.

The United States had long systematically exploited the island's resources and its people.[3] First, Puerto Rico was transformed into a one-crop economy: sugar. Sugar companies gobbled up the land, wrecking the small coffee and tobacco growers who were the backbone of the island's economy. In their place arose a vast agricultural proletariat whose members worked for the sugar companies for only a few months of the year. The second government strategy was to encourage Puerto Ricans to leave their homeland and settle in the United States. Two million people, almost 40 percent of the island's population, had moved to the United States by 1960, but this movement solved none of the island's problems. It did help provide cheap labor for the mainland United States, however. Migrant workers received $1.30 an hour for farm work, much of which was stolen by the growers. As garment workers in New York City in the late 1950s, Puerto Ricans worked as cleaners for as little as $32.50 a week under union contract. Low-income levels in Puerto Rico were at least partly related to the low wages Puerto Ricans were forced to accept in New York City. The same logic may also have applied to rural blacks who moved north.

Another ill-advised government strategy was to encourage U.S. companies to help build the Puerto Rican economy, but this, too, had disastrous results. Through the 1990s, American corporations controlled 85 percent of Puerto Rican industry, were exempt from federal taxes, and extracted huge profits. And, while new U.S. factories created 37,300 jobs by the early 1960s, 16,000 jobs in Puerto Rican-owned factories were lost during the same period; these firms could not compete and were driven out of business.[4]

Companies with high research, development, and marketing expenses but low production costs farmed out factory production to wholly owned subsidiaries in Puerto Rico, then transferred the patents and trademarks from their U.S. headquarters to the subsidiaries, as well, thus shielding all revenue from federal taxes.[5] The tablets in the drug prescription bottle may have cost only pennies to manufacture in Puerto Rico, but the lion's share of the $20 price tag, which included research, development, and marketing costs, were all tax exempt under Section 936 of the IRS Code. By 1974, more than 110 of the *Fortune* 500 companies had Puerto Rican subsidiaries. By 1976, Puerto Rico accounted for 40 percent of all U.S. profit in Latin America.

The new jobs created by the new factories hardly dented the soaring unemployment caused by the mechanization of agriculture and the
flight of impoverished people to the cities. At the time when new U.S.
investment reached its peak, the greatest number of Puerto Ricans in
history migrated to the United States. This confluence of events could
well be the forerunner of a global phenomenon.

Another part of the problem was the high cost of living in Puerto
Rico. Since its early days as a U.S. possession, Puerto Rico has been
bound by laws that require that all trade between the island and the
fifty states be carried on U.S.-made ships, manned by U.S. crews. Puerto
Ricans ended up paying as much as 25 percent more for imported
goods than the rest of the world (which transports most cargo on Pana-
manian- and Liberian-flag freighters). The tuna caught by Puerto Rican
fishermen was exported to the U.S., processed, and then re-imported
for consumption by Puerto Ricans at high prices. In Barcelonetta, fishermen's livelihoods were destroyed by pollutants dumped in the river
by pharmaceutical companies. The petrochemical industry, accounting
for a third of all U.S. investment, provided a grand total of 7,700 jobs.
The oil refined in Puerto Rico was exported to the United States; the finished products were then sold from the United States to Puerto Rico,
again at high prices. Sugar cane production in one plantation dropped
from forty to thirteen tons per acre because of its proximity to one of
these refineries. In the late 1960s, a huge new superport refinery was
being pushed by the United States. It would triple U.S. corporate investment, take a great deal of land, pollute vast areas of land and sea,
and increase unemployment, rather than alleviating it. American Metal
Climax (AMAX) and Kennecott Copper were negotiating strip mining
rights in Puerto Rico's central mountain range, a deal that would return
$1 billion in profits to the companies and little to the island.

As part of the strategy to enrich U.S. corporations at the expense of
the Puerto Rican people, new oppressive measures were being contem-
plated by congressional corporate interests under the guise of giving
the island more freedom.[6] Under a plan to transform the present "Commonwealth" to a "Free Associated State," Puerto Rico would have entered into a permanent compact with the United States that would have
imposed "fiscal, financial, and economic austerity" on the Puerto Rican
working class for the foreseeable future and would have intensified re-
pression of the growing independence movement on the island.[7] In the
early 1970s, a bill introduced in Congress would have exempted Puerto

Rican workers from minimum wage and environmental protection laws. Another congressional committee, the Committee to Study Puerto Rico's Finances, issued a report that recommended "painful austerity," including a wage freeze on all government employees, reduction if not suspension of minimum-wage standards, givebacks of workers' hard-won fringe benefits, elimination of subsidies on publicly owned utilities, and bigger tax incentives to industry, all this to "attract" investors and to hold labor costs below those on the mainland. The outcome of these proposed measures is unknown.

In addition to the sugar catastrophe, U.S. control has dealt further blows to Puerto Rican agriculture. Seventy percent of the land in Puerto Rico is not being cultivated or is poorly used because Puerto Rico cannot impose tariffs or protective quotas on its own agriculture. Egg production in Puerto Rico, for example, depends on the productivity of hens in Miami, Florida. When there is a surplus in Florida, eggs are sent to Puerto Rico at half price, wiping out the Puerto Rican egg farmers. When there is a shortage, local egg production laboriously starts up again, only to be wiped out by the next American surplus. This is, unfortunately, a worldwide phenomenon, and measures to alleviate the resulting hardships are sorely needed.

Though out-migration in the early 1970s was moderate, the Puerto Rican government adopted a new program to reduce the island's population from 3.2 to 2.2 million. This was to be achieved partly through continued migration and partly through the sterilization of Puerto Rican women. By the early 1970s, some 200,000 Puerto Rican women had been sterilized, almost a third of those of childbearing age. Reports in the early 1970s put sterilizations at more than 1,000 a month in rural areas alone. Between starvation and sterilization, the only escape was to leave the island.

The plight of Delta blacks and Puerto Ricans is no different from that of hundreds of thousands of Jamaicans, Haitians, Dominicans, Trinidadians, and other Caribbean peoples whose lands were similarly exploited and who have contributed large numbers of legal and illegal immigrants to our shores. More recently, immigration officials estimated the number of illegal immigrants in the New York metropolitan area at a million. Mexicans have also entered the United States in substantial numbers, in addition to the millions of native Chicanos in the southwestern states, many of whom are discriminated against and kept illiterate.

Refugees from many European nations and other countries have also arrived on our shores. And there were poor whites, coming from places such as eastern Kentucky, a coal-mining region that included thirty-two of the 1,000 designated disaster areas in the country. In the late 1960s, despite massive out-migration, 65,000 jobs were needed in eastern Kentucky. Like Delta blacks, the miners had little formal education and few skills. Starting before World War II, they moved to Baltimore, Pittsburgh, Detroit, Philadelphia, and other cities in search of a new life.

Life has been hard for these migrating peoples. Unfamiliar customs, languages, cultures, and people and the strains of finding work and holding the family together are often overwhelming. Yet, out of the chaos, most whites will finally get the chance to assimilate, if not in this decade, perhaps in the next. For the poor minorities—the blacks, Puerto Ricans, Mexicans, Indians, Chinese, and other peoples of color—the ways to assimilation have been severely restricted.

THE UPPER WEST SIDE STORY

The Upper West Side of Manhattan (the area west of Central Park) was the port of entry for hundreds of thousands of Puerto Ricans entering the United States and, at one point, had all the earmarks of an emerging ghetto. Many East New Yorkers came through the Upper West Side. Weakness in the housing market provided an opening wedge for the ghetto creation process. Puerto Ricans were pitilessly exploited, forced to live in shameful and often inhuman conditions. Perhaps worst of all, their experience shows the lengths to which the larger community will go to preserve "valuable" real estate "for whites only."

In the nineteenth century, the Upper West Side was built up primarily with single-family homes, ranging from luxury mansions to the brownstones that carpeted most of the area.[8] The brownstones were too big, too expensive, and too difficult to run as single-family homes. Lodgers were taken in to help with the upkeep, and soon whole floors were being rented to other families. Later, brownstones were built as multiple dwellings, and the rest were sooner or later converted to rooming houses or smaller apartments.

Widespread dissatisfaction with the brownstone led to the apartment house as we know it today. In 1879, the first luxury apartment building, the Dakota, was built on Central Park West at 72nd Street. One of the most luxurious apartment houses ever built, the Dakota had six apartments on a floor, fourteen-foot ceilings, four main stairways and passenger elevators, four service stairways, and three service elevators. Apartments ranged from seven to fourteen rooms and averaged 5,000 square feet each. Amenities included a public dining room, laundry rooms, and a floor for maids and other servants.

Other luxury buildings followed, and, by the early 1900s, an Upper West Side address represented the peak of fashion. As apartment houses came into general favor, space standards were sharply reduced so that middle-income families could afford them, but through at least the early 1920s all the apartments were designed with at least six rooms. Brownstone owners left their buildings in droves for the new apartments.

Yet, the apartment houses, even the most luxurious, did not take much account of children's needs. The historian Alan Burnham's report, "The Dwelling in Greater Manhattan, 1850–1950, Part II 1850–1890," has few references to children, and most of those give the impression that children were a necessary evil.[9] The lack of facilities for children is glaring by contrast with those available in suburban communities. As the post–World War II housing shortage eased, therefore, upper- and middle-income families began moving to new developments in city and suburbs. As the large families moved out, small adult families moved in. Between 1940 and 1950, the size of the average Upper West Side household fell from 3.2 to 2.2 persons per household (one of the most precipitous drops in U.S. Census history).

As this tumultuous transition was taking place, Puerto Rican families with children were also moving in. Not all of the Upper West Side was plush; the growth of the Puerto Rican population got its start in a tenement area to the northeast, already overcrowded back in the 1900s. As upper- and middle-income families moved out of the Upper West Side, Puerto Ricans got a foothold in the adjoining area.

Starting in the late 1940s, tens of thousands of Puerto Ricans came directly to the Upper West Side, remained for a few weeks or months to get their bearings, then moved on to other neighborhoods. At one point, buses engaged by rental agents met planes from Puerto Rico at Kennedy Airport, offering a free ride to the Upper West Side and a guaranteed room (at an outrageous sum for the week).

Many landlords (and tenants of large apartments) greedily rose to the challenge of housing the newcomers. They harassed and coerced their rent-controlled tenants out so that more Puerto Rican tenants could be housed at higher rents. Landlords turned vacant apartments into furnished rooms, renting each room to a Puerto Rican family. One landlord increased his rent roll from $107,000 to $296,000 annually in a single year by converting apartments to SRO (Single Room Occupancy) units.

Maintenance was neglected throughout the Upper West Side after the war, but the owners of brownstones, tenements, and better apartment houses in and around the Puerto Rican concentration were especially negligent.[10] Tenants were asked to fix up their own apartments, halls went unpainted, elevator service was curtailed or elevators were made self-service, and exterior maintenance was neglected.

The housing that thus became available to Puerto Ricans carried a high price tag.[11] In one census tract south of the tenement area, surveyed in 1953, Puerto Ricans made up 32 percent of the population. Half the families were living in better old-law[12] tenements and half in furnished rooms. Space in the old-law tenements was adequate, but rents averaged $80 a month, while average earnings were only $60 a week. Of the furnished rooms, two-thirds rented for $54 or more a month, with some as high as $154 a month. Only two-fifths of the tenants were employed; an additional fifth was unemployed, and the rest were on welfare. Here, the rent-to-income ratio was close to 40 percent. A quarter of the furnished-room tenants were families of three or more living in 1 or 1.5 rooms. Tenants were unanimously dissatisfied with their quarters and their rents, but they had little choice.

The overcrowding, the constant moving in and out, the aggressive and expanding Puerto Rican presence, the bodegas, record shops, and other Hispanic stores, and the strange language and culture frightened and upset the aging and "genteel" middle-income population. White tenants, particularly those who had no direct contact with Puerto Ricans, were hysterical on the subject of crime and safety in the streets. Meetings on crime in the early 1950s regularly attracted crowds of about 500 people. In discussions, meetings, and interviews with tenants, the white community invariably blamed the victimized and exploited Puerto Ricans for the destruction of the area.

As contact between whites and Puerto Ricans increased over the years, appreciation of the Puerto Rican culture and people replaced much of the hysteria and fear of the 1950s. In those early days, however, the white community felt itself cut off from many of its "own" facilities. The West End Presbyterian Church, at Amsterdam Avenue and West 105th Street, for example, long a pillar of the community, was now in the "bad" area; attendance dropped sharply.

Most schools in the northern sector were also in the "bad" area. In some of them, Puerto Ricans made up half the enrollment. Language was only one of the resulting problems. Puerto Rican (and white) transiency resulted in yearly enrollment turnover of 50 to 90 percent in some of the schools. Educational quality plummeted. Many families sent their children to private schools so that they would not be exposed to "foreigners" and "low" types. One "bright" spot was the Joan of Arc Junior High School, recently built in the "good" area on the site of the West Side Tennis Club (the last private recreational space on the West Side). It became the common ground for meetings aimed at reducing Puerto Rican-white tensions.

The growing Puerto Rican presence was an important factor in the pattern of Upper West Side population shifts in the 1950s. Interviews in 1953 with brownstone rooming-house occupants (then predominantly white) showed a high level of dissatisfaction with their quarters.[13] They wanted to move into more modern, elevator apartments at reasonable rents. Tenants in the apartment buildings liked their quarters well enough, but only 27 percent liked living on the West Side.

Many were able to satisfy their desires. Large numbers of apartment house tenants and young couples in brownstones moved from the Upper West Side to newer developments in the city and suburbs. As examples, proportionately twice as many families moved from the Upper West Side as from other areas in Manhattan to the massive 16,000-unit (white-only) Stuyvesant Town development in downtown Manhattan and to Fresh Meadows, a 3,000-unit development in Queens. The Upper West Side accounted for 8 and 10 percent, respectively, of the total tenancy in these new projects.

As many as twice the number of households moved to these two developments from the area in which Puerto Ricans lived as from other parts of the Upper West Side. This resulted in a substantial number of vacancies. Nor were whites moving into the vacancies. An analysis of the young men who moved from the 63rd Street YMCA (in the southern part of the Upper West Side) showed that a majority moved into other Upper West Side buildings, but few moved to the areas to the north.

Through the 1950s and early 1960s, Puerto Ricans and other minorities filled the vacancies left by whites. Landlord neglect and rental exploitation increased; housing conditions got worse, while rents spiraled upward. The area began to collect the least stable elements of the black, white, and Puerto Rican populations. Recent migrants, alcoholics, drug addicts, second- and third-generation welfare families, and newly released mental patients were thrown together in disastrous concentrations. Black homosexuals, lesbians, and transsexuals, long oppressed in their search for personal freedom, found it in and around the Trianon bar on Broadway in the West 90s. On the corner of West 95th Street and West End Avenue, four buildings contained 328 welfare families; alcoholism, prostitution, and drug addiction were pervasive in three of them. Almost the whole building at 317 West 95th Street was occupied by newly released mental patients referred by DOSS (Department of Social Services) Special Services staff. According to DOSS estimates, half the mental patients discharged in 1963 ended up in West Side SROs.

This destructive social mix became possible because of the 20 percent vacancy rate in SROs and rooming houses. The high vacancy rate, in turn, was a result of the exorbitant rents, the irresponsible management, the pressure of social pathologies, and the transience of the tenants. In some buildings, welfare tenants were regularly assaulted and robbed. A suspected pyromaniac, a child of six treated for a narcotics injection, and an abandoned child of three lived in other buildings. Mental patients suffered relapses; elderly people starved in their rooms because they were afraid to go out.

Throughout this period, most of New York City's substantive actions were directed against the Puerto Rican community. Early in the 1950s, the city yielded to powerful real estate and influential citizen pressures to redevelop part of the tenement area, the most concentrated part of the Puerto Rican presence. While local real estate interests could not control the wild profiteering in Puerto Rican occupancy, they were vigorously opposed to the idea of a Puerto Rican community and worked toward its elimination.

The redevelopment program displaced 5,000 mostly black and Puerto Rican families for a Title 1 luxury development and a public housing project. These projects did not have the desired effect. Instead of leaving the West Side, the displaced site tenants moved west and south, merely adding to the pressure on adjacent areas. After years of community complaints, the city did outlaw the creation of new SRO buildings in 1954,[14] but it was not until January 1, 1965 (some eleven years later), that the city finally made occupancy of SROs by families with children under sixteen illegal.

In the late 1950s, the West Side Urban Renewal Area, south of the original redevelopment site, was designated for renewal as a further effort to stem the Puerto Rican tide. This new plan, covering twenty square blocks, called for the displacement of 9,000 low-income households, 5,000 of them Puerto Rican and 4,000 Irish, black, and others. In their place, 6,700 new middle-income and luxury units were to be built. Another 3,000 units for middle-income and luxury use were to be created by rehabilitating brownstone furnished roominghouses; more than 3,000 high-rent apartments along Central Park West and vicinity were to be conserved. Thousands of units in better old-law tenements occupied by Irish and Puerto Rican families at reasonable rents were slated for demolition. Only 1,000 units of new low-rent housing was projected (later raised to 2,500 after protracted community struggle), compared with the 9,000 low-income households being displaced.

Once the twenty-block area was designated, and before the acquisition of the affected properties, conditions became intolerable. Ninety percent of the buildings were irresponsibly managed, compared with 60 percent in the northwest area. With the help of alcoholic and drug-addicted superintendents, with some housing so deteriorated it could not be recovered, with alcoholism estimated by residents at 60 to 80 percent of the adult population, whole blocks became virtually unlivable. More than one renewal area block was characterized as "the most dangerous block in the City of New York." A 1964 survey identified 123 SRO buildings and 480 roominghouses with from 6 to 300 units in each.[15] In one building, tenants had only sticks of furniture, inoperative toilets, hot plates, and tiny, hotel-sized refrigerators for families of five. The median period of unemployment for household heads was two years; the average unemployed individual had been out of work for five. Stores closed down as leases ran out, further depressing the area. Neither shopkeepers nor owners would invest in improvements.

Despite years of controversy over the amount of low-rent housing to be built and other issues, the urban renewal plan finally moved forward in 1963. Brownstones projected to remain were bought up by young, white, middle-income families even before the plan was officially adopted; the buildings' Puerto Rican tenancies were terminated and the structures converted to duplexes or small apartments at high rents. These new owners and the hundreds who followed them became vociferous proponents of the urban renewal plan. They formed block associations to police the area, became active in West Side politics, and supported the plan at hearings and meetings.

During the 1960s, thousands of families and businesses were moved out, and whole blocks and other sites were cleared. Gone were the Puerto Rican bodegas, barbarias, ferreterias, sastrerias, and restaurantes so gradually (and painfully) built up over the past decades. The Puerto Rican community also lost many of the social, political, and religious ties it had so laboriously put together. Before the close of the decade, the Puerto Rican community had suffered an almost fatal blow.

Out of these bitter ashes rose the new splendor. By the early 1970s, a wholly different atmosphere had been created. Instead of the aging tenements and drab stores, there was a new community of high-rise buildings with posh stores and restaurants advertising roast beef dinners at $9.50 (pricey at the time). At the entrance to one middle-income project, a neatly lettered sign declared, "No Dogs or Non-Residents Permitted." Of the 8,500 new and rehabilitated units, low-income residents had gotten a bare 1,900. Most of the rest went to middle- and upper-income white families.

When it became clear to site tenants that even the promised 2,500 low-rent units were not going to materialize, 208 Puerto Rican and other Hispanic families, aided by El Comite (a Dominican activist group), Columbia University students, Operation Move In, and other tenant groups, squatted in new, still vacant, luxury apartment buildings on the renewal site. The Housing Development Administration vowed to evict the squatters and threatened mass arrests if there was resistance.[16] In a few days, with hundreds of police taking part, the city did (peaceably) evict the squatters. After another year of confrontation, the city agreed to add another 150 units of public housing, but even this tiny addition to the low-rent total was challenged in the courts, with the white middle-income plaintiffs charging that 150 more units of low-rent housing would "tip" the area.

By the early 1970s, the Puerto Rican population tidal wave had definitely subsided. From the 1950 total of 20,000, the area's Puerto Rican population on the Upper West Side grew in the early 1960s to a peak of close to 50,000, then dropped sharply to its 1950 level by 1970. Along the way, the concentration of Puerto Ricans in the area known as "San Juan

Hill" were also displaced for what is now Lincoln Center. Other factors in the decline included lower rates of in-migration from Puerto Rico, newly available housing in the expanding Bronx and Brooklyn ghettos at lower rents, the prohibition on families with children in SROs, and, prominently, attention by owners to an improved market for white middle-income occupancy. As a result, Puerto Ricans were harassed and encouraged to leave to make room for high-rent renovations for the white, upscale housing market.

At the end of the transition, the Puerto Ricans were in firm possession of only part of the area they had occupied in 1950, an area in which 50 percent of the buildings needed extensive rehabilitation or clearance and another 30 percent required at least moderate rehabilitation. Puerto Ricans were not responsible for the housing destruction that took place; they were steered to the West Side and forced to live in overcrowded conditions in largely neglected buildings at excessive rents.

Puerto Ricans were not destined to hold the West Side. City officials and powerful West Side real estate interests felt the area was too valuable a location for the poor. As the situation developed, ways of dealing with it developed as well. The various real estate interests gradually coalesced around a plan to contain the Puerto Rican advance and to exploit the Puerto Rican people, gradually making their stay untenable, and ultimately pushing them out. In effect, that is just what happened.

Though the West Side did not surrender to the pressures of the minority population wave, parts of Brooklyn did. Hundreds of thousands of blacks and Puerto Ricans moved to Brooklyn during the 1950s, 1960s and 1970s, a wave of banker/broker/speculator–inspired destruction paralleling their advance. Bedford-Stuyvesant became all-black at the cost of several thousand units; almost two-thirds of Brownsville was destroyed or burned out during those turbulent decades. East New York was also overrun. Like an out-of-control brush fire, the ghettoization of East New York consumed everything in its path.

3

The Ghettoization of East New York

BLACKS AND PUERTO RICANS ended up in East New York because it was one of the few parts of the metropolitan area into which they could move. Segregation—American style apartheid—created the conditions that put East New York and other vulnerable communities at risk. The actual process started with bank redlining and property neglect as blacks and Puerto Ricans began to move in, continued with blockbusting and vicious exploitation, resulted in the undesirable concentration of welfare and poor families, and ended by overwhelming the community's ability to cope with the resulting problems. The machinations of the real estate fraternity, the racism and greed of the banking industry and the indifference of government officials all contribute to the creation of ghettos, which can be described as the destroyed remains of once viable communities.

APARTHEID, AMERICAN STYLE

While urban ghettos were expanding by half a million persons a year, only 40,000 blacks were moving into the suburbs.[1] The exclusion of blacks and other minorities from the suburbs was maneuvered by the national organizations of real estate interests who control our federal housing programs. Chief among these groups was NAREB (National Association of Real Estate Boards) with 1,100 local boards as members, the NAHB (National Association of Home Builders) with 11,000 members, the National Association of Lumber Dealers, and the Producers Council (which represents powerful materials interests). Federal involvement in housing during the depression of the 1930s gave rise to this lobby (termed the most dangerous in Washington by President Truman), whose prime objective was to mold federal housing programs to their own advantage.[2] Led by NAREB, the lobby proceeded to dominate the preparation of real estate texts and the establishment of university real estate courses, to coordinate and direct the activities of local real estate boards and builders, and to pursue white exclusivity as a central theme.

In essence, white exclusivity was the device used to lure the affluent to the suburbs. The automobile was ready and the railroads wanted more riders, but only small numbers of moderate-income families were moving to the suburbs. Substantial black movement to the cities and even into white areas after World War II despite threats, violence, and local real estate codes, helped to make the suburban alternative seem attractive.

In February 1937, *Good Housekeeping* magazine gave a "shield of honor" to ten exclusive suburban communities, applauding those communities that had the "right" groups and the proper "restrictions" and that had achieved an admirable "social standing."

To further cater to the prejudices of the nation, NAREB and its partners added nationality, religion, and income to the exclusivity package. In a final blow, the lobby incorporated its racist doctrine in the now-infamous 1935 FHA (Federal Housing Administration) Underwriting Manual, which guaranteed mortgage insurance only for segregated developments.[3]

As a result, blacks were excluded from the suburban boom that followed World War II. Although the federal government had subsidized some 10 million units by 1965, only 2 percent of these were made available to nonwhites, and much of this housing was on a segregated basis. FHA discrimination continued, though the racist provisions were stricken from the manual in the late 1940s.

In 1965, President Lyndon B. Johnson issued an executive order directed precisely at the problem of racial segregation. The order opened occupancy in white areas to minority people. Its purpose was to prevent the ghettoization of East New York and dozens of other minority communities in the nation's big cities. The FHA and federal banking agencies arbitrarily exempted one- and two-family homes from President Johnson's executive order. Nor has the FHA ever invoked Section 102 of the executive order to bring about the desegregation of millions of sales and rental units under its jurisdiction.

FHA policies continue to discriminate against older urban neighborhoods, as well as female-headed households, blacks and other minorities, and low-income people. New York City, with 3.7 percent of the nation's population, received only 2.1 percent of FHA loan insurance.[4] FHA and the banks have "pulled" upwardly mobile, predominantly white families with male heads of household out of the city and "pushed" low-income, predominantly black and minority families into the central cities. The private sector, federal housing agencies, and local governments have all failed to guarantee the civil rights of all citizens, and to preserve and revitalize urban neighborhoods by providing long-term capital.

CREATING GHETTOS

In the cities, both federal and local governments, influenced by real estate interests, pursue racist policies. Estimates of segregation in public housing run as high as 90 percent, and even HUD admits to 70 percent segregation by calling projects integrated if they have more than a few black (or white) families. "Liberal" New York City approved Metropolitan Life's white-only middle-income project of 16,000 families (Stuyvesant Town and Peter Cooper Village) in 1943; even by the late 1970s, fewer than thirty black families lived in the two complexes. Of 111 New York City middle-income projects, which accommodate 80,000 families, 79 percent were segregated (occupancy 90 percent or more black or white) in 1965.[5] Real estate boards also tightened their hold on real estate transactions and sharply reduced selling to blacks in white areas.

The way the East New York ghetto developed is typical of ghetto creation all across the country. When minority families move into the big cities, they head for the existing ghettos, where they join in a desperate search for shelter, a sort of musical chairs with a severely restricted supply of housing constantly affected by abandonment, demolition, conversion, and other changes. It is a highly transient population. In Chicago and Los Angeles, more than a quarter of the nonwhite families moved from one house to another in 1965, most of the moves by the newest and poorest residents. They moved from one-room units to two-room units, or (we can hope) to an apartment, or they moved because they were robbed or assaulted, or they were evicted because they couldn't afford the high rents, or they skipped to avoid paying them. Thousands of families went from one horrendous housing situation to another in the generally unfounded hope that conditions couldn't be as bad in the house on the next block.

Minority families were seeking to improve their conditions against impossible odds. Nearly 42 percent of nonwhite homes across the country lacked a flush toilet in the early 1960s, compared with 10 percent of white homes. By the end of the 1940s, overcrowding declined to 5 percent for whites but rose from 11 to 19 percent for nonwhites. Even blacks with higher incomes were unable to find decent housing. In 1960, almost half of Chicago's black families with incomes above $7,000 (a decent wage at the time) lived in substandard dwellings compared with only 6 percent of whites. In Washington, D.C., even among blacks earning $10,000 a year or more, 25 percent lived in overcrowded facilities.

Better housing was available in white areas but was not open to blacks. Realtors would rarely show a house in a white area to blacks (or houses in black areas to whites). Blacks who did manage to buy a house in a white area were upper or upper middle class.[6] In most cases, blacks who bought houses in white communities were hounded right out again or made so uncomfortable that few other black families would venture into the neighborhood. Cross burnings, arson, vandalism, bombings, shootings, beatings, and threats were the typical tactics employed in white neighborhoods, and they were reported in the nation's press with dulling regularity for decades.

Somehow, the police never seemed to intervene effectively. They often stood idly by, on occasion waiting until a full-scale riot involving hundreds and even thousands of people developed (as in Chicago, Detroit, Cicero, East St. Louis, and Miami in the 1950s) before they acted, or they actively sided with the white community. In one incident in Chicago, police were reported showing young white men how to make Molotov cocktails. In a 1974 case in Philadelphia, after a black family's home was vandalized and almost wrecked by six white men, the black family itself was arrested. While they were in jail, their house was burned to the ground. White hostility was so well known in black communities, that only the most desperate or courageous blacks even thought of trying to find a house in a white area.

As a result, minority newcomers and the existing ghetto population were forced to stay in or adjacent to the existing ghettos. In Syracuse, in 1950, 83 percent of the black population lived in three of the city's seventy-six census tracts. By 1960, the black population had tripled, but 95 percent of blacks still lived in those same three tracts. Segregation and overcrowding increased while blocks were grudgingly yielded to the growing black population. All but 1,500 of Boston's 63,000 blacks lived in the contiguous neighborhoods of Roxbury, North Dorchester, and South End. A special federal census taken in the Los Angeles area after the Watts riot in 1965 found segregation increasing in each of the seven neighborhoods that make up the black ghetto of South Los Angeles, despite the existence of 200,000 apartment vacancies in the greater Los Angeles area.

With 4 million blacks and millions of other minority people pouring into existing ghettos in cities across the country, there nevertheless had to be an expansion of black living areas. This was done by expanding the ghetto into adjacent white areas. The policy dates back at least to 1917 (and probably much earlier), when the Chicago Board of Realtors declared: "It is in the interest of all that each block be filled solidly [with Negroes] and that further expansion shall be confined to contiguous blocks. . . ." The Board, which at least up to 1962 was all white, no longer makes a copy of this statement available in its office, but the policy has never been rescinded or repudiated.[7] None of the Board's 1,700 members violates it.

Blacks could move successfully into adjacent areas only after explosive pressures had built up in the existing ghetto. Black unemployment, already twice that of whites, often doubled again as newly arrived migrants could not find work. High unemployment, high rates of transience, and overcrowded housing meant more people on the streets, and more antisocial behavior. Senseless man-in-the-house welfare regulations encouraged the dissolution of the rural family structure. Overcrowding also forced young people to leave their homes and to take up life in the streets or in vacant buildings. Alcoholism, drug addiction, and prostitution increased; muggers, petty thieves, and pushers multiplied and began to terrorize the community. Garbage loads were heavier, but less refuse was picked up; street conditions were appalling. Policing became less effective and more vindictive. The ghetto became desolate and dangerous.

This explosive situation spilled over into the neighboring white community. Desperate middle-income househunters visit brokers, while poor black renters haunt the adjacent white streets looking for a place to live. Black children enroll in neighborhood schools and begin to use neighborhood parks. Banks redline the area. Landlords neglect their properties, whites move out, and blacks move in. Real estate speculators and blockbusters move in and speed the transition. Youthful vandalism escalates to armed robbery, and stores begin to close. Before long, another neighborhood is added to the ghetto.

REDLINING

Redlining is the withdrawal of mortgage money from a community. Banks prefer to lend their money (the deposits of their urban customers) to suburban borrowers and generally restrict lending in older urban neighborhoods. They typically reject loan applications for mixed-use buildings, residences near industry, multifamily housing, and older buildings. It doesn't matter if there are no abandoned buildings or apartment vacancies in the neighborhood. As soon as it appears that blacks or other minorities are moving into an area, the banks promptly redline it, whether or not it conforms to their loan requirements. While redlining has been outlawed, the discriminatory practices continue.

Profit in real estate is usually derived from the ability of an owner to sell or remortgage a building, enabling the owner to benefit financially. If an owner cannot sell or refinance because of bank disinvestment, his investment has gone sour. He either sells out to a speculator who will exploit the property, or personally starts seeking a higher (short-term) return by "milking" the building. Tenants move out and are replaced by minority families at higher rents. Maintenance and services are further reduced, eventually leading to abandonment.

The key factor is whether or not the banks continue to provide financing. As John Bunting, of First Pennsylvania Bank and Trust, stated, "We [the banks] determine who will succeed and who will fail."[8] Indeed, banks determined that racial change from white to minority portends decline, that integration cannot succeed, that women heads of households were risks, that certain geographic areas of the city and building types were undesirable. They set in motion and have reinforced by their actions a self-fulfilling prophecy; the withdrawal of mortgage money actually causes decline.

Redlining was the signal for the start of blockbusting and its associated ills, as described later. All the groups that could not find conventional means of financing fell prey to the private mortgage market, which made financing available at exorbitant rates. The "white" alternative, as the savings banks' ads indicated, was to move to the suburbs.[9]

THE TIPPING POINT

Real estate interests tried to sugarcoat their apartheid policies by promoting the "tipping point" theory. They told us that white neighborhoods "tip" from white to black when white tolerance for living with blacks is exceeded. The theory states that, as the black population rises above a certain percentage (generally estimated at between 17 and 30 percent), the remaining whites leave because they cannot or will not tolerate such a high percentage of blacks. Several studies have shown the concept to be mythical, with so many exceptions and flaws as to be valueless.[10]

Nevertheless, the "tipping point" theory persists. A whole typology of neighborhood succession has been developed and has assumed, in the minds of the general public and of government officials, the stature of physical law.

Blacks and whites can and do live together in greater proportions than the 17 to 30 percent black levels projected by real estate interests. Despite overwhelming segregation in public housing projects, many New York City projects have had mixed occupancy for decades. Just south of East New York, Starrett City's 14,600 units have been integrated since its construction in the early 1970s. The 2000 U.S. Census found the population of Starrett City to be 32 percent white, 42 percent black, 18 percent Hispanic, and 8 percent other ancestries. Despite high indices of racial segregation, researchers found mixed occupancy in dozens of census tracts in both northern and southern cities.[11] Many more would be mixed occupancy if it were not for the policies and practices of the real estate industry, government agencies, and the elite arbiters of social mores. As with the "blacks like to live with blacks" theory, and the "blacks depress home values" theory, the "tipping point" is merely another racial gambit masquerading as social reality.

As the black tidal wave crested in the ghetto and built its explosive pressures, and as the edges of adjacent communities began to be occupied by blacks, the banks, brokers, and various government agencies swiftly redrew their white-only boundaries. One or more adjacent streets or whole neighborhoods were marked for black use. Restrictions against renting or selling to blacks were lifted; whites were encouraged to leave and discouraged from coming in; city services were permitted to deteriorate. Open season was declared on the community, and both blacks and whites were mercilessly exploited.

All this happened long before the mythical "tipping point" was reached. The white community affected was not a party to the decision. It was not the limit of white tolerance that "tipped" the area; it was American-style apartheid. FHA restrictions, bank redlining, and an army of real estate brokers dedicated to racial change were the overwhelming forces that "tipped" the community.

One of the more reasonable ways of looking at a "tipping point" was contributed by the housing expert Elizabeth Wood.[12] She criticized public housing officials and others who wanted to set a 20 percent limit on black occupancy to prevent projects from going all black. Reminding the officials that experience with such formulas shows that they solve nothing, she posed the more pertinent question of how many elderly, large families, children, welfare families, families of low income, or problem families a project could absorb. "A balanced neighborhood," says Wood, "is one in which the mixture is not in the process of self—destruction." It was a wonderful, if generally ignored, observation. If ghettos were not typically overburdened with desperate welfare and poverty-stricken families, they would be far better and safer places in which to live. Thus, it is not just race which characterizes ghettos; it is the concentration of poverty, as well.

One would think that white community residents threatened with total racial shift would rise up and demand that blacks be permitted to move into vacancies in other parts of the city, if only to keep their own community from being sacrificed. The sad thing was that none of them did. Their ire was directed against the incoming minority and (sometimes) against the real estate interests and the city that sold them out. On the issue of racism, they were silent. They remained loyal to the racist creed, even as it destroyed their communities.

BLOCKBUSTING IN EAST NEW YORK

As described in chapter 1, wholesale changes from white to black and Puerto Rican had taken place throughout the area by 1967. The opening wedge came in the tenement area,[13] where maintenance and services had suffered since World War II. As blacks began to move into the tenement area in the late 1950s, the banks redlined the area. Tenement landlords could neither refinance nor sell their buildings to legitimate buyers. Many began to milk their buildings, harassing their white tenants out in order to get rent increases from blacks and Puerto Ricans. They then cut back on services to their minority tenants. Others sold to slumlords or leased to opportunists who milked both buildings and tenants; banks followed the same route with their foreclosed properties. Physical conditions rapidly deteriorated; vandalism, crime, and violence multiplied, and abandonments, fires, and burned-out buildings followed. White owners of two- and four-family houses in and around the tenement area were frightened and alarmed.

This was a perfect setup for blockbusters who descended on the area like the plague. Working on the fears and prejudices of white owners, a horde of brokers and speculators flooded "ripe" blocks with scare literature, hinting that "the time to sell is now." A black family or two was moved into a block and often deliberately paraded by the speculators. Agents offered ridiculously low prices for houses over the telephone, further worrying owners. Agents then came around in person, offering quick cash, sufficient for a down payment on a house in a "safer" area. Owners sold.

During this initial stage of the racial shift, a black or Puerto Rican family with an income of $7,000 (a lower-middle-income wage in those years) and modest savings could buy a two-family house in East New York. A blockbuster might purchase a house worth $15,000 for $12,500, resell to a black family for $17,500, and pocket the difference. In the active blocks, from 30 to 40 percent of the properties changed hands in a year.

Typically, the second-floor apartment would be rented to a welfare family. (Another working family able to afford the $125 rent would buy its own house.) Whites did not rent in the changing area, leaving the rental field open to minority welfare clients. The second-floor apartment had to stay rented to a paying tenant in order for the owner to keep up his payments, especially if he had been persuaded to take an improvement loan in addition to the mortgage. One broker estimated that more than half the new homeowners were victimized by improvement schemes.[14] Even with the second floor rented, many minority owners couldn't afford to make needed repairs to plumbing and heating systems or to exteriors. The default rate in 1967 was estimated to be an unusually high 15 percent.

The larger part of East New York lay east of the tenement area. It was fully built up, primarily with one- to four-family houses, and was less than 5 percent minority in 1960. All but 30 percent of the housing required only minor to moderate repair. Housing quality was mixed, with values ranging from $12,000 to $25,000 for a one- or two-unit house, with better and poorer, older and newer parts.

Despite these favorable conditions, banks redlined the whole area in the early 1960s, except for FHA-insured homes. Few East New York buildings met FHA requirements, however. Houses with "railroad" apartment layouts, windowless rooms, apartments above a store, or with nonfireproof party walls that were too close to a commercial structure, were ineligible. Buyers were therefore forced to seek more expensive financing from private mortgage companies. While white home buyers could afford to avoid areas where excessive prices and loan rates were being charged, black people had to buy houses where they could find them. Even FHA-insured houses were more expensive.

Unlike banks, mortgage brokers were often actively involved in buying and selling houses, as well as in making mortgage loans. As both speculator and investor, they demanded a higher rate of return for their correspondingly greater risks. Their presence often led to higher sales prices to people of lower economic levels, and they were not unduly bothered by declines in maintenance because of their short-term interest and the possibilities for repossession of the property in case of default.

When selling a property, if a speculator (or mortgage broker) was unable to arrange for a substantial bank mortgage, he would still agree to sell the house to a family that didn't have sufficient money for a reasonable down payment. The speculator accepted a smaller amount, giving the purchaser a purchase money mortgage (a contract to buy the house) for an inflated amount and at a higher than normal interest rate. The buyer was then responsible for paying the higher mortgage payments plus normal house maintenance costs. If the buyer missed a single payment, through unemployment or loss of a tenant, he forfeited the contract; the speculator repossessed the property and repeated the process.

To capitalize on the prospects for racial change, brokers stopped showing houses in East New York to whites. Some brokers claimed that whites did not want homes in the changing area; others claimed that families had to pay twenty points (a loan of $15,000 became a mortgage of $18,000, with $3,000 going into the mortgagee's pocket) to get a mortgage. This was compared with only eight points in Rugby (an area just

beginning to change in East Flatbush) and three points in all-white Farragut, south of Rugby. Black families had to pay the premium because
they had no alternative, but whites could go to other areas. Even FHA
insurance was difficult to get unless one dealt with FHA-favored firms.
At its height, 200 firms were willing to sell to blacks in East New York,
but few if any could be found selling to minority families in Flatlands,
Canarsie, or the adjacent communities in Queens.

As the area became more black and Puerto Rican and the number
of welfare families increased, the area lost its attractiveness even to
moderate-income blacks. Houses were then sold to even lower-income
families. Whites were paid still less for their houses, and blacks were
charged more. Lower down payments were accepted through the use
of high-cost purchase money mortgages. Given the higher cost of owning and the lower incomes of owners, the default rate continued to be
high. While homes continued to be sold to minority families, though
at a slower pace, the percentage of minority ownership didn't rise
along with sales. The departure of higher-income blacks from the area
and the high rate of foreclosures kept the homeowner total well below
25 percent.

The shift from white to black followed a seemingly inexorable
course, even against stiff white resistance. After the first wave of blockbusting, the rapidly expanding black and Puerto Rican population ran
headlong into a prospering Italian community. Racial antipathies and
the deteriorating quality of life decided the issue. The riot in the Italian
area in the summer of 1966, with Italian youths battling black and
Puerto Rican youths, followed by confrontations and more rioting in
the summer of 1967, resulted in the wholesale out-migration of the Italian community. Black and Puerto Rican occupancy passed the 80 percent mark that same year. An entire shopping street—blocks of stores
and fruit and vegetable stands typical of Italian communities—was
abandoned in the space of two years.

Sales, which had been very active in East New York early in the
1960s, had slackened considerably by 1965–66. The two or three finance
companies that regularly handled mortgages in East New York had become more particular about granting loans. Blacks and Puerto Ricans
with enough income to legitimately buy houses no longer found the
area attractive. Finance companies limited loans to better parts of the
area and refused to make loans on properties with stores or even those

within 100 feet of a commercial street. While some brokers claimed it was impossible to get FHA insurance north of New Lots Avenue, others claimed it was still possible if you contacted the right broker.

Whites forced from their homes to create the new black ghetto also suffered financial and social losses; they too lost a community. They were also pawns, their displacement adding to the demand for more new, exclusively white suburbs. The banks and blockbusters gained, of course. Over the past several decades, perhaps 25 percent of New York City's population (white and minority) has been subjected to these upheavals and community-destroying tactics, and a terribly high price has been paid to "keep blacks in their place."

In reviewing these practices, it must be noted that they are one answer to the problem of finding more homes for blacks. Even if the default rate is 15 percent, a sizable number of blacks have nevertheless successfully bought new homes, something they would have found hard to do without blockbusting, private mortgage financing and other less-than-desirable practices. What is undesirable is the creation of social and economic ghettos through the use of segregation and blockbusting techniques, and the extra burdens put on black and Puerto Rican homeowners and renters in areas where mortgage money is not readily available.

EAST FLATBUSH

From East Flatbush, new details became available on the initial stages of ghettoization and how difficult it was to stop it.[15] In this case, minority school enrollment, as well as a housing market weakness, provided the opening wedge. Essentially all white in 1960 (no census tract had as much as 1 percent nonwhite residents), the racial composition of the community began to change shortly thereafter. The pressures came from Crown Heights and Bedford-Stuyvesant to the north, and from the Brownsville ghetto to the northeast, and from parts of Flatbush to the southwest, where a few blacks had gotten a foothold. (In 1969, Flatbush boundaries were euphemistically described as "where the Negroes aren't.")

The initial changes took place in the northeast, the area of poorest housing. Conventional mortgages were already difficult to obtain by 1960, nor could legitimate buyers be found. While the area contained many two-family houses, four-fifths of the residents were renters, primarily in multifamily walkups and large apartment houses. By 1967, substantial deterioration had taken place in the multiple dwellings, and the minority percentage reached the 25 percent mark. Of twelve typical buildings surveyed in 1967, ten needed extensive work in entryways and halls where worn stairs, leaking skylights, broken mailboxes, and sagging floors and ceilings were found.[16] Apartment interiors were also in poor shape. In three-quarters of the units, at least 25 percent of walls and ceilings needed replacement; half needed new window frames and sashes. Bathroom equipment was largely old; high-tank-type toilets predominated. Wood kitchen cabinets were rotting, and stoves were in poor shape. Electric wiring was inadequate in all buildings. In seven of the twelve buildings, tenants complained of do-nothing landlords, and several complained that heat and hot water had been completely turned off on occasion. Landlords were generally willing to make stop-gap repairs, but no significant improvements had been made in years. Only a third of the tenants were black and Puerto Rican, and these were mainly wage earners.[17]

The average rent for minority families was $90 per month compared with $80 for whites, partly because of the effects of rent control. As apartments became vacant, the rents rose. Blacks and Puerto Ricans were happy to obtain the vacancies, but whites were obviously not. In many cases, landlords lowered the rents in order to attract white families. Other landlords felt their investment had collapsed and followed the same paths as their East New York counterparts, paths that would ultimately lead to abandonment.

The school situation added to the pressures. Starting in 1960–61, East Flatbush had been the recipient of minority children through busing and open-enrollment programs. It had a surplus of seats, and there were serious shortages of classrooms in both Brownsville and parts of Flatbush. From 8 percent of East Flatbush enrollment in the 1960–61 school year, minority enrollment climbed to 46 percent in 1967–68.

As minority pupil enrollment in the northeast schools rose to more than 70 percent, white families with children began to move out and were replaced with younger black families. By 1965, blacks made up less than 25 percent of East Flatbush's northeast population, but because of the busing of youngsters from Brownsville and heavy white enrollment in parochial schools, minority enrollment in two northeast schools reached 90 percent. Real estate interests were quick to exploit the situation. A swarm of brokers and speculators in the northeast and Rugby began buying houses from whites and selling them to blacks; the banks did their part by withholding mortgage funds.

With more blacks visible in the community and the banks and brokers encouraging a racial shift, owners were pressured and panicked into selling their homes. The techniques were similar to those used in East New York. Church Avenue sported some sixty real estate offices, about double the number required for normal real estate transactions. One broker's sign advertised his practice as "Selling to A-1 Puerto Rican Families" before local protests forced the sign's removal. All denied blockbusting.

Yet blockbusting was going on in East Flatbush, and groups like the Rugby Neighborhood Council organized against it. In a heavily Jewish part of the community, Rugby community leaders were hoping to establish an integrated community but were opposed to the panic-inducing and sell-only-to-minorities policies of the real estate and banking fraternities. They brought postcard solicitations and other evidence of blockbusting to the State Commission on Human Rights in 1968. The situation was then put before John P. Lomenzo, New York's secretary of state, who undertook an investigation.[18]

In December 1969, Lomenzo penalized a number of Brooklyn real estate brokers and salesmen with fines, license revocation, and the return of profits totaling more than $6,000 for a variety of offenses. Rose Perlstein, a broker, lost her license for blockbusting. She had generated fears by making persistent calls to solicit homes for sale with the knowledge that a black family lived on the block. She had, in fact, paraded a black family up and down the block. Brokers for one house misrepresented the salaries of the purchasers on applications for FHA loan insurance and were forced to return profits on the sale and commissions and to pay $500 in fines or have their licenses revoked. Cases of two other brokers were turned over to the U.S. Attorney. The penalties were puny, but they may have served to prevent even worse excesses.

The flight of whites was of great concern to the clergy. Two orthodox Jewish rabbis, fearing the elimination of their congregations through swift neighborhood change, asked all congregants preparing to put their homes up for sale to come to them. The rabbis, by advertising in the Jewish press and other journals that served the Orthodox Jewish community, and by word of mouth, succeeded in turning over nine houses and thirty-five occupants during October and November 1967.

The new occupants, of course, were Jewish and sustained the strength of the congregation.

While this method was plainly discriminatory, it did counter-balance the brokerage firms whose business was increasingly (and sometimes exclusively) aimed at the minority market. A home-finding service, open to all, operated by the community, is one method of coun-teracting discriminatory and destructive practices. One such service, the Laurelton Home-Finding Service of the Laurelton Fair Housing Committee in Queens, operating through the Jewish temples in the area, provided thirty people to take calls and show houses every Sun-day. Through ads placed in the *New York Times*, they claimed to have changed the percentage of white buyers from 20 percent in 1966 to 50 percent in 1967. Despite this valiant effort, Laurelton was almost all black by the early 1970s.

The majority of residents were not panicked by blacks moving into the community. For a sizable number, however, the time to move had already come. Of 377 households throughout East Flatbush that were asked, in 1967, "Are you planning to move in the immediate future?" 14 percent answered yes. The highest percentage of yes responses came from families in the northeast. All the younger white families inter-viewed wanted or were intending to move. They were interested in paying $10 to $33 more per month for "better" areas in Queens or Long Island. Including the elderly who also planned to leave, a total of 25 per-cent of the northeast residents intended to move out, almost double the percentage in Rugby and quadruple that in Farragut.

As the whites moved out, a steadily increasing proportion of sales were made to black and Puerto Rican families. Whites were not pre-vented from buying in Rugby and the northeast, but terms were stiffer and the prices were higher. Blacks would pay the higher prices; whites didn't have to. In 1967, brokers indicated that three-quarters of sales in the northern half of East Flatbush and a quarter of sales in the southern half were being made to minority families. They considered the entire area to be "changing" or "ripe for change," and many predicted flatly that East Flatbush would go all black in a decade or two.

Community leaders blamed the city, as well as the real estate fra-ternity, for the racial shift. Their case against the city went back to the 1960 Board of Education Report, "Blueprint for Quality Education," which announced the open enrollment and bussing programs. That 1960 report called East Flatbush a "changing neighborhood" before changes had begun to occur. Community leaders were convinced the city had sold them out. The educational "tipping" produced neighborhood "tipping" as the city had known it would, the leaders said, and, since the report was published, the community had been treated like a stepchild. Few improvements were slated for the community in the city's capital budgets, and city services were deteriorating. "Brownsville has garbage pickup seven days a week," screamed one community leader, "but our pickups have declined from three to four to only two days a week."[19]

The city, when asked to help the community, was blind to the school integration issue, as well as to the depredations of the real estate fraternity. Officials saw East Flatbush as no worse off than dozens of other communities. "The community isn't in such bad shape" or "higher priorities exist elsewhere" was their stock answer to appeals for help. As for more progressive technicians, they felt that East Flatbush whites would simply have to learn to live with blacks, and, if they couldn't, the area could go all black, for all they cared. This was (and is) a basic point, to be sure, but it ignores essential truths about the situation. Whites weren't being given that choice by the real estate fraternity, and the city's policies and lack of action were only aiding and abetting the apartheid policies of the realtors.

Under attack by the real estate interests and ignored by the city, it is no wonder that communities like East Flatbush turned to the only weapon left in their arsenal: overt racial hate. This has been a potent weapon in cities across the country and has kept blacks and other minorities from moving into white communities in an uncountable number of cases. In the early 1960s, a cross was burned in front of a Farragut home bought by a black family. This incident, and other expressions of racial hate, helped to keep Farragut white through much of the 1960s.

By the late 1960s, however, there was a whole real estate system arrayed against the community, transforming its racial composition against its will. In this situation, the "rules" did a flip-flop. Police no longer condoned or encouraged cross burnings, bombings, and the like. They suppressed them vigorously.[20]

In Farragut, however, the spirit of racism died hard. Its Community Action Committee was fanatically determined to maintain the status quo. It was a strong supporter of the police and crusaded fiercely against new expressways, new housing, new schools, or anything else that might bring more black people into the community. "We're the last holdouts before the suburbs," shouted a community leader to the cheers of his listeners.[21]

In areas where the battle to remain white-only was lost, as in East Flatbush, these strategies no longer worked. When a black broker showed a house to a black family in 1968, neighboring residents came out to yell at them: "We don't want niggers here." The house was sold to a black family, nevertheless, and, according to the broker, whites on the block were "moving out left and right." By 1970, the northeast area was 55 percent nonwhite, double its percentage in 1967. Rugby more than doubled its minority population, to 25 percent. Even in Farragut, the minority percentage rose to 10. The transition continued.

POSTMORTEM

When white America adopted its policy of white exclusivity, it may not have foreseen the results. Blinded by its prejudices, it may have failed to calculate the size of coming minority migrations or the shape they would take. Perhaps it didn't know how the ghettos would grow, fester, boil over, and explode. Perhaps no one could have predicted the viciousness of the exploitation as the ghetto expanded or the accompanying destruction of white, as well as black, communities. The growth of huge minority enclaves, some of them containing hundreds of thousands of people, separating and isolating center cities from suburbs, may also have been unanticipated.

If the nation was unaware of these implications when it all began, it isn't now. Not since the riots of the 1960s. Yet nothing has been done to change the situation. The architects and executors of our housing policies—the real estate fraternity and our governments—are fully aware of the situation but refuse to change it. Nor can they hide behind the excuse that only a few in their profession are involved in racial change; every broker, builder, and banker who accepts white exclusivity is equally guilty of these racial crimes.

From the news media, one could easily get the impression that government was trying hard to find answers to the problems of older communities and ghettos, but without much success. The reality was that government was invisible for all practical purposes—except for aggravating the situation by its neglect. Government's failure to deal with the real issues—the depredations of the real estate interests and the mindless concentration of welfare and problem families, as well as its willingness to write off the devastated communities it created— has resulted in the creation of many scars and open tears in the urban fabric.

4

Destruction of the "Target Area"

THERE HAD BEEN widespread deterioration throughout East New York by the dawn of 1967, but the area hardest hit was the "Target Area," part of the tenement area west of Pennsylvania Avenue. Thus, while conditions throughout the community are reviewed in this chapter, most attention is paid to the Target Area—which became the focus of improvement planning and activity. The disastrous housing conditions in the Target Area and how they got that way are therefore analyzed in some detail. It was the Target Area that the community unanimously selected to receive the bulk of new and rehabilitated housing being offered by the city.

It is hard to describe the chaos of life in the Target Area, portraying its full measure of deterioration, congestion, instability, and destruction. Some of the community's emotional intensity during that period is reflected in the early meetings of the planning committee. Many years ago, while the experience was still fresh in my mind, I wrote up a description of the first meeting with landlords. This chapter starts off with that description, as I wrote it then.

LANDLORDS' MEETING

Outside, it was bitterly cold, the wind swirled the falling snow against my face; it was hard to breathe.[1] Hell, I thought, as I struggled toward the Community Progress Center, nobody's going to be at the meeting. After all the effort to get a decent turnout of property owners—the flyers, the mailings, the efforts of local housing groups—it was going to be a bust.

Inside, I was shocked. The place was jammed with people, 125 of them, I was told later. And, as I soon realized, half of them were landlords. Leo Lillard, the planning committee's newly elected chairman, had no sooner opened the meeting and introduced me as consultant when the complaints began crashing over me like the waves at Coney Island's high tide.

Vito Batista, a Brooklyn assemblyman, and Lee Sterling, citywide advocate for small property owners, started things off with a bang. "Mr. Thabit," Vito thundered, without waiting to be recognized, "tell City Hall that rent control is killing the small property owner. These good people are dying here. They can't keep their properties in repair because they can't charge a decent rent. Banks won't give them mortgages, and the city keeps fining them for violations. What the hell's going on?"

While Vito pauses for effect, Lee Sterling steps up to the mike. "NO MORE RENT CONTROL," he shouts over and over again. Pretty soon the hall is vibrating with landlord chants of "NO MORE RENT CONTROL" and Lee's follow-up message, "CUT PROPERTY TAXES."

Now the tenants are on *their* feet, shouting at the landlords. "We know you, YOU RUN A PIGSTY," yell several tenants. "When are we gonna get HEAT and HOT WATER?" yell a dozen more. Bedlam.

Somehow, through it all, Leo Lillard remains calm. After a few chaotic minutes, he stands up and raises his hands out toward the crowd, then lowers them, then up and down again, up and down, "That's enough, that's enough," finally quieting the crowd.

He addresses Vito Batista and Lee Sterling. "Mr. Batista, Mr. Sterling," he says, "tha . . . than . . . thank you for coming tonight and giving us your views." (He stutters a bit when he's excited.) "But we have a lot to do to . . . to . . . tonight, and if we're gonna save our community for the benefit of tenants and landlords, we better get to it."

Finally Batista and Sterling leave to a smattering of applause at the back of the hall, and the landlords take up the attack. I have barely gotten through my opening about the reason for the meeting (which was to offer landlords the opportunity to get a municipal improvement loan at low interest) when landlords reveal their own agenda—which has little to do with rehabilitating their buildings.

"I have two buildings on Hinsdale Street. Take them now, pay me later. I can't take care of them anymore. The tenants are not paying the rent. Last week, vandals stripped the plumbing from a vacant apartment on the third floor. They left the water running, and two apartments below the empty got full of water and the tenants moved. Out of twenty-four apartments in my two buildings, I now have only twelve tenants."

The tenant chorus: "You're a lousy landlord. Your buildings haven't had heat and hot water all year. And you never fix anything that goes wrong."

"Why can't the city leave us be? Every week, the inspectors come around and find violations. Why not? All my tenants are welfare tenants; they don't care about the building. I fix things and they break them. Is it my fault? Down south they never saw a toilet, and they come up here and throw chicken carcasses into the toilet and clog it up."

Another landlord: "Yes, that's the trouble. All we're getting is welfare tenants. Wherever people are being displaced, and the Welfare Department needs housing for them, they send them here. We've gotten hundreds of tenants from Brownsville, just west of here. The Housing Authority is tearing down blocks after blocks to put up new high risers, and the Welfare Department is relocating them all here."

After half a dozen more complaints about welfare tenants, I pondered solutions. It wasn't a good idea to concentrate a poverty-stricken population as heavily as was being done in East New York. The same thing had happened in Brownsville to the west.

"Maybe we can appeal to the Welfare Department to stop sending welfare clients to East New York," I said. "They already threaten to overwhelm social services and schools, as well as overcrowd the housing."

"NO, NO!" The landlords are screaming. "We NEED the welfare tenants. They're the only ones who will live here!"

The meeting gradually disintegrates. One not highly regarded contractor, George Jaffee, came to the front after the meeting and said he was interested in the Municipal Loan program. He pursued this objective, became interested in the whole improvement effort, and over the next few years rehabilitated half a dozen buildings under the Municipal Loan program.

LANDLORD-TENANT RELATIONS

The average white landlord, who might have barely gotten along with his aging Jewish tenants, failed miserably as a landlord of minority tenants. He believed blacks and Puerto Ricans would destroy his property, steal his fixtures, and not pay their rents. Many believed that blacks should be satisfied with the kind of housing they (the whites) had lived in forty years earlier (cold-water flats) and should be content with even less. "What did they have down south?" demanded one landlord, "Whatever they get here, it's better than they had. They've got no kick coming." With this mental set, half the landlords refused to make any repairs, to provide decent stoves or refrigerators, or to provide steady heat and hot water; 10 percent threatened eviction when pressed for repairs or services. Landlords also became angry at normal wear and tear and pressed overbearingly for their rent.

Naturally enough, tenants responded negatively to such treatment. While some welfare clients were docile and uncomplaining, others did not hesitate to take out their frustrations on both landlord and building. Some airmailed the garbage (threw it out the window), defaced the building, threatened the landlord (one elderly landlady was murdered by her tenants), refused to pay the rent and waited till evicted, or took other retaliatory action. All this made the landlord hesitant to enter his building to investigate complaints or to make repairs. He may even have become afraid to collect his rents. When the situation reached this point, the building could quickly be destroyed.

Welfare tenants were particularly subject to landlord vitriol. Though all landlords welcomed them as tenants because "nobody else will live in this area," landlords accused welfare tenants of withholding rents, committing acts of vandalism, and setting fires. A typical commentary was "The engine company keeps its trucks in the street; as soon as it comes back from one call, it goes out on another." Landlords wanted an end to rent control (which they claimed kept them from dispossessing unruly or undesirable tenants), a reduction in taxes, and police aid in keeping vandals at bay.

As the problems multiplied, many landlords tried to sell but found no legitimate buyers. The area had long since been redlined by the banks. Some finally unloaded their property to avaricious exploiters (black or white) who purchased houses (usually housing two to four families but often larger) with a minimum down payment. They then leased apartments to welfare clients through fronts, acting as rental agents (to get the agent's fee), at somewhat more than the going rate (because welfare paid more). They got the agent's fee and the tenant's security and rent and sometimes could almost cover their down payment with this money alone; performing minimum maintenance, moving welfare tenants from one building to another (to get more fees), effecting instant evictions, and pursuing other shady practices brought them high returns and prospects for ballooning their original investment. When city agencies finally caught up with such profiteers or their buildings were abandoned by tenants or vandalized, they simply walked away from them. A few welfare investigators were suspected of being in collusion with such profiteers.

The situation was not much different when landlords sold their property to someone who specialized in operating slums. Slumlords were simply more systematic in their exploitation of the property. They knew how far they could go in neglecting repairs without having their rents reduced; they knew the welfare bureaucracy and how to exploit it; they knew which tenants could be browbeaten. They were tough and wouldn't let the threat of physical violence stop them from evicting families that didn't pay the rent or were especially destructive.

Landlords who took out loans to improve their property were heavily penalized for their trouble. Since the banks would not increase the first mortgage, they were forced to seek second and even third mortgages. A second mortgagee, because of the higher risk, inflated the amount of the second mortgage to give him the higher return he insisted on. Thus a mortgage would be made out for $10,000, but the owner getting the loan might receive only $6,000. If the income was insufficient to maintain the building and to make the increased payments, the building would be neglected; both the tenants and the landlord would suffer.

Many landlords wanted out and wanted the city to take their property. They were close to hysteria at the two special meetings held for property owners, feeling badly used by both tenants and the city. One owner complained that vandals had stolen several thousand dollars' worth of materials being used in rehabilitation; others countered that he had stolen them himself and criticized him for not having a watchman. There were some landlords, primarily owner-occupants and those who had been able to make peace with their tenants, who wanted the area fixed up and rehabilitated. If they could get rid of the vacant buildings, get some new housing, and rehabilitate the remainder, they thought the area could be made attractive once again.

Exploration of the situation with landlords, tenants, community leaders, and the Area Services staff indicated that East New York's multiple dwellings could not be improved without a basic change in the ownership and management structure, as well as heavy investments in physical improvements. The combined effects of absentee landlords, small holdings, racism, lack of management experience, security problems, and speculation were to immobilize the area against any purely local efforts to improve it.

VACANT BUILDINGS AND LAND

A basic part of my firm's planning effort in East New York was to assess conditions in the community, including housing quality, community organization, social services, education, recreation, and transportation. The results of these surveys and investigations were presented to the community to help give the participants an idea of the overall picture, and as a prelude and guide to the planning to follow.

One of the first surveys to be completed and presented to the community was that of vacant buildings and land.[2] This survey identified almost twenty-five acres of vacant land throughout East New York and an additional twenty-eight acres in open space uses, some of which could be made available for development. While the bulk of this land was in small parcels, parcels of more than an acre were found in the Linden Boulevard area, and some opportunities for assembling sites with little displacement also appeared in the northwest quadrant. The basic idea here was to stage construction, building relocation housing for families who might be displaced for Target Area reconstruction, after which the Target Area rebuilding could take place. Unfortunately, it did not work out that way.

In addition to the vacant land, a total of 350 vacant buildings were found in the first survey. Most were scattered throughout East New York, and they were already weighing heavily on the community psyche. Residents feared vandalism and fires most of all, and building maintenance began to suffer throughout East New York.

The greatest concentration of vacant buildings, seventy-five of them, were found within the Target Area. These seventy-five buildings amounted to 17 percent of the Target Area properties, with more becoming vacant all the time. During the next four months, an additional twenty buildings were vacated in the Target Area, bringing building vacancies to 21 percent of the total.

One promising note was the decline in the rate of buildings being vacated during the summer months of 1967. This could have been partly a result of the Vest Pocket Housing and Rehabilitation Program.

Owners may have kept up their properties, hopeful of getting higher acquisition awards if their property was taken by the city while occupied, rather than vacant. Others may have been strengthened in their resolve by the promise of improvements in the area. Building owners were also fearful of the stepped-up demolition program, which could wipe out any hope of recovering their investment in a vacated building.

Nonetheless, the sheer numbers of vacated buildings and the rate at which they were becoming vacant raised serious questions about the efficacy of a Vest Pocket Housing and Rehabilitation Program of limited magnitude. Would the area continue to disintegrate while a rebuilding program was being implemented? Could vandalism be curbed and crime and fire rates sufficiently reduced to attract sponsors of middle-income housing, as well as tenants? One way or another, the questions would be answered.

HOUSING CONDITION BY BLOCKFRONT

Simultaneously with the vacant land survey, we undertook a survey of building conditions throughout East New York. Surveyors rated entire blockfronts on the basis of the exterior condition of the buildings. Since buildings in very different condition are regularly found on the same blockfront, the rating concentrated on measuring the percentage of buildings requiring a certain kind of treatment.

The results were illuminating (and depressing). In the highest rating category, where only minor repairs were needed, a disappointing 22 percent of the blockfronts qualified. In a reasonably well-maintained community, 80 to 90 percent would fall into that category. Rated in poorer condition was an additional 49 percent of the blockfronts, all of which needed more substantial maintenance and repair work, reflecting several years of neglect.

Fully one-fifth of the blockfronts had more serious problems, with most of the buildings needing extensive rehabilitation, though up to 20 percent of such a blockfront could be in good shape. Finally, in the last 8 percent of blockfronts, 40 to 80 percent of the buildings required gut rehabilitation or clearance.

With few exceptions, the better housing was found among the one- and two-family structures. Blockfronts with the highest ratings were invariably free of multiple dwellings. The interiors of multiple dwellings

were somewhat poorer than their exteriors would indicate (an impression reinforced by later interior surveys), while the one- and two-
family homes were in somewhat better shape. Despite this, even in the
one- and two-family areas, the bulk of the buildings required substantial work.

DESTRUCTION IN THE TARGET AREA

In the Target Area, where multiple dwellings and high densities were
concentrated, the poorest conditions were found. A planning surveyor
who rated building conditions in the most devastated part of East New
York in November 1966 wrote, "This looks like a redevelopment site in
the process of being cleared. Half the people have moved out, the rest
are in the process of moving."[3] He found furniture mixed with snow
lying in the streets, several weeks of accumulated debris and broken
glass on the sidewalks and in the streets, and dozens of vacated,
burned-out, and destroyed buildings, mostly small apartment houses,
their doors open, their windows smashed, standing there in mute re-
buke. At this point, almost 100 buildings out of 450 in the twenty-one-
block sector were vacant.

Following the blockfront surveys, building-by-building exterior
surveys were made in selected parts of the Target Area, followed by an
interior survey of selected buildings. Ten building types were identified
and surveyed in detail. A survey of tenants in the inspected buildings
was also conducted.

At the start of this intensified analysis, an imposing amount of information on vacant and partially occupied buildings was in hand. This
included a list of buildings on which searches and precepts (in preparation for the issuance of demolition orders) were being prepared by the
Department of Buildings, as well as building violations information. In
the assembly of this material, the staff of the Area Services office was an
invaluable resource, supplying details on buildings and landlords.[4] We
also had expressions of interest in rehabilitation under the Municipal
Loan program from a few landlords, as well as statements from many
landlords who wanted nothing more than to be bought out.

Initially, some fifty buildings were selected for detailed interior
surveys. In the end, thirty-five of these buildings were thoroughly inspected inside and out; the other fifteen buildings were vacant and

boarded up or were otherwise not easily entered. Following is a summary of the conditions found:

Exteriors: Of the fifty buildings, twenty-eight needed extensive repairs to restore the building to serviceable condition, or reconstruction of most if not all of the facade.

Public Spaces: Twenty-three of the thirty-five buildings whose interiors were inspected needed reconstruction of halls, ceilings, and floors.

Bathrooms: Half the seventy-two bathrooms had no sinks. Of sixty-one bathrooms rated, only one had tile floors or wainscoting on the walls. Fifty-two of the bathrooms required new fixtures; forty-nine required new plumbing. Only 17 percent of the bathrooms were rated acceptable.

Kitchens: Half the kitchen fixtures were in reasonable condition, but 70 percent of the plumbing needed replacement.

Apartment walls: Almost 70 percent (fifty-two of the seventy-four walls inspected) required complete replacement. An additional 10 percent needed replacement of up to 25 percent of the wall. Only thirteen of seventy-four apartment walls required only patching and painting.

Apartment floors: Almost half the seventy-one floors rated required complete replacement. A third required partial replacement; the remaining eighteen floors were rated in good condition.

Buildings surveyed were carefully selected to be representative of the most frequently found building types in the Target Area. The building types in the best condition constituted only 12 percent of the total, and most such units were found primarily on shopping streets, which were to be avoided by the plan.[5] When these types were excluded, conditions in the remainder of the buildings were found to be much more serious. For example:

Exteriors: Seventy percent were rated 3 or 4.

Public spaces: Eighty-three percent were rated 3 or 4.

Bathrooms: Only one of forty-four bathrooms' fixtures was adequate; 90 percent required new plumbing; 60 percent had no sinks.

Kitchens: Ninety percent required new plumbing.

Apartment walls: All apartment walls were rated 3 or 4.

The still-occupied buildings had been neglected for decades. More than 70 percent of the roofs needed replacement, evidence of twenty or more years of neglect. Landlords had been neglecting their buildings since World War II, claiming that continuing rent control and low rents prevented them from keeping their buildings in repair. The landlords were not losing money but were angry because they weren't able to charge what the market would bear. To summarize, the buildings were already in terrible shape when blacks and Puerto Ricans got there.

As blacks began to move in, the landlords intensified their efforts to get their white tenants out so that they could raise the rents. The tenants were reluctant to leave; they were working-class people and couldn't really afford to move. It took the terrible condition of the housing, the increased harassment, the rapid spread of the minority population, and the riots to finally force them elsewhere.

Once a busy shopping street, Sutter Avenue had become little more than a convenience shopping area, patronized primarily on weekends, with a growing number of vacant stores. Livonia Avenue, another shopping street in the past, was in somewhat better shape thanks to the fabulous success of the Fortunoff stores, but it was also on the downgrade. (Fortunoff's moved to Manhattan a few years later.) The community wanted these shopping streets improved and supermarkets and other new stores brought in. The future of Pitkin Avenue stores (another well-regarded shopping street), as well as of those on Blake and Dumont Avenues, was also in serious question.

The residents were overwhelmingly dissatisfied with their housing. Of seventy-four tenants interviewed, a third intended to move immediately or as soon as they could manage it. The average family had been in its apartment only sixteen months (compared with five to ten years in stable areas). Families wanted more space, a better apartment, and a better neighborhood, and many were looking for lower rents (they paid an average of $70 in 1967). A quarter of the families were willing to pay even higher rents if they could find a decent place.

Tenant interviews corroborated the incredible transience in the area. Fifty-nine of seventy-four tenants had been in their present apartments less than two years. The average length of stay in East New York was about four years. Of sixty-five tenants responding, forty-five had moved into East New York from outside the area. Sixteen of these had come from Brownsville, nine from Bushwick or Bedford-Stuyvesant, seven from elsewhere in Brooklyn, four from Manhattan, three from the Bronx, one from Long Island, one from Puerto Rico, and two from upstate New York.

This tendency to move in and out and around did not seem to be diminishing. When asked whether they would move if better housing were available in another neighborhood, the response was overwhelmingly yes. Three-quarters of the tenants would move. More than half would pay an average of $15 a month more for a decent apartment. The range of increases they would pay ran from $5 to $50.

Since the average yearly income was $4,200 for these tenants and they were paying an average of $72 per month rent, their willingness to pay more reflected the inadequacy of their present quarters. Tenants' complaints about their housing were typical of households living in the worst conditions. Only half the landlords made repairs when asked, and the general condition of the buildings indicates that only minor repairs were made in any event. In one case, a tenant was threatened with eviction after asking for repairs; utilities were shut off in five other cases.

That we were dealing with the very poor was indicated by the high percentage of unemployment recorded in the interviews. Aside from twenty-nine persons with jobs, fifteen respondents were unemployed but not on welfare, another twelve were on welfare, and five were living on social security or disability pensions. All of those interviewed, whether working or on welfare, were mainly interested in having a decent apartment in a decent neighborhood. (If housing in white areas had been more open to minorities, their needs could have been more easily satisfied and the transience and instability sharply reduced.)

While it usually takes some years for the final 10 to 15 percent of the white population to move out of an area that becomes 100 percent minority, this transition took only two months in East New York; the result of a riot between blacks and Puerto Ricans. There was no love lost between the two groups; they didn't even live in the same buildings.[6] In some parts of the area, you had to "show respect" to whomever laid claim to a particular piece of sidewalk. A black community leader tells of being stopped by a Puerto Rican group in front of a bodega:

"You gonna show some respect?" asks a small Puerto Rican brandishing a .38 pistol. The loungers draw in close, enjoying the confrontation.

The tall, elegant black opens his long overcoat, draws a .45-caliber pistol out of his waistband, and grins, "You want to play with that .38? Fine. I'll just play with this .45." He waves it slowly back and forth. The crowd draws back with a gasp, the Puerto Rican's .38 vanishes, and smiling broadly, he makes a sweeping gesture with his left arm up the street. "Pass right on through, my man. My street is your street."[7]

Excessive densities, lack of recreation facilities or jobs, street congestion, drug trafficking, and competition for housing were among the obvious causes of conflict.

Violent racial conflicts did occur, as reported by the *New York Times*.[8] In mid-July 1966, a water bag hurled by a white Puerto Rican burst near a black Puerto Rican baby. Soon after, a black youngster was shot in the back; three Puerto Ricans were knifed in the back. On the next night, Betty Powell was shot in front of her house on Alabama Avenue. Soon, hundreds of police and riotous youths roamed the streets, terrorizing nearby residents. Forty black tenants moved early the following morning from 397 and 401 Alabama Avenue, just after the departure of Puerto Rican residents from an adjoining building at 389 Alabama Avenue. Neighbors attributed the troubles both to Puerto Ricans who did not live in the area but sought to keep the community enraged and to Black Muslim families who lived in 397 Alabama Avenue.

During and after the riots, dozens of buildings were vacated, vandalized, and burned out, sparking a panic that drove out blacks as well as whites, poor as well as better-off families. As apartments became vacant, they were systematically vandalized. Plumbing was literally ripped out of the walls, with water flowing full force out of the broken pipes. If the apartment was on the top floor, the building was flooded, and the remaining families were often forced into the street. At the height of the destruction, buildings were being vacated at the rate of one every two days. This was the last straw for the remaining whites, and the area went from 90 to 97 percent minority during the late summer of 1966. Barely 200 white homeowners and tenants remained. From overflowing occupancy a few months before, the vacancy rate following the riot and its aftermath soared to 15 percent throughout the tenement area. The sector swiftly became a welfare dumping ground.

CONTINUING NEGLECT OF THE GHETTO

Early in our analysis of East New York's conditions and needs, the community presented its view that East New York was a step-community, lacking in almost every desired service and facility. Existing facilities were either poorly equipped, difficult to gain access to, understaffed, or staffed with hostile and indifferent people. Such new facilities as were being built neglected essential services and equipment (new schools without gymnasiums or equipment for hot meals, for example). Nor were schools being built fast enough to keep up with the growing demand.

Not only did the banks and the FHA redline the area while blockbusters ran roughshod over the landscape, but city services and needed capital improvements suffered, as well. In many parts of the surrounding community, schools, day-care centers, libraries, health centers, and playground facilities were being built, but few such items were earmarked for East New York.

The East New York community was understandably outraged by the city's 1967 capital budget. Two of the items had to do with an already completed school and a playground for P.S. 328. The remaining items were a laughable addition to the already scarce supply of community facilities for 100,000 people. They included a vest pocket park on New Jersey Avenue; a new swimming pool measuring 50 by 100 feet; negotiations for space for a welfare center to be located in the community; and an annex to P.S. 158, to be housed in a former synagogue. A temporary swimming pool, also in the capital budget, was installed in Linton Park for the summer. On the darker side, a proposed library to replace the existing one, still far from the heart of the area, was struck from the executive budget.

HOUSING IMPROVEMENT PROGRAMS

That little was being done about housing conditions in East New York was not surprising, but it was still shocking in an area of such desperate need. The community's request for middle-income and public housing had gone unanswered till now, nor was urban renewal offered as an option—which may have been a good thing, since renewal has often destroyed low-income communities rather than helped them. Middle-income programs such as Mitchell-Lama had been used in several areas, with little impact on the real problems ghetto communities face. A study of the planning needs of twenty-six local communities revealed the shortcomings of many government housing programs.[9]

The study roundly criticized massive public housing projects such as the 3,000-unit Fort Greene Houses in the University-Clinton area of Brooklyn. This immense project, all low income and mostly minority occupied, provided an almost impenetrable social and economic barrier in the larger community. Brueklyn Houses and other massive projects in Brownsville were having a similar effect in that community.[10]

An aversion to huge projects was not the only criticism of public housing. In some communities, even vest pocket housing and rehabilitation proposals of the New York City Housing Authority were viewed with alarm. At least one group with a strong tenant orientation had rejected such proposals, primarily because the Authority's "slum clearance" bias resulted in the selection of sites from which large numbers of people had to be displaced.[11] In many ways and in different situations, public housing has fallen short of giving satisfaction.

Until July 1, 1967, an Area Services Program served thirty-one blocks in the East New York Target Area and further south. Operated by the Bureau of Neighborhood Conservation of the HRB (Housing and Redevelopment Board), the program was designed to enforce housing and health codes in areas not being renewed and to assist landlords in removing violations and making repairs. No housing or health inspectors were assigned to the East New York office during the course of this study. The local staff worked with landlords and tenants and passed complaints on to the appropriate departments. Much of its work was concentrated on developing block associations with the help of Vista volunteers.

On July 1, 1967, the Area Services office was closed, and some personnel were transferred to Project RESCU (Repair Emergency Service Coming Up). This locally staffed operation was opened in an office on Bradford Street. Inspectors were assigned to this project, checking the findings of local staff to see whether emergency repairs were needed. Local residents were employed by the program, not only as inspectors but also as repair assistants. Sixty youths were in a repair training program. This was one of the more promising operations in East New York, though its scope was limited. If it showed real effectiveness, however, experience suggested that it would be discontinued, possibly because it demonstrated that effective intervention was possible after all.[12]

Parts of East New York, Brownsville, and Bedford-Stuyvesant were designated as a demolition program area financed jointly by the city and the federal government in 1967. The grants financed the demolition of unsafe buildings and were under way in East New York. Within the target area, the demolition staff had placed almost 100 buildings in an "unsafe building" category. Early in the program, demolition orders were issued for five of these buildings, with uncounted others to follow. The program encouraged many owners whose buildings were vacant and open to board up windows and doors. While it did rid the community of eyesores and fire threats, many buildings that could have been recovered and rehabilitated were demolished through the program and lost forever to the community.

While the demolition program was being set in motion, little attention was being paid to the basic housing problems. Redlining was in place; blockbusters continued their depredations and exploitation. In neither case did the city take the necessary steps to stop the practices. Unscrupulous and exploitative landlords remained an uncontrolled menace. The city did not drive such landlords out of business, nor would it take over their buildings. Its receivership program was token; its code enforcement effort remained without teeth; its rehabilitation program was barely off the ground five years after its initiation.

In response to the riots, the city finally began to recognize the needs of its ghettos. Mayor John V. Lindsay concentrated most of the city's housing resources in the riot-torn areas of the South Bronx, Bedford-Stuyvesant, and East New York. For East New York, 2,000 units of new and rehabilitated housing were promised under the city's Vest Pocket Housing and Rehabilitation Program. As described in greater detail in chapter 7, the community used these units largely to rebuild the Target Area, first, by reducing the concentration of the poorest families in the Target Area and, second, by adding moderate income housing to the Target Area mix.

How to deal with the violent and destructive sides of ghetto youth and the largely unresponsive uniformed services were among the other tough questions faced by the community. By 1967, the problems were still developing. Few answers were forthcoming.

5

The Uniformed (and Other) Services

IN SOME SENSES, a special zone of misbehavior was created in East New York, not only among some of its residents but also in the performance of its government services. In explaining the devastation and shell-torn look of ghetto communities, residents felt that the uniformed services (sanitation, police, fire) no longer responded to community concerns, that the services rendered were of inferior quality, and, all too often, that service levels had been sharply cut. Such falling service levels accompanied (and sometimes preceded) the movement of blacks and other minorities into aging neighborhoods. Sanitation services declined; growing school needs were neglected; parks deteriorated. The police became brutal and aggressive; they appeared to be in collusion with drug sellers. The whole situation deteriorated from one in which misbehavior was the exception to one in which it became the norm.

During the city's fiscal crisis in the 1970s, East New York was more than ordinarily battered.[1] Huge potholes went unrepaired. The Housing Authority's Linden Houses suffered the loss of fifteen provisionals (nonpermanent workers) who were doing all the grounds maintenance. Playgrounds and parks were unsupervised and rarely cleaned because of a 50 percent reduction in the workforce. In May 1975, the Children's Room at the New Lots Public Library was closed, and despite a United Community Centers (UCC) campaign to force its reopening, it never did. Most social service and health needs went unsatisfied.

By July 1976, 50 percent of the guidance staff in Community School District 19, along with about 200 teachers in twenty-five elementary and junior high schools, had been lost, resulting in higher class sizes.[2] Crossing guards were also terminated. The cuts in education were deepest in minority communities.

In July 1977, the city dropped two buses from the B-83 line from East New York to downtown Brooklyn. The result was a nine-minute wait between buses during morning rush hours. The remaining buses were so crowded that by the time the B-83 progressed from Ashford

Street (the beginning of the line) to Vermont Street, six blocks away, passengers waiting at Vermont Street were left on the sidewalk.[3] The cuts in bus service and the loss of 4,500 transit jobs was part of the city's solution to the fiscal crisis.

Not only local ghettos were made to suffer in this way. Whole cities have been subjected to disproportionate budget cuts. When blacks became the majority in central cities like Detroit and Newark and whites had completed their withdrawal to the surrounding suburbs, virtually all structural supports for interracial cooperation ended. Whites looked out for their own interests, regardless of the impact of their actions on blacks. Because allocating more money to black areas meant increased taxes and lower net incomes for suburban whites, racial segregation gave white politicians the perfect setup for limiting the flow of dollars to black-dominated areas. When state budgets had to be trimmed, white legislators, who represented a majority of the states' voters, cut the funding to the black-controlled central cities most sharply.

White politicians in New York City were also administratively and politically insulated from black voters and had no direct political interest in black welfare. While the ghetto population in East New York contributed heavily to the area's maintenance problems, the short staffing of—and studied neglect by—the uniformed and other services deserve much of the blame for the result.

Determined effort and enough resources could have produced a far different outcome. The streets didn't have to be dirty; youthful vandals did not have to roam destructively throughout the community; the trees, parks, housing, and other facilities did not have to be neglected. Health and social service needs could have been met. Even educational requirements could have been satisfied by putting new construction on a fast track, using available options creatively, and adding personnel and responsive programming (see chapter 9).

Incredible as it may seem, when the city did put its mind and muscle into it, it demonstrated how communities like East New York could be serviced, and how impressive the results could be.

THE CRASH CLEAN-UP CAMPAIGN

The Crash Clean-up program was ordered by Deputy Mayor Robert Price on February 11, 1966, fulfilling a campaign pledge by Mayor John

Lindsay. Assistant Commissioner Sid Davidoff, of the Buildings Department, was selected to coordinate the program. Twelve city departments were deployed on forty city blocks in the East New York tenement area bounded by New Lots, Sutter, Pennsylvania, and Van Sinderen Avenues. The local office of the Housing and Redevelopment Board's Neighborhood Conservation Bureau served as headquarters.

A scant two weeks later, on February 23, 1966, Mayor Lindsay released a report on the progress of the Crash Clean-up program.[4] The involvement and contributions of the Departments of Sanitation, Police, and Fire are detailed below. In addition to those efforts, Buildings Commissioner Charles Moerdler reported that, in the first full week of operation, the Buildings Department had completed inspections of 5,471 apartments and uncovered 8,075 violations in 617 buildings. Only thirty-eight dwellings remained to be inspected by Building Department crews.

By the end of the Crash Clean-up campaign, precepts for demolition of eighty "unsafe" buildings had been filed, and twenty-seven buildings had been boarded up. The Department of Real Estate, acting under the leadership of Assistant to the Commissioner William P. Tobin, deployed a ten-man crew from its Emergency Repair Program, which agreed to demolish the eighty buildings. To ensure swift and appropriate action, the department was in the process of razing three of the unsafe buildings. Its crew had worked closely with the Sanitation Department. The inspectional forces were withdrawn as soon as the crash effort was concluded, however, leaving most of the housing in the same condition as it was found.

Other examples of poor normal service were negatively documented by the special efforts made during the Crash Clean-up campaign. A site for a vest pocket park was selected and blacktopped, but the equipment for the park still had not been delivered three years later. Three hundred trees were pruned during the campaign, but nothing was done about the condition of the parks.

A modicum of health services was also brought into the area. More than 3,000 persons received X-rays, blood tests, polio vaccine, and tests for venereal disease and diabetes from a healthmobile. In addition, 415 health violations were found in 101 of 149 stores inspected, as well as 14 violations for short weight, failure to post prices, and meat tampering. Curb repairs were made, 449 holes in the street were repaired, and 640 sidewalk violations were recorded.

There is little doubt that the zeal displayed during the crash clean-up campaign was needed in East New York on a day-to-day basis. Added personnel and constant attention were essential to meet the community's multiple needs. The following sections describe how the uniformed services did their jobs, before, during, and after the Crash Clean-up campaign.

SANITATION SERVICES

Almost a year after the Crash Clean-up campaign, during the 1967 Christmas holidays, garbage was not collected in parts of East New York for nine days. A neighborhood newsletter issued on January 19 headlined its story, "REVOLT-ING." When the cold snap broke, the situation had not materially improved. Though the better streets in East New York were being swept, the tenement area was ignored. Although there was a six-day-a-week pickup schedule, garbage was collected only twice a week. Granville Payne and other irate residents picketed, demonstrated, and sent telegrams but never got more than temporary satisfaction.

The Department of Sanitation could do a good job. It showed what it was capable of doing following a riot in the summer of 1966 (months after the Crash Clean-up campaign in February and March). "In the aftermath of the riots," one report put it, "some sections resembled ghost towns. Accumulated debris lay untouched. Disemboweled cars and shattered glass blanketed the streets. There were dozens of vacated, burned out and destroyed homes and stores, their doors ajar, their windows smashed."[5] By 6:45 A.M. the day after the riots, the streets had been swept clean for the first time in months. The mayor's visit to the area during the riots the night before undoubtedly inspired the swift action.

A petition signed by hundreds of residents was sent to Samuel J. Keating, commissioner of the Department of Sanitation, at the end of 1967. It was circulated by the United Block Associations of East New York, whose president, Granville Payne, implored the commissioner to institute six-day-a-week garbage collection and associated improvements. There was no official response to the petition.

Another United Block Associations flyer, dated February 28, 1968, called for the Association to be "an independent voice in our community to demand our rights to city services (taken for granted in non-ghetto communities), and also to find the answers for the many wrongs we see all around us." The flyer announced a meeting on March 4 at the New Lots Public Library. The call to action was signed by Granville Payne and Bruce Rawlins, cochairmen.

In response to community urging, my firm looked into the quality of sanitation services in East New York as part of our work for the Model Cities program (see chapter 9). I met with Department of Sanitation representatives J. T. Lennon, director of operations, and George J. Ambrosecchia, of his staff, early in 1968. I was told that the entire area was in an alternate-side (no parking on alternate days) mode, but it was not well enforced by the police. Part of the area was in a six-day collection area, principally west of Wyona Avenue. I passed on the community's complaint that there was no six-day service, that residents were not served at all for more than a week during the holidays, and that Tuesday's collection had been missed. The department was not doing its job. Lennon countered that the community was not doing *its* job, and both men seemed to feel that otherwise things were okay. Because community complaints had not made much of a dent in their thinking, it seemed obvious that the district needed a shaking up, and I said so.

Seeing that I wasn't buying his argument, Lennon brought up the subject of the Crash Clean-up campaign, saying that when more men and equipment were made available, they were able to do a better job. They always ask for more men and equipment, he said, but don't get it. The inevitable assignment of insufficient equipment and personnel to poor communities made its way into the discussion.

Exaggeration of the amount of service given to the community was visible in departmental reports made prior to the Crash Clean-up campaign.[6] The reports stated that parts of the Target Area had pickups three times a week and parts had daily pickups using five trucks and fifteen men, with good results except for holidays and snow emergencies. I countered that the community had never received such service levels. On the other hand, the Department reports also acknowledged deficiencies; throw-out bulk, mechanical cleaning, manual sweeping, litter patrol, flushing, and towing of abandoned cars were all rated poor, with insufficient personnel assigned.

Early in the Crash Clean-up campaign, during the week of February 21–26, many improvements were reported: "For scheduled bulk, added three truck shifts; throw-out bulk, added one truck shift; mechanical cleaning, added tn-weekly;[7] litter patrols, added two truck shifts, two collector trucks, all with good results. For abandoned cars, added one truck shift, one tow truck; manual sweeping, made daily, one man, fair results. For cleaning yards and alleys, etc. four truck shifts, four cut-downs, and four men. All with good results."

During the following weeks, more improvements were noted. At the height of the project, seventy-eight men and six officers were used. For the last four days, forty men and five officers were used. Abandoned cars were no longer a problem; ditto mechanical sweeping. More manual sweeping was used. Signs that present staff was doing more were evident in throw-out bulk and mechanical sweeping results.

In each week, ninety-five New York City Buildings Department men also cleaned alleys and yards.

Maurice Spadaford, borough superintendent for Brooklyn East, signed each day's report with "Upon completion of street cleaning operations in any area, appearance is good. The next day, operations have to be repeated due to the habits of the residents. Constant, day to day, services would have to be rendered to maintain the degree of cleanliness required in the area."[8]

The Sanitation Department also reported that strict enforcement of alternate-side-of-the-street regulations by the Police Department during the Crash Clean-up campaign had enabled it to more effectively clean the streets.

In addition to its other efforts, the department had scheduled rubbish removal on a six-day basis. In one week, twenty-four truckloads of rubble had been cleared from six empty lots; nine abandoned cars were towed away; all streets had been washed, sidewalks swept, and summonses for improper garbage disposal issued.

Ambrosecchia said he had been in East New York about five weeks after termination of the Crash Clean-up program and found conditions good, though they had probably deteriorated since (it was now early 1968). The idea behind the program was to clean up the area; maybe it would stay clean. The program ran from February 11 to March 11, 1966.

The lack of sufficient equipment and manpower and the tendency of many of the personnel assigned to East New York to put in less than a full day's work were responsible for the poor state of sanitation in the area. While the poor habits of many residents contributed heavily to the result, they only highlighted the desirability of, perhaps even the necessity for, a joint Sanitation Department and community effort to improve conditions. Sid Davidoff, the Crash Clean-up coordinator, was convinced that the department had made a mistake in not involving the East New York community in the clean-up program.[9] If it had, he said, he believed the program would have had more lasting results.

Davidoff also felt that lower-level sanitation workers and police did not give the services they were supposed to give—and reported falsely to their superiors that they did give. He was also convinced that a lot of administrative red tape could be cut, citing the towing away of abandoned cars as an example. It can take a month to get an abandoned car towed away, but it took only one day during the Crash Clean-up campaign. Normally, a policeman fills out a form and turns it in; the form goes to headquarters, gets transferred to Sanitation Department headquarters, and makes its way down to the district, and the car finally gets towed away. While the clean-up program was in progress, the police handed the form directly to the coordinator, who handed it to sanitation men the same morning, and the car was towed away. Davidoff believed that neighborhood city hall coordinators could perform this kind of function.

A clear example of service cutting in the Sanitation Department took place during the fiscal crisis of the early 1970s. Garbage pickups were reduced to two times weekly south of Linden Boulevard and three times weekly to the north.[10] While most districts suffered service reductions, the ghettos were hardest hit.

THE NEW YORK POLICE DEPARTMENT

If there was an obvious lack of communication between the community and the Department of Sanitation, the breach was wider between the community and the police. While the Sanitation Department was accused of lying down on the job, the police were accused of harassment, as well. When irate residents called the Department of Sanitation about overflowing garbage cans in front of absentee landlords' buildings, the department referred the matter to police, who promptly ticketed cars parked in violation of alternate-side regulations but did nothing about the offending landlords. Also, normally, police did not enforce the alternate-side regulations, making the job of the Sanitation Department that much more difficult. When citizens complained about poor police work, they were likely to be harassed by visits from other police officers. Fires in vacant buildings were known to have burned for half an hour (watched over by police) before the first fire engines appeared on the scene. This practice was apparently an attempt to render such buildings useless to vandals and addicts, but it destroyed a great deal of housing in the process.

Police, fire, and sanitation staffs were mostly white and appeared to be as prejudiced against blacks and Puerto Ricans as were the landlords. They looked for failure, saw it in the filthy streets and high crime rates, and concluded there was no reason to extend themselves on behalf of the population. When police were seen drinking beer in their patrol cars or cooping (sleeping) in out-of-the-way places by citizens who had tried in vain to get prompt police response to the acts of vandals and thieves, bitterness and cynicism were the most likely reactions. Nor was the situation lost on youths and vandals.

The police were not as responsive to complaints as they should have been; yet they harshly ruled the streets, deciding which laws to enforce and when to enforce them. If offended, they would arrest a person for drinking beer on the street, yelling, playing a boom box, or even hanging out with a bunch of other kids. Those arrested were frisked and if they were carrying weapons, got more serious charges lodged against them; they were interrogated about other crimes. Residents distrusted the police and told them nothing; they were fearful of the drug dealers, as well. Drug dealers often avoided being caught in raids; it was as if they had been tipped off by the police.

In 1967, one out of three victims of murder, rape, felonious assault, and robbery in New York City was attacked in one of six police precincts, of which East New York's 75th precinct was one.[11] In 80 percent of such cases, the offenders and the victims were either in the same family or neighbors. A related survey of 10,000 American households by the National Opinion Research Corporation found that three and a half times more rapes, three times more burglaries, and twice as many aggravated assaults occurred as were reported to the police. Serious crime was rampant in East New York and other ghettos, but police attention to such crimes was never fully responsive.

In a single month in 1971, the New York City Police Department recorded more than 66,000 robberies, a "large proportion" of which were street crimes caused by youngsters who were raised in families where "some form of child abuse had been practiced," a police spokesman said.[12] At the same time, a visible police presence on East New York streets was almost nonexistent. Thus, while city policies in East New York concentrated youth from the poorest (and most abusive) families, creating a breeding ground for criminals, the police followed their own special rules, which did nothing to counter the criminal tendencies of the community's youth.

Many of the findings in the report of the National Advisory Commission on Civil Disorders, issued in 1968, could appropriately be used to describe police work in East New York.[13] Much of what follows was drawn from that report.

The commission cited deep hostility between police and ghetto communities as a primary cause of the disorders surveyed by the commission. In Newark, in Detroit, in Watts, in Harlem—in practically every city that had experienced racial disruption since 1964—abrasive relationships between police and African Americans and other minority groups had been a major source of grievance, tension, and, ultimately, disorder.

As the symbol of the entire system of law enforcement and justice, the police become targets of grievances against assembly-line justice in teeming lower courts; against wide disparities in sentences for similar crimes; against antiquated correction facilities; against the basic inequalities imposed by the system against the poor—to whom, for example, the option of bail meant only jail.

As Dr. Kenneth B. Clark told the commission: "This society knows . . . that if human beings are confined in ghetto compounds of our cities, and are subjected to criminally inferior education, pervasive economic and job discrimination, committed to houses unfit for human habitation, subjected to unspeakable conditions of municipal services, such as sanitation, that such human beings are not likely to be responsive to appeals to be lawful, to be respectful, to be concerned with the property of others."

In addition to a widespread belief that police brutality was a fact, blacks complained of harassment of interracial couples, dispersal of social street gatherings (often groups of youths), and of blacks being stopped while walking the street or driving without obvious basis. Verbal discourtesy was also noted. All such behavior, the commission said, was reprehensible.

Roving task forces or stop-and-frisk quotas were unacceptable. The commission suggested that abusive officers be reassigned elsewhere, that officers be screened for ghetto work, and that incentives be given for outstanding police work in ghetto communities.

The commission noted the lack of civilian complaint review procedures as well as police harassment. It also proposed that community police officers increasingly be used to patrol and learn about the community, and deplored the lack of blacks on the police force. (Blacks make up an average of 6 percent of police forces in major cities, compared with the black population percentage of 23 percent. As of 1968, only 5.4 percent of the NYPD was nonwhite.)

During the Crash Clean-up campaign, however, the Police Department took an entirely different tack. It assigned foot patrolmen to the seven foot posts on an around-the-clock basis as well as a motor patrol. During the thirty-day period, only forty-four arrests were made in the area, compared with four times that many in a typical month. Clearly, greater police presence (and perhaps more professional police conduct) was responsible for the reduction in arrests. More coverage was clearly required in East New York, where people could least afford the injuries and losses from robberies, beatings, muggings, rapes, and other outrages against persons and property. When the crash program ended, the extra personnel were also removed, and the crime rates reverted to normal.

The pattern was similar elsewhere. Residents of a large area in the center of the black ghetto in Hartford, Connecticut, were victims of more than one-third of the daylight residential burglaries in the city; yet only one of Hartford's eighteen patrol cars and none of its eleven foot patrolmen were assigned to the area.[14] White areas got greater coverage even though blacks called the police six times as often to report criminal acts.

East New York failed to get its fair share of police attention. By 1977, as one result of the fiscal crisis, the 75th Precinct had lost seventy policemen. To jump ahead to the present, in 1999, East New York's 75th precinct, with 2.8 percent of citywide felony complaints, was assigned only 1.5 percent of the uniformed precinct police force, just over half of what its crime rate merited.

THE FIRE SERVICES

In an era of fiscal austerity and declining urban resources, the political isolation of blacks made them extremely vulnerable to cutbacks in governmental services and public investment. If cuts had to be made to balance strained city budgets, it made political sense for white politicians to concentrate the cuts in black neighborhoods, where the political damage would be minimal.

The destructiveness of this dynamic has been forcefully illustrated by Rodrick Wallace and Deborah Wallace, who traced the direct and indirect results of a political decision in New York City to reduce the number of fire companies in black and Puerto Rican neighborhoods during the early 1970s.[15] Faced with a shortage of funds during the city's fiscal crisis, between 1969 and 1976 the Fire Department eliminated thirty-five fire companies, twenty-seven of which were in poor minority areas located in the Bronx, Manhattan, and Brooklyn, areas where the incidence and risk of fire was high. Faced with the unpleasant task of cutting services, white politicians made the reductions in segregated ghetto and barrio wards where the political damage would be minimal. Black and Puerto Rican representatives were unable to prevent the cuts.

As soon as the closings were implemented, an epidemic of building fires occurred within black and Puerto Rican neighborhoods.[16] As housing was systematically destroyed, social networks were fractured, and institutions collapsed; churches, block associations, youth programs, and political clubs vanished. The destruction of housing, networks, and social institutions, in turn, caused a massive flight of destitute families out of core minority areas. Some affected areas lost 80 percent of their residents between 1970 and 1980, putting a severe strain on housing in adjacent neighborhoods, which had been stable until then. As families doubled up in response to the influx of fire refugees, overcrowding increased, which led to additional fires and the diffusion of the chaos into adjacent areas. Black ghettos and Puerto Rican barrios were being hollowed out.

The overcrowded housing, collapsed institutions, and ruptured support networks overwhelmed municipal disease prevention efforts and swamped medical care facilities. Within affected neighborhoods, infant mortality rates rose, as did the incidence of cirrhosis, gonorrhea, tuberculosis, and drug use. The destruction of the social fabric of black and Puerto Rican neighborhoods led to an increase in the number of unsupervised young males, which contributed to a sharp increase in crime, followed by an increase in the rate of violent deaths among young men. By 1990, this chain reaction of social and economic collapse had turned vast areas of the Bronx, Harlem, and Brooklyn into "urban deserts," bereft of normal community life.

Despite the havoc that followed the reductions in fire service, the cuts have never been rescinded. Though segregation paradoxically made it easier for blacks and Puerto Ricans to elect city councilpersons by creating homogeneous districts, those elected were isolated, weak, and unable to protect the interests of their constituents.[17]

Not only did white politicians see little benefit for themselves in promoting black welfare, but a significant percentage were also racially prejudiced and supportive of policies injurious to blacks. To the extent that such racism existed, the geographic and political isolation of the ghetto made it easier for racists to make blacks easy targets for racist actions and policies. Poorer as well as better-off blacks made some gains; government willingness to expand welfare rolls during the 1960s and 1970s was a response to the growing power of the black vote.

In 1965, there were some 400 fires in the Crash Clean-up area, up to half of them in vacant buildings. During the Crash Clean-up campaign, the Fire Department completed 144 inspections and supplied a trailer for the dissemination of fire prevention information. This also would have been a good time to convene a brain-storming session involving the Fire Department, the NYPD, city housing agencies and the community on how to help preserve vacant buildings.

TOWARD SOLUTIONS

Any basic improvement in ghetto conditions requires that white society begin to accept its responsibility for those conditions. Whites are not simply putting extra dollars in their own pockets by their penny-pinching and discriminatory funding of ghetto communities; they are also actively responsible for the continuation and even worsening of ghetto conditions. If whites can be made to comprehend this and its long-term negative implications, it will be possible to return equitable funding to ghetto communities and to make some real progress. More active use of the courts and more creative protest movements could also pay big dividends.

Whether or not whites come to their senses, conditions in East New York could have been improved in the 1960s and 1970s by joint city-community efforts. A 1965 summer clean-up campaign in Bedford-Stuyvesant, sponsored by the Brooklyn Congress for Racial Equality (CORE), demonstrated that even streets such as those described in this chapter could be cleaned up and maintained.[18] By putting teenagers to work on the streets and communicating with residents, by enlisting the cooperation of the police and inspectional forces, by mounting a total effort, it was possible to clean up the neighborhood and keep it clean as long as the project lasted and the city cooperated.

A cooperative effort by the agencies and the community would have been the healthiest and most productive kind of action. The community's ideas and approaches to combating problems related to crime, sanitation, health, housing, recreation, welfare, education, and other areas could only have been helpful in what was a chaotic and volatile situation. The centralized bureaucracies had neither the flexibility, the imagination, nor the will to pursue solutions, nor could they readily perform their duties in difficult situations with inadequate forces. Working cooperatively with the community would have made a difference.

Close cooperation between city and community forces is a logical step leading to more local control of municipal services. While it does not yet affect the uniformed services to any great degree, some progress in empowering the community to participate in its own management has been made during the past two decades. In housing development, in the provision of social services, in health and education, local community efforts are proving to be as good as (if not better than) centrally provided services (see chapters 7 and 14).

On analyzing the Detroit riots, the planner and sociologist Irving Rubin found that it was better-off blacks that rioted.[19] They were totally fed up with being restricted, manipulated, neglected, and abused. Rubin called for changing the way American society treats blacks and for allowing blacks to control their own communities. It is an idea we must begin to take seriously; the establishment of local community governments with responsibility for municipal housekeeping and service functions should be high on every community activist's agenda.

6

The Youth of East New York

IN THE MID-1960s, there were a lot of young people in East New York. The average age was only eighteen years, compared with the twenty-five to thirty-five years in typical city neighborhoods. About 45 percent of the population lived in female-headed households, primarily large ones. Welfare families accounted for 30 percent of the population, averaging one adult and four children each. Not much adult supervision—or even adult presence—was available for this mass of young people.

While a good high school education can open the way to a decent job, the ghettoization of East New York overloaded the school system. By 1968, 6,000 pupils were on short time (less than a full school day) in thirteen schools. Portable classrooms were placed in six schoolyards, and 674 children were being bussed. About 30 percent of Jefferson High's students dropped out (or were expelled) every year; inferior administration, negligent teaching, and overcrowding were all to blame; racism was very much a factor. Fewer than a third of the students earned an academic diploma, and many if not most of these were white.

Little has changed since. In November 1996, Jefferson High was cited as one of forty-five city schools that had to shape up or face possible closure.[1] The school's reading, writing, and math scores were well below standard.

THE JOBS PROBLEM

As East New York kids reached their teens, there was more and more pressure to earn money. Many teenagers (unwanted or thrown out of their homes) needed a place to live and jobs that paid enough to live on. Others had to help support their families; some started families of their own. They wanted to be part of the community, but society didn't encourage teenagers to live on their own or to head families.

Local job opportunities were rare. There were few stores or other commercial establishments that had jobs for young people. In the 1960s, a local minister who offered several summer recreation jobs to youths for 50 cents an hour had twenty applicants for every job available. At the time, fewer than 40 percent of the household heads in East New York were gainfully employed. Welfare provided no pocket money, and adult drinking and drug abuse helped keep the cupboard bare.

For the average minority teenager, menial, part-time, temporary, low-wage, and dead-end jobs were all that were available. Adult blacks were little better off. Half as many nonwhites as whites held white-collar jobs.[2] Nonwhites were operators and laborers almost twice as often as whites and were service workers three times as often. Those with high school diplomas got almost twice as many full-time jobs as those without.

For a poorly prepared ghetto youngster, the job hunt could be totally devastating. Consider a typical young man in his late teens. He didn't have a high school diploma; he had dropped out years ago. He had applied for jobs and found that people didn't understand what he was saying. He had a tough time filling out an application, and nobody offered him any kind of a job. He looked into his future and saw nothing out there. He got the message: he stopped looking.

JOB TRAINING

Programs such as the Neighborhood Youth Corps provided low-paying service jobs in local and state government agencies. Hard to find, these positions taught work discipline, required few skills, and provided a little desperately needed money.

Real job training programs, especially good ones, were even more rare, never serving more than a tiny minority of needy youth. And, while such programs supplied needed skills, many young people had a hard time staying with them to completion.

An especially useful study that explored the attitudes and motives of Manpower Development and Training Act (MDTA) trainees and dropouts highlighted the problems.[3] There were thirty-six representative interviews, three dropouts for each completer, and three males to each female. Right off the bat, we find that only a third of the trainees completed the program. The desire to do better than one's parents was there, but the path to that goal was rock strewn and unclear. Many wanted the results of training but weren't ready to commit the time and effort required.

Many of those who dropped out had no history of working at all and no role model, such as a father who worked and supported the family. Inexperienced teachers sometimes precipitated dropouts by demanding that students progress faster than they realistically could. Feeling that they had failed themselves and the school, potential dropouts rarely discussed their problems with counselors.

While the trainees generally understood that hard work was necessary for success, many carried scars—of discrimination, humiliations, violence in the streets, and going back even further for some, the castrating oppression in the South. They needed counseling or psychotherapy to alter certain basic attitudes toward the world that interfered with their ability to develop and use their skills.

Most interesting was the high percentage of mothers who were widowed, separated, or divorced but who had held their families together. These women showed remarkable independence and resourcefulness in supporting their families after separation. Young males from such families generally completed the course or dropped out for good reason (illness in the family or financial problems).

The Job Corps was another type of program with promise. It removed young men and women from the perpetually disruptive environments in which they were born and raised and gave them a chance to break with their past. It gave them job training, though not always for the right kind of work. At least some East New York youth found their way into the program.

According to Congresswoman Shirley Chisholm, the Job Corps taught many of its members to get along with people of different racial, ethnic, and religious backgrounds. [4] Many of the girls at the Poland Springs Job Corps site, to give one example, came from trying, unpleasant community settings such as East New York. "They are tense, difficult, explosive young people. To see white, black, and Puerto Rican mingling freely and naturally in a relaxed and amicable way is a very impressive thing," said Chisholm. In this and other ways, she said, young people were beginning to mature through the Job Corps.

The Job Corps also provided many of its trainees with the first medical and dental care they'd had in years. In fact, half the trainees had never seen a doctor or dentist before.

"The Corps could be improved if administrators paid attention to what the kids want, not just to a bureaucratic agenda," said Chisholm. There were not enough recreational activities, not enough social life for a group of young women living in a remote area for a year or more, far from home.

DELINQUENCY—A HISTORICAL NOTE

It is not surprising that delinquency was high. It traditionally accompanies all newly arrived immigrant groups that find themselves in a strange locale. Back in the 1850s, it was Irish youth 12 to 24 years of age who were described as "thieves, cutthroats and murderers . . . roving in gangs from Corlears Hook to Canal Street and even onto Broadway."[5] Nor were blacks always lowest on the totem pole. According to an 1857 State Assembly commission report, "in some of the houses built for tenantry, Negroes have been preferred as occupants to Irish or German poor. . . ."[6]

Delinquency had not been a big problem in Puerto Rico, but it became one when Puerto Ricans arrived here. The language barrier made progress in school or anywhere else very difficult. Winter weather was chilling; housing was mean and expensive. Puerto Rican cultural values (male dominance, family authority, females as property) got an explosive shock in the New World. The independence, self-reliance, and assertiveness of American women and children were viewed as signs of sinful disrespect. Yet these "sins" were swiftly adopted. Children developed the smarts needed to survive violence in the streets and were equally "smart" at home.

Women and girls shook loose from the old norms. "I don't want you to pick me up after school anymore," said a twelve-year-old to her mother. "Nobody's mother picks them up." Discipline broke down; the men walked out or turned abusive; family disintegration and alienation between the generations followed all too easily.

For black children, racial hatred and discrimination was a typical diet. The heady dose of liberation blacks felt on moving north was quickly diffused. If they moved into a largely white area such as East New York or neighboring East Flatbush, whites called them "nigger" and screamed, "Go back to Africa" at them. They were harassed by cops. Every black child knew that Medgar Evers was assassinated by whites. In early April 1968, they all heard about Martin Luther King's murder, too.

What did all this spawn? These already troubled children were moving from a hostile but familiar environment (maybe the adjacent Brownsville ghetto or Manhattan's West Side) and were thrown into the even more threatening and volatile East New York. The tendency was to be aggressive, to respond in kind to violence, to join gangs for survival. Violence became epidemic; everyone was afraid; survival required so much of one's available energy that delinquency found a foothold and flourished. Little energy was left to prepare for the future.

The resulting disaster certainly wasn't all the youngsters' fault. A self-fulfilling prophecy was imposed on the young at far too early an age. The impoverished community's needs were enormous but largely ignored. Overwhelming needs for day care, more schools, health care, and other social services went unheeded. Nor has time healed the wounds. If anything, the problems of youth in East New York are even more serious today, thirty-five years after it all began.

PREJUVENILE DELINQUENCY

Even before we get to actual delinquency and crime, family breakups and calamities put many East New York youngsters in jail. Half the 100,000 children placed in prison-type institutions such as the city's Youth House every year were guilty only of being homeless, parentless, or friendless and were placed there by the courts until a final disposition of their cases was made.[7] While most families even in the ghetto did their best to provide their children with a decent and loving home, ghetto communities such as East New York contributed a major share of such inmates.

These children behind bars were just that: children. Eight-year-old Wayne kept "Peppers," a stuffed orange dog, on his cell bunk and crayons on a table next to his toilet. Kitty, Lupe, and Inez, from intolerable home and school situations, had their dolls and posters with them while they waited behind high wire fences and electric gates in state training schools for girls.

Children who were jailed were generally not helped to read. Illiteracy ate away at them and was one of the prime causes for children's breaks with school, family, and, ultimately, society. Many such children became juvenile delinquents, and up to 85 percent of juveniles repeated crimes after their incarceration. (In one Massachusetts facility, the rate of recidivism for boys under twelve was 100 percent.)

These were children whose state governments paid an average of $10,000 per child per year in the 1960s to keep them locked up. In March 1967, there was a plan to open small, twenty-five-bed community-based detention centers for children in all five New York boroughs to relieve overcrowding at Youth House, then under investigation on charges of brutality, sexual abuse, overcrowding, and neglect. The children in these proposed community-based shelters would continue to attend public schools. Nice idea, but, as with so many nice ideas, no action was taken. Space was not found, or the required staff could not be lured; the money was ultimately put to other uses.[8]

THE GANG CULTURE

With little adult supervision, young people gravitated toward peer group cliques and gangs where they found acceptance and identity. In 1967, the *New York Times* reported, Jose Colon read in the papers about Mayor Lindsay's calling the Devils (an East New York Puerto Rican gang) "a very bad crowd."[9] "They're not a gang," Mr. Colon said in response. "They're just kids. They run around the street; they don't do any damage. They're just kids who have to stick together. They can't walk down that street alone."

The children may have formed a gang to defend themselves, but gangs were also dangerous. Black homeowners along New Jersey Avenue accused the Puerto Rican band of vandalism and assaults, maintaining that it hurt property values. A picture accompanying the story showed about ten children climbing all over a trashed car. The Devils also tangled with a band of Italian youths from a housing project across Linden Boulevard.

Outside a neighborhood meeting at which residents demanded protection from the Devils, a patrolman became involved in a struggle with fifteen Puerto Rican youths across the street. Participants at the meeting rushed over to help; two of them were stabbed. Three Puerto

Rican youths were arrested for the assault. What are you supposed to do, the kids said, when the police put a choke hold on you!

According to the police, the Devils had twenty-five to thirty members, ten or twelve of whom were arrested in 1967 on charges ranging from glue sniffing to possession of stolen property. Quite possibly, the police arrests were partly punitive and were designed to demean and intimidate the gang. For their part, the Devils claimed 100 members and called their leader Mr. X.

A social worker asserted that only four of five of the older Devils were violent and that kids, some as young as ten years old, followed in admiration of their "elders'" fierce defiance of police and homeowners alike. The homeowners, whose cellars were being flooded by hydrants turned on by the kids, met with the gang and offered "to do something" for them, but the offer was rejected. The youths said they wanted respect. The confrontation ended in acrimony. "Every turkey has its Thanksgiving," said one youth.

ON THE STREETS OF EAST NEW YORK

I'm driving home from one of the weekly planning meetings. A gaunt, sneaker-shod teenager is squeezed into an H-shaped column, which holds up the elevated subway line overhead. It is midnight and cold. He stands perfectly motionless in the recess of the column, trying to become one with it. His eyes move alertly. Maybe he waits for an unwary passerby to mug. Perhaps he wants the comfort of the steel. Why is he there? Does he have a home? What accounts for this apparition, this young avenging angel? This totally isolated young man is one manifestation of the ghetto tragedy.

For the great majority who never got a chance at job training and for those who were poorly prepared, multiple failures and/or inner rage often frustrated any attempts to get along in society. Turning to crime often seemed the only way out of poverty and dependence. In the mid-1960s, teenage youths would walk down a street of two-family homes, ringing doorbells until they found one with nobody home. They would break a pane in a door and walk in. Neighbors would phone the police, who did not appear for an hour (often they would not respond at all). Meanwhile, the youths had burglarized the household and gone.

Literally hundreds of stores were vacated in East New York during the 1960s, but minority merchants had not replaced white ones. The fear of being robbed, vandalized, burned out, and shot had stripped the area of most commercial and retail uses except in peripheral areas and on major commercial streets. The few stores in the heart of the residential community were mostly tiny grocery stores or bodegas serving the immediate vicinity. Perhaps three-quarters of the money available for retail goods in the community had to be spent outside it.

It is frightening to contemplate the level of violence that existed in East New York.[10] In 1974, a commercial photographer who had just finished taking pictures in an apartment was set upon by three youths. His cameras were smashed, he was stripped of his clothing, his hands were tied behind his back, and he was thrown bodily out of a third-floor window to the street below. He suffered multiple serious injuries. The youths then stole his car. What could he have done to provoke such violence?

Fear for the safety of persons and property was great. In the industrial quadrant, businesses hired special guards to protect their premises and worried about whether employees could get safely to and from work. Landlords lived in fear of vacancies, since they were almost certain to attract vandals who would rip out the plumbing and fixtures and terrorize the remaining tenants. Parents worried about their daughters walking in the streets or in schoolyards in broad daylight; stories of muggings and rapes were common.

In the tenement area, where black and Puerto Rican youths engaged in turf wars in the summer of 1966, followed by pitched battles between Italian youths and blacks and Puerto Ricans, virtual martial law was declared as police swarmed the streets of East New York. By late fall, hundreds of black, Puerto Rican, and the few remaining white families had moved out of the area, touching off a wave of vandalism and crime that lasted well into the winter. By November, there were a hundred abandoned buildings and a 15 percent vacancy rate in the twenty-one-block area.

Unrest simmered throughout the winter. In May 1967, John Williams, executive director of the Council for a Better East New York (CBENY), declared, "The situation is . . . highly explosive, a potential volcano. . . . We are sitting on a vast reservoir of idle youth, and there is no program to meet their needs."[11]

"After last year's riots," said Frank Rivera, a TV personality-turned-activist and director of the United Negro and Puerto Rican Front, "we got five play streets and buses to take the children to parks and the beach. This year, not even that. And everything that caused the riots last year is still here." Though seventeen groups submitted proposals to the city for meaningful ways to deal with the needs of youth, as of the middle of May 1967 none had been funded.

In mid-June 1967, before the summer was fairly under way, a youth was stabbed in a racial incident in Linton Park in which black youths taunted white youths, not far from the scene of the previous year's riots. The whites chased the black youths; sixteen white youths were arrested following the incident. Vinnie Jones, executive director of United Youth in Action, and other community leaders worked hard to defuse the situation. The following day, bricks and bottles flew again as fifty white youths paraded around the park, shouting, "Two, four, six, eight, we don't want to integrate." They carried signs reading, "Down with black power" and "Whites were born free—Blacks were born slaves—Let's keep it that way." No further incident occurred. Still later that summer, police dispersed large groups of youths who were congregating near the riot area. Capricious arrests and harassment by police did nothing to improve the short tempers of youth.

In 1967, I drove past a roaring fire on my way to a planning meeting. There were no fire engines present, only a lone police car, blocking off the street. As it happened, the meeting had been aborted, and, after trying unsuccessfully to locate it, I turned around and drove home. I passed the fire again, half an hour later, and the first fire engines were just arriving, the fire roaring triumphantly away. I learned that fire companies typically responded to a blaze only after it had burned for a half hour or more, ensuring the destruction of the building's habitability. On the basis of my experience, I concluded that the fires were watched over by police, who would call the Fire Department in when a fire showed signs of getting out of control. Some 400 fires and more than 1,000 crimes (about a quarter of those that actually occurred) were recorded in the tenement area alone.

THE NEED FOR RECREATION

One of the keys to reducing youthful delinquency and crime is the socializing influence of recreation, the replacement of gang behavior with social behavior. Young peoples' recreation needs and desires are generally ignored and neglected, and the lack is most keenly felt in the ghetto.

As an example, public dances in East New York could have defused a lot of the anger and frustration on all sides. One of the books on the Watts riots of 1965, a minute-by-minute account, strongly hinted that if a dance for young people suggested by several young black leaders had been held at the start of the second evening, all or most of the violence (more than thirty dead, hundreds injured, 4,000 arrests, and hundreds of millions of dollars in damage and looting) after the first night could have been avoided.[12]

In the 1960s, NO DANCING was a common sign on juke boxes all over the city. It was (and is) nonsensical to have a law requiring a cabaret license before anyone can dance in public in this city. You could dance in any bar or soda shop before the cabaret laws were passed after World War II. You can do that now anywhere else in the civilized world. To curb the excesses of a few, a whole city's passion for dancing was hobbled. Dancers of the city, UNITE!

While the local community made heroic efforts to bring meaningful recreation activities to East New York, the city ignored all pleas for help. Centers like the Brownsville Boys Club were badly needed; the director of the YM-YWHA at the edge of East New York felt that the community needed another four centers like his, including swimming pool, gymnasium, bowling alley, meeting rooms, and lounges. A little ambitious, perhaps, but right on target.

At a meeting of East New York's United Youth in Action, the teenagers wanted all those things and more: handball and basketball courts, guards to take care of parks, lights for night activities, trees, a bowling alley, a "place with concessions that sells things . . . a kind of candy store, lounge or cafe, a hangout," amusement-park type games, a "discotheque with psychedelic lights."

Neighboring East Flatbush white youths wanted the same things as East New Yorkers, including places to hang out and dance. As one sixteen-year-old put it:[13]

> Our parks and playgrounds and community centers aren't fun, they don't meet our needs. We could use better bus services, and night centers in schools. We need the Farragut pool (a local swimming pool threatened by redevelopment). We need clubs and cafes on Utica Av-

enue, places to listen to music and dance, instead of drug stores and pizza places. And cops shouldn't bother us so much.

TODAY'S EAST NEW YORK—THE HARD ROAD BACK

According to the *New York Times* edition of November 17, 1996, the youngest ex-cons faced a difficult road out of crime. They got out of jail still young enough to go back to school; if they did go back, they were more likely to get a diploma or, failing that, at least a job.

But prison has not been the place to turn around the lives of youthful offenders. A survey of 100 youths six months after their release from Rikers Island found that twenty-two had been rearrested, and twenty-five had gone back to school, with four already having dropped out. About two-thirds of juvenile offenders were arrested again within eighteen months of their release.

Home and street life threatened to unravel any progress they might make and lured them back to criminal pursuits. Many were refused enrollment in their old high schools, especially if they'd caused trouble in the past. Others had family responsibilities, which interfered with pursuing that elusive diploma.

More useful have been programs like City Challenge.[14] Youths were enrolled in City Challenge as part of their criminal sentence. The program, started in Bedford-Stuyvesant, was a boot camp that took youngsters for five months, schooled them, kept them focused, and helped them with their living arrangements and family problems. Tim, a young man enrolled in the City Challenge program, went further with his school work than he ever had before. Counselors helped Tim persuade his mother to get AIDS treatment and arranged for a foster home when he informed his counselors that his father was dealing crack.

But, when the youngsters had served their time and left the camp, it could get rough. When Tim's City Challenge sentence ended, he was sent to a large public high school. He cut classes and came to the attention of the "special ed" (enforcement) section, and the pressures got so bad that he just quit school. Over the summer, he was charged with a misdemeanor for being in a car where a gun was found. But he really wanted to make it. He stopped hanging out and started doing needed work on his foster family's garage. He wanted to get back into the City Challenge program.

Spurred by recidivism, jail crowding, and cost (up to $90,000 a year for a youth in jail), the *Times* story said that correction and schools officials were trying different ways of luring young ex-cons back to school. But it wasn't easy without spending some money, and not enough was being allocated for the purpose. Extended City Challenge–type programs, reinforced with stipends as needed, should have been available to all youthful offenders, and to noncriminal dropouts, for that matter. Many more kids would have been able to stay in school if they had had a little money.

While there are pros and cons to this idea, I believe that jails should also be established in the local community for nonviolent youthful offenders as an alternative to sending them to some faraway detention center. A youngster or teenager could go to school or work in the community by day and sleep in the detention center at night. This would keep the young person in the community, help in his rehabilitation, and reduce the drift toward isolation and estrangement. It would also save money in jail construction and operating costs.

Lisa Lovejoy was sixteen when she helped two other girls attack and stab a man nearly to death in a Queens subway station (he had tried to rape one of them).[15] She served a year in jail. When she got out, she was placed in a large public high school, but that didn't work. School officials then recommended placement in the Murray Hill Borough Academy, which has only 135 students. The school had strict attendance requirements and provided counseling and a jobs program. Lisa, who saw a parole officer once a week, managed to do well, using the school as a partial escape from life's hardships: her brother's murder, the fatal shooting of her boyfriend, the pressures from "the fellas" to sell drugs or to sell "her little bit of stuff." "I don't want to be out there collecting cans . . . selling drugs . . . selling my body. I don't want that to be me." Lisa graduated in June 1997.

TODAY'S EAST NEW YORK—A VIOLENT PLACE

Violence is still pandemic in East New York; it touches all aspects of community life. Gangs are even more violent and have expanded their drug selling, prostitution and other criminal ventures. What was true thirty-five years ago is even truer today. Places like the Cypress Hills Houses, a vast housing project on the eastern edge of East New York, and Unity Plaza and Brownsville Houses, on the western edge, were some of the most dangerous spots on earth.[16] In 1992, eight people were murdered in the Unity Houses complex alone; one building was so deadly that the Housing police called it "the slaughterhouse."

A burner, a jammie, a bis (for "biscuit"), a kron, a four-fifth (.45 caliber), an oowop—there are a score of ever-changing names for the gun, the most recent scourge of Brownsville and East New York, the one single element that has changed a desolate existence to a nightmare.[17] The gun is the drug of choice for the young now, releasing them from the shadows of doubt into the white light of power and respect or death. Trying to control the contagion of weapons, Thomas Jefferson High School installed metal detectors at its doors.

Sharron Corley is a teenager who had some acting talent and personality, and he wanted to make it big.[18] But standing in the way was the culture of the streets, where you had to show you were not a victim and were part of what went down. Every time this young man left home, there was the possibility that he would not come back. He was alive, but always close to death. So he ingratiated himself with a gang, stole coats and other clothing from Bloomingdale's to prove he was worthy, and then did six months for stealing a coat from a kid who fingered him from photos shown by the police. He had jobs and he left them, then transferred to the Satellite School, determined to make it.

Sharron's decision to transfer from Jefferson High to the Satellite School is neither capricious nor unusual. Things are so wild in Brownsville and in East New York that more and more students opt to attend schools in distant communities, even in neighborhoods that are also rough in order to cut down their chances of catching a bullet, either as a bystander or as the object of a vendetta. Mothers play a deadly game of chess with their kids. When parochial schools still existed in East New York, more than a few black families converted to Catholicism so that their children could attend them. Some, like Nettie Epps, sent her son Trevor (who fingered a killer to police) to South Carolina for the school year to get him out of harm's way. Margaret James sent her son to South Carolina, but he couldn't stand the quiet and came back to Brooklyn and very serious trouble, ending up in jail for thirty years for selling heroin and cocaine. Others don't have the resources or family to make such tactical maneuvers.

Sharron enrolled in a theater class. One exercise found Sharron cast as a witness to a street crime. A lady screams, "Help me, please!" as a mugger grabs her bag in which her rent money is stashed and then heads toward Sharron, who is ready for anything and not a victim to be bothered by anyone. The mugger passes Sharron who steps smoothly aside, and the thief is gone. His classmates nod approvingly. In the students' eyes, to help someone in trouble is misguided and dangerous. A sad commentary on the local value system—bolstered as it is by government neglect.

Five hundred mostly black and Puerto Rican freshmen arrive every September to go to Jefferson High, many of them from social work caseloads.[19] That suggests that 500 should graduate every year. Of the graduating class of 120, maybe only seventy-five have fully earned a diploma. The rest have to go to summer school to get the extra credits they need. If you eliminate the Dominicans, Guyanans, Jamaicans, and Barbadans, you are left with perhaps twenty-five African American graduates.

Mrs. Beck, the uniquely passionate principal of Jefferson High during the early 1990s, tells her basketball players that they won't be on the team if they don't attend classes and get the grades needed to qualify. They must go to class; they must go to study hall. And she won't have them on the team if they embarrass the school in any way. They shouldn't wear hats because it makes them look like hoodlums. "You are not hoodlums. You are talented stars." But the boys wear hats and hoods to have some protective coloring as they walk home through hostile territory. The ski masks and goggles the kids in Crown Heights took to wearing gave the chilling impression that they didn't want to be identified.

Vassar gave two Jefferson High girls scholarships. Both had high grades but combined math and verbal SAT scores of only about 750. The Vassar standard was about 1250. The 750 score was not just low; it was very low. The low scores spoke of the war zone conditions they came from. The best and brightest of Jefferson High could barely qualify for a good private college. Worse yet, there was a probability that these young women would never make it through Vassar.

Violence erupts out of nowhere! Milton Lowers was shot along with his friend Rodney James when they made the mistake of visiting the Linden Houses. As they left 570 Stanley Avenue with a girl friend, they were followed and shot by a young man named Randolph, who knew that Lowers was a friend of Dupree's; Dupree is known as Lhalil's man, part of a rival gang. That was all it took—the wrong friend, the wrong project. Lowers was hit in the left thigh, his femur shattered; James received one bullet in the stomach. A dozen more .45 shells blasted the trunk and back window of a faded green Cadillac that sat by the curb. The shooter was ultimately caught at Rikers Island, where he had turned himself in on a prior charge.

If the idea behind criminalizing ghetto youth is to separate them from the mainstream, the effort is having the opposite effect. Ghetto youngsters are a driving force behind pop culture throughout the world.[20] Young white kids watch with rapt attention everything they do and say. If they wear their baseball caps backward, their trousers low and loose, kids in the suburbs are quick to emulate. In a year or two, lines outside trendy clubs in Paris and Tokyo are filled with would-be home boys in backward caps and droopy pants. The droopy-pants look comes out of the house of detention, where belts are confiscated to prevent suicide and mayhem. Bizarre, but true.

TODAY'S YOUTH—AT HIGH RISK

Though juvenile (youth under sixteen years of age) arrest rates are very high in East New York, they mask the true extent of violence in the community. Only four of the city's fifty-nine community districts amassed more than 350 juvenile arrests in 1996; East New York was among them, with 402 arrests in that year.[21] Total juvenile arrests dropped to 304 in 1997, 283 in 1998, and 266 in 1999; possible explanations for the drop include a continuing decrease in the number of young people or a reduction in the attention being paid to their escapades.

East New York youth ages sixteen to twenty were the targets of 994 felony arrests and 836 misdemeanor arrests in 1996. In 1998, there were 949 felony arrests and more than 1,100 misdemeanor arrests. Felony arrests dropped in 1999 to 840, a drop more than offset by an increase in misdemeanor arrests to 1,285. The increase in misdemeanor arrests was due to "Operation Condor," in which police were given arrest quotas to fill. At least for older youth, the beat goes on.

A more complete picture of East New York violence appears when the children themselves are asked about it. A 1994 survey of 850 sixth-, seventh-, and eighth-grade pupils in East New York's Intermediate

School 302 showed that 33 percent of the children claimed to have "badly beat" someone in the previous four months. Twenty-six percent said they had carried a weapon at least once during that period. Fifteen percent claimed to have robbed someone, and thirteen percent said they had been arrested.

Given psychological testing, half the students exhibited symptoms of severe posttraumatic stress syndrome, a relentless cycle of recalling, then repressing the memory of a traumatic incident. Another 27 percent showed mild to moderate symptoms. Less than a quarter of the students seemed to be at peace with themselves. The community's basic fight-or-flight pattern has continued to feed on itself for the past thirty to thirty-five years with no letup in sight.

In 1995, Mary Ann Fenley, spokeswoman for the U.S. Centers for Disease Control, reported that, "murder is the second leading cause of death for fifteen to twenty-four-year-olds, second only to car accidents, and the rate is increasing. If you take children and place them in settings where there are high rates of conflict and threat and hostility," she went on, "their bodies will react to living in that sort of environment."

Across the nation, health statistics show increasing levels of youth depression, suicide, and, as the East New York survey shows, posttraumatic stress syndrome.

Youths join gangs for a variety of reasons, all stemming from the hopelessness of their situation—badgering by police, scorn from their teachers and all of white society, and, all around them, poverty and violence.[22] Many kids who belong to gangs believe that the gang loves them and will take care of them. They are brainwashed and gradually withdraw from family and other friends and society and depend completely on the gang. Many, if not most, such gang members end up dead sooner or later. Even if they want out, they often feel it is too late, that they are tied to the gang forever.

Sometimes, the police ask gang leaders to let a kid out of a gang because he wants to go straight; sometimes they let him. A kid can leave a gang, but he may have to move out of the neighborhood and go to a different school to escape. Gangs rarely try to follow such kids and punish them for leaving if they go far enough away.

Young people need counselors to help them. They need help recovering from addiction and from substance abuse and help to straighten themselves out. They need to get completely away, totally out of the culture. Once they solve these problems, they can become mentors of other youth. Mentors meet once a month or more with the youngsters, help to aim them in the right direction, go places with them, and provide someone to talk to. They give moral support, help with career and educational choices, and so on. It does a lot of good, and the agencies, such as Catholic Charities, that sponsor such programs try to match volunteers with the right kids. Hundreds more volunteers are needed.

While taping teenagers who were trying to make it back into the mainstream, Zachary Brown, of the New York City Department of Health, found that the young people saw violence as the most rational response available.[23] A quick and violent reaction may dissuade future attacks by onlookers. Young people's life experience indicates that this is the most effective strategy, since it is the same strategy used by those in power in their lives—their parents and the police. A beating subdues most impulses and is faster and easier than an explanation. At the same time, many wished they'd had some adult presence in their lives to point them in the right direction. They mostly drifted into doing bad things through peer pressure. Brown also found that when kids tried to go straight and make it back into the mainstream, they were the most vulnerable. It was all too easy to forget the violence all around them and think that they were now immune. They were no longer always on the defensive; they were caught without firearms, or they walked through previously hostile territory unprepared. Many became victims of their old gangs or friends.

Zachary was going to film some of these teenagers and gave them improvisations to act out. All these teens had had antiviolence training and appreciated it. In one scene, each teen was told that his jacket had been stolen, and that he had rushed home and run into his house. Once inside the house, he was to improvise. More than one youth ran into his house and yelled out, "Where's my bat?" The moral was that antiviolence training is all right but that it takes more than a brief exposure to overcome the violent reactions that permeate everyday life.

How to steer children away from violent behavior? One suburban Philadelphia elementary school-based program provides conflict resolution training for all children, starting in kindergarten. Parents of children who still exhibit behavioral problems in first grade or beyond are encouraged to enroll themselves in counseling classes while keeping their children in a program of weekly counseling, academic tutoring, and social-skill-building "friendship groups." Most children reportedly succeed early in overcoming their own hostile impulses.

Should conflict resolution be a required course in East New York? You bet your life it should!

7

Vest Pocket Planning

IT IS AGAINST the background of the six previous chapters that I undertook to develop a housing improvement program for East New York. On November 9, 1966, I was standing with Eugenia Flatow, Mayor John Lindsay's Assistant for Program Planning, as she announced the beginning of the city's Vest Pocket and Rehabilitation Program in East New York. She introduced me to the 150 residents as the planning consultant who would work with them on the plan.[1]

For perhaps the second time in my experience as a planning consultant, I was being employed by the City of New York to prepare a renewal plan that met with the approval of the local community. Usually, I was on the other side, opposing the city's plans, which displaced the poor for luxury development. Because of the summer's riots in East New York, the city was going out of its way to do things the community's way.

Blacks and whites were well represented at the meeting. Leaders of antipoverty programs, block associations, settlement houses, churches, institutions, city agencies and community organizations were in attendance, as well as tenants, homeowners, landlords, and businessmen.

Community people spoke up, angrily recalling promises made—and broken—by the city in times past. "It takes a riot to get you down here, and after the fuss dies down you disappear and leave things as they were." Some recited the community's long list of needs and concerns, urging the city to keep its promises now, before it was too late. "It's already too late," others said. "East New York is already dead."

At this point, East New York was both in poor physical shape and socially unstable and threatened to deteriorate further. The rate of juvenile delinquency had risen rapidly over the past ten years, as had rates of welfare dependency, crime, and fires. In Brownsville, where rates had risen similarly a decade ago, they had not declined after peaking; they continued on a high plateau. In areas such as Brownsville and East New

York, the malignancies fed on themselves; outside help was needed to break the cycle.

This was the situation with which the community, and its consultants, had to grapple. Community organization was in a fragmented and transitory state; only a few organizations had been in existence for more than two or three years. At this first meeting, the assemblage elected Leo Lillard, a young black activist, as chairman, and Sara Ross, an outspoken white liberal, as vice-chair. Before the meeting ended, Leo proposed that anyone attending the planning meetings would be considered a member of the planning committee. The idea was adopted unanimously.

When I was introduced, I stated that the objective of the program would be to locate between 800 and 1,000 units of public housing, combined with an equal amount of middle-income housing, that would help restore East New York's attractiveness as a place to live. The major question to be answered by our studies and community preferences was where to concentrate the rebuilding effort. We promised to work with the community, to undertake studies and to map conditions, to help develop nonprofit housing sponsors, and to keep the community informed.

EAST NEW YORK'S PLANNING ACTIVISTS

To understand East New York's planning process, it is useful to know something about the major players, because it was primarily these people whose views, interplay, and ultimate consensus determined the outcome.

In any discussion of East New York's movers and shakers, Leo Lillard, a black activist, stood out, first because everyone recognized that he would not personally benefit from anything that happened and second because people would follow his lead. Leo was direct and to the point, kept his eyes on the goal, and, if unsure of something, took the trouble to learn about it. Almost before the vest pocket planning program had gotten off the ground, Leo enrolled in Hunter College's Graduate School of Planning and quickly earned his master's degree. He became fully conversant with the planning process, made many suggestions in both the vest pocket and Model Cities planning programs, produced more than one plan of his own, and helped keep the planning effort on track.[2]

Though he never hesitated to expose wrongdoing, Leo was always careful to give someone an out or to propose a solution that would allow the person to save face. He made a few mistakes; he was, after all, human. Yet he came close to being an ideal leader.

Sara Ross was middle aged, white, probably a member of the Communist Party, an indefatigable worker, a liberal, a welcomer of blacks to the community, an apologist par excellence: "We didn't have a riot. It was just an incident." A long-time resident and homeowner in East New York, she had community improvement as her basic agenda, and, though not rigid about where to put new housing, she favored rebuilding in the tenement area. Elected to co-chair with Leo Lillard, she often took minutes of meetings, as well.

When we first started work in the community, David Stoloff, of my staff, met with John McGrath, president of the East New York Savings Bank, and persuaded him to map the bank's loan commitments in East New York. Though the bank had already redlined the area, McGrath was astonished at how deeply invested in the community the bank was, and he became a strong supporter of the vest pocket planning effort. It was around that time that he hired Marshall Stukes to oversee the bank's interests in East New York.

Marshall Stukes was one of the regulars and served on the executive committees of both the Vest Pocket HUPC (Housing and Urban Planning Committee) and the still-to-be-formed East New York Nonprofit Coordinating Committee (ENYNPCC). Marshall was black and leaned in the direction of black power, though his position as a vice president of the East New York Savings Bank kept him circumspect. Much later, as if to emphasize his separatist leanings, Marshall joined Louis Farrakhan's 1998 Million Man March in Washington, D.C.

Granville Payne, a homeowner, was president of the United Block Associations. A black man, Granville, incensed by the poor sanitation services given to the community, organized the United Block Associations, circulated petitions, and led protest rallies in front of Sanitation headquarters. All this proved fruitless; sanitation services remained terrible. Yet Granville Payne persisted, became a stalwart contributing member of the vest pocket planning committee, more than once chairing meetings in Leo's absence. So great were his contributions to the community that New York City Councilwoman Priscilla Wooten got City Council approval to subname Pennsylvania Avenue Granville Payne Boulevard.

Another major supporter of the planning committee's work was Leo Fiorentino, a small Italian man who couldn't stand racism in any form. He made many speeches at committee meetings, deploring the violence between blacks and Italians, and worked hard to bridge the gaps between races and ethnicities. He, too, was recognized for his work by the community; one of the NYCHA housing projects on Pitkin Avenue was named in his honor.

Bill Wright was an ambassador without portfolio, a black wheeler-dealer who also had the best interests of East New York at heart. Though not a member of the vest pocket planning committee's executive committee (quickly formed by Leo Lillard), which held a meeting December 22, 1966, Bill Wright, then a youth program director, and Virginia Dawkins, director of the East New York Area Services Project of the HRB (New York City's Housing and Redevelopment Board) also showed up. To the idea of building on vacant land south of Linden Boulevard and integrating that part of the community, Bill Wright and others said they didn't want to run from bad conditions; they wanted to build for their own community, solve the problems where they were, and develop pride in race and community. The blacks present didn't think the city was interested in integration but did believe it was ready to invest in community facilities and housing. The meeting ended with the feeling that most attention should be given to the Target Area, with some given to deteriorated parts east of Pennsylvania Avenue.

On the other side of the argument stood Evelyn Millman, president of the board of the United Community Centers (UCC), which was wholly committed to integration. The UCC sought to develop a coalition of working-class blacks and whites along Marxist lines, successfully organized young people, and was an important activist neighborhood organization.[3] Millman favored building public housing south of Linden Boulevard to integrate white Canarsie to the south. She also favored building garden apartments in the Target Area as a way of reducing the density. This was not a bad idea, but the housing need was perceived to be so great that it was not seriously considered.

Frank Rivera was a Puerto Rican activist. A few years earlier, Frank had been a television reporter, but he gave it up to help the struggling East New York community. He became Director of the Council for a

Better East New York (CBENY), and vigorously supported every progressive idea or needed program. He, too, favored rebuilding in the Target Area as a first priority.

Vinnie Jones, executive director of the United Negro and Puerto Rican Front, was another of the major players. He typically assigned an aide or a protégé to represent the organization on committees but hovered in the background, watching everything like a hawk. When he did speak, people listened.

Juliet Greene, a middle-aged white woman, was a strong supporter of the planning effort, as well as the relentless force behind the drive to get a real health center for East New York. She made regular trips to a clinic at Brookdale Hospital three miles away and was outraged by the circuitous and time-consuming trip that she always faced.

Paul Gertz, a Jewish shopowner, represented the commercial interests on the committee but was a very dedicated member of the committee as well. The same could be said for Don Haymes and Nicholas Van Valen, both white, both active church members.

Among the most active organizations were CBENY, the East New York Civil Rights Association, the United Block Associations, United Community Centers, the United Negro and Puerto Rico Front, United Youth in Action, and the Louis Pink Tenants Association. Representatives of many churches and synagogues attended one or more meetings, and several religious institutions ultimately became housing sponsors.

To be candid, blacks and black interests dominated the planning effort. Though many Puerto Ricans attended the sessions, including a few organizational leaders like Gilberto Matos and Al Sanchez, most were not very active in the decision-making process (Frank Rivera was a sparkling exception). Similarly, while many whites attended the meetings and spoke up as much as anyone, black thinking and interests dominated the discussions. It was not that other needs or ethnicities were ignored, just that the blacks were more attuned to active involvement in the organizational and planning work.

VEST POCKET PLANNING

The first planning meeting, held on December 10, was announced at the kickoff meeting in November. About fifty people showed up, representing a variety of organizations and individuals. Most of those attending were black; many were Puerto Rican, and there were fewer whites, mostly Jews and Italians. My short presentation repeated the objective of the program and expressed the hope that the planners and the community would reach agreement on the decisions to be made.

At this first session, people again voiced their grievances and frustrations, pointing to issues other than housing that needed to be addressed. Many of the community's needs (aside from housing), such as better sanitation services, police protection, schools, recreational facilities, and a hospital, health center, and an outpatient facility were raised, many more than once. More than one person brought up the Parks Commissioner's visit to East New York the previous year, which, they emphasized, was the last they'd heard from him.

They were tired of surveys and analyses; they were suspicious of the city and its consultants. They wanted to know right off whether this was really going to be planning by the community or community manipulation by the city. "Why don't you tell us what your plan is," several said. "You know you wouldn't come into East New York if you weren't sure of what you were going to do." We answered that the studies now being undertaken would help both of us to make the needed decisions.

We met again on December 19, 1966. Again, we were asked what we had in mind, but our surveys and studies were just getting under way. As the meeting developed, a host of issues aside from housing surfaced. Numerous proposals and questions were of concern to many of the attendees, whose input touched on a number of other areas, including these:

- A new Jefferson High School field, some twenty blocks away, is being proposed: "That's too far."
- Will the community get Model Cities money?
- East New York should have its own college.
- We need an educational park.
- Is urban renewal slated for Area 15 in Brownsville?
- Is an industrial park really being proposed for the industrial area in the northwest?
- When are we going to get the swimming pool we were promised?
- A youth center is desperately needed.
- We need a health center or a hospital.

- We should get rid of the terrible factories along Van Sinderin Avenue.

The best location for new and rehabilitated housing did get some attention, with some people wanting to act in the worst areas, while others favored areas east of Pennsylvania or south of Linden Boulevard. As previously noted, representatives of the Target Area wanted the new public housing to be built in the area to house present residents. Other interests, primarily from east of Pennsylvania Avenue, wanted the public housing put elsewhere and the tenement area rebuilt with middle-income housing and more parks and recreation space.

After my own windshield survey of East New York, I had three thoughts: (1) give community organizations 1,000 units of poorly run property to manage, and, as they gain experience in maintenance and operation, give them funds with which to rehabilitate the properties; (2) there is an unrelieved boredom, a sameness, in East New York, and perhaps some sense of place can be created with parks, squares, and the like; (3) young people need programs and space to do what they want. They should be given a youth center and operating funds in exchange for community service.

On December 28, the full committee met again. Leo Lillard spoke of the need for a block-size community center, perhaps on Sutter Avenue, Hendrix Street, Blake, and Schenck Avenues. There was more discussion on the siting of public housing, with the United Community Centers favoring going south of Linden Boulevard in order to integrate, but the difficulties and opposition one could expect were also discussed. I raised the possibility of inserting public housing "fingers" into the area, and the discussion that followed made people aware of the subtleties and the difficulty of integrating and/or siting public housing in that largely white area. In addition to issues raised at the previous meeting, a whole new set of concerns and ideas was voiced:

- We need a high school.
- We should have a community college in the industrial quadrant.
- We should put a shopping center and theater in the worst area.
- We should add a play area to P.S. 174, which has none.
- Don't follow Brownsville's example of putting public housing in the worst area.

- Garbage has been sitting out in the streets for seven days.
- Children will be bussed into a new school.

At the meeting, I discussed relocation problems and said that we would recommend the staging of development. I also said that the problem with developing middle-income housing was finding nonprofit sponsors. People immediately came up with suggestions including Fortunoff's, St. John Cantius Church, the East New York Savings Bank, the State, County, and Municipal Workers Union (many residents of East New York were civil servants), and several community groups.

On January 4, 1967, my staff met with a youth committee of the United Negro and Puerto Rican Front. In addition to their recreational needs (discussed in chapter 6), they felt isolated from the community; yet were asked to pay their own way or to pay room and board, or they were forced to live alone, but there was no recreational space just for them. If they had a place of their own, they would not be into vandalism and thievery. They were very open to the idea of living quarters for young people. They also had many complaints about the way the schools were run; they experienced a lot of hostility toward blacks from many of the teachers.

That same night, we met with the community committee. About twenty-five people were in attendance. By then, my office was deeply into its surveys of housing condition, community organization, vacant buildings and land, city-owned property, public improvements, and more. We presented a map of community facilities, which suggested that East New York was underserved in a lot of ways. Two empty synagogues were suggested as possible community centers. On a staff level, we came to the conclusion that the community needed at least the following: a health center, a day-care center (it actually could have used a dozen), a recreation center, a library, and at least one more park.

Gradually, a basic approach to the vest pocket plan was emerging. It involved the rehabilitation or clearance of many of the tenements west of Pennsylvania Avenue and their replacement by both public housing and low-rent and middle-income rehabilitation and new construction. Pitkin Avenue east of Pennsylvania was also considered as a possible public housing site; there was dilapidated housing along Pitkin, and the construction of some public housing there would relieve the pressure on the tenement area.

The community was not too receptive to the idea of more parks, but it did want to see improvements made to the existing ones. "Parks should be open day and evening," they said, "and lit with floodlights." We hoped they would be receptive to at least one additional park space in the Target Area, sweetened with a proposed amphitheater and wading pool.

At the January 12, 1967, meeting of landlords (reported on in chapter 4), some twenty-five landlords took municipal loan forms, but only one or two were ever returned filled out. At a second landlords' meeting on February 17, from the 400 letters sent out, perhaps fifty landlords showed up at the meeting. About ten took municipal loan forms, but, in the end, only five landlords representing sixteen buildings expressed an interest in the program. George Jaffee, perhaps because of his determination, was one of the few successful applicants. Regrettably, most of those proposing to rehabilitate their structures were among the worst landlords.

While we were making steady progress with the community committee, the low level of support services was causing the process to stumble. Quality secretarial help was not available; minutes got garbled. Potential nonprofit sponsorship was proceeding poorly. The Area Services office (our unofficial headquarters) was not staffed and was often unable to mail out the hundreds of notices for meetings. We could not leave maps there for public examination because they were too valuable and security was nonexistent. As a result, the larger community was not being kept fully informed about or involved in the planning process.

On January 18, 1967, we met with Morris Eisenstein, director of United Community Centers (UCC), and Evelyn Millman, president of its board. They were very interested in the youth center idea and wanted to sponsor one or more, possibly on a site near New Lots Avenue. They also wanted more communication, said they would try to get CBENY to provide some services, and wanted the whole community to understand what was going on. They also wanted to see sanitation services and other services improved.

By January 22, 1967, my office had completed many of the needed surveys and had already shown a few to the community committee. On this night, the Vacant Buildings and Land map and the dramatic Housing Conditions map were shown. While everyone knew the general condition of buildings in the community, the maps showed just where the worst conditions were: concentrated in the Target Area and liberally distributed among other parts of East New York, as well. During the evening, at least half of those attending the meeting went up to the map, looking to see how their blockfront was rated. Just by looking at the map, it was easy to pick out likely sites for vest pocket action.

The city's offer of housing resources to the community included funds for rehabilitation, as well as for new construction. While the detailed housing condition surveys (described in chapter 4) showed that almost all the buildings in the Target Area required extensive rehabilitation or clearance, it became important to identify which of those buildings could be rehabilitated and which were best torn down and rebuilt. To make that decision, we undertook an architectural analysis of the rehabilitation prospects of eight of the ten building types in the Target Area. Several of them, including A, B, D, E, and F, emerged as good rehabilitation prospects, some because they were basically well designed and others because their relatively small apartments could be reconfigured to provide larger units. In D-type buildings, for example, though room and apartment sizes were small, the building configuration was amenable to an increase in room size and a reduction from six to four apartments per floor.

By presenting the findings of our surveys and the implications of alternatives, we were gradually accepted as negotiators and catalysts of community consensus. Questions on whether to rehabilitate or redevelop a potential site were quickly resolved. Still, a basic question remained and was frequently asked during disagreements: "Are you going to do what we tell you, or are you going to do it your way if we disagree?"

Generally, it was sufficient to suggest that both the community and the planner should vigorously discuss the issues, gradually reducing the points of difference until they reached agreement. This worked well enough, but close to the end of the planning period, when the location of a proposed park remained unresolved for a number of weeks, with community people on one side and consultants on the other, the question was asked once again.

Granville Payne stood up. "Mr. Thabit," he began, in his gravelly voice, "if we can't agree, will you propose our park or your park?" After a long moment, I said, "We'll propose your park, but we may not like it." This drew both applause and laughter, eased tensions, and led the way to a rapid consensus on the park question. Just a few years later, I couldn't remember what the argument was about or whose view prevailed.

In my firm's interim report, *A Planning Approach to East New York*, we proposed that a concerted effort be made to prevent the continued influx of welfare families into the area. The area should be designated a Saturated Area, the report stated, and moving in more such families would do more harm than good. Within the area of concentration, the needs were already overwhelming. According to our estimates, almost 5,000 East New York families were in need of human rehabilitation, including child care, health care, welfare, employment, education, and youth assistance. While the report was distributed to many city officials, as well as to the community committee, the suggestion was universally ignored.

At the weekly meetings in February, mostly in freezing weather, reports on progress were presented, many plan features were put in place, and many detailed decisions were made. One of them concerned whether to propose new commercial development on Sutter Avenue. Bill Wright was pushing the idea for the merchants. But the site was also ideal for new housing, and, under the housing finance programs then in use, housing and shops could not be mixed. As we leaned over the maps, I said, "if we go with the new shops, we'll have to cut back on the amount of new housing." To his credit, Bill Wright withdrew his support for the store frontage. "Well," he said, "If it's a choice between more housing and more stores, I'm not going to stand in the way." He was willing to make a buck when possible, but not at the expense of an improved community.

As the weeks progressed, the planning committee took on a more permanent form, officially calling itself the East New York Housing and Urban Planning Committee (ENYHUPC), and began to see itself as more than an ad hoc group. It held executive committee sessions before the Wednesday night meetings, prepared agendas, presented recommendations, invited government officials and outside experts to explain their programs and approaches, and spread word of its work throughout the community. Mailings were sent out, delegations went to city agencies, and the community and consultants were kept advised of developments. The Area Services office, directed by Lillie Martin, was of great assistance throughout the effort.

At the meeting on March 1, Joe Christian, executive director of the

New York City Housing Authority, appeared and was grilled about what the NYCHA would build and how it would build it. Great emphasis was put on the need for large apartments (surveys found that 45 percent of the households in the Target Area were composed of six or more persons). Christian appeared sympathetic. After a lot of questioning, Christian agreed to a tour of Housing Authority projects. It was set for March 11.

Between December 1966 and April 1967, seventeen Wednesday-night meetings with the ENYHUPC (Housing and Urban Planning Committee) were held at the Community Progress Center at 505 Sutter Avenue. Most of these nights were bitterly cold, or there was a half-foot of snow on the ground, or freezing rain was falling. News of shootings or other violence, building vandalism, or disastrous fires punctuated each meeting. Sirens were a constant accompaniment to the discussions.

More than 250 people attended one or more of the seventeen planning meetings, according to the attendance sheets. The "faithful" of the committee, those who came to at least five meetings, numbered eighteen persons. Another twenty-eight came to three or four meetings, while twenty-four came to at least two. Members of at least thirty community organizations and churches came to at least one meeting, most to two or more. Representation was equally divided between the areas east and west of Pennsylvania Avenue, and among blacks, Puerto Ricans, and whites.

Four community organizations had representatives at all the meetings: United Community Centers, United Block Associations, United Negro and Puerto Rican Front, and the Council for a Better East New York.

On April 11, 1967, the ENYHUPC mailed out a report to the community in which it stated that a mailing list of 175 individuals and organizations had been compiled, with notices sent out in advance of each meeting. It reviewed the progress made and the form of the plans produced, dealt with relocation, the use of Pennsylvania Avenue as a street for community facilities, and ended with a call to action.

On April 18, 1967, the final community-approved Vest Pocket and Rehabilitation Plan was presented to city officials. In brief, the plan proposed the following:

1. Construction of 810 units of new public housing
2. Construction of 460 units of new middle-income housing

3. Rehabilitation to produce 1,020 apartments, 560 of which would be public housing
4. Creation of a park of almost two acres in the Target Area, with a community center and a day-care center in it
5. Construction of several small parks to provide school play space
6. Transfer of four buildings suitable for community use to community control
7. Construction of a health center
8. Construction of a swimming pool
9. Development of a library and arts center
10. Creation of a staged relocation plan
11. Creation of a youth and recreation center

The presentation was well received by Eugenia Flatow, Bob Hazen, the director of development for the HRB, and other officials, and plans were made to move toward public hearings and sponsorship. Official interest was concentrated on the housing proposals; except for the health center, the community facilities proposals were largely ignored.

On May 17, 1967, at a meeting of potential housing sponsors at the East New York Savings Bank, it was decided to consolidate the rehabilitation portion of the plan, consisting of thirteen small sites, into six project areas. It was also revealed that an organization of sponsoring agencies was in the process of formation and that some fourteen churches and other entities were interested in sponsoring new and rehabilitated housing.

Meetings in June dealt mainly with plans for the new park. At the meeting on June 21, two architects showed their ideas for development of the park. One of them, Sy Breines, was very impressive; people liked the way he conducted himself.

At the July 12, 1967, ENYHUPC meeting, preparations were made for a rally in favor of the Thabit plan. The purpose of the rally was to impress city leaders and legislators with the community's support for the health center and for the Vest Pocket plan. Also discussed at the meeting was the reluctance of banks to give loans in East New York and how to spread the word about the Thabit plan throughout the community.

On October 18, 1967, ENYHUPC approved George Jaffee's plan to rehabilitate several properties on Site 1 under the municipal loan program. While he did not have a great reputation in the community,

Jaffee attended many of the planning committee meetings and seemed genuinely interested in the community improvement effort. He promised to do a good job and was one of the few private contractors interested in the municipal loan program, prompting HUPC to approve his application. He did a fairly good job of rehabilitating those buildings, justifying the confidence placed in him.

HEALTH PLANNING

Just how complex and difficult it is to put a needed community facility in place is exemplified by East New York's fight for a health center.[4] Juliet Greene flew the banner for a health facility for East New York from the earliest meetings of the planning committee. On February 1, 1967, Greene persuaded the group to turn down an offer by HIP to establish a 5,000-square-foot health center, saying that East New York needed more. She became chairperson of the Health Committee and doggedly pursued all possibilities for establishing a health center in East New York. As part of the planning effort, Site 41 at Pitkin and Pennsylvania was selected for the health center, which gave added impetus to the project.

On May 17, 1967, the Health Committee issued a report, containing a letter from Mrs. McLaughlin of the Health Department suggesting that the Health Committee be enlarged, allowing the group to bring greater pressure on city officials. She informed the group that $240,000 was being allocated for research on the health center and that $2 million would be allocated to East New York for its construction.

At a meeting of the Health Committee, on January 18, 1968, with representatives from Brookdale Hospital, discussion centered around starting up health center activities even before the building could be constructed and on whether local people could be trained to do the jobs that needed doing. The associate director of ambulatory care service at Brookdale said that Brookdale was willing to be the backup hospital for the center, but he wanted to know whether the city was going to cover the costs. There was no answer to this. While the core of the facility's proposed services were internal medicine, gynecology, obstetrics, and pediatrics, the need for dental care, narcotics treatment, and podiatry was also mentioned.

On February 7, 1968, a meeting on health took place at the Browns-ville Health Center at which architectural and construction issues took center stage, though an affiliation contract with Brookdale Hospital was also mentioned. Whenever the possibility of a new hospital for East New York was mentioned, officials felt it should be located elsewhere. The idea of an interim storefront facility was also shot down by health professionals. A working committee was set up as a subcommittee of the Brownsville Health Planning Council including Dr. D. Trice of the Health Services Administration, along with representatives of Brook-dale, ENYHUPC, the East New York Community Corporation, CBENY, youths, Hispanics, private doctors, and other groups. Juliet Greene was to set up the committee.

On February 28, Greene sent a fine single-spaced letter to a large community mailing list, telling everyone that East New York was going to get a health center, inviting people to join the health committee, and setting March 5 as the date for the next meeting. Few if any new persons showed up at that meeting. Leo Lillard brought up the issue of com-munity control, but, since a hospital would be responsible for care, the best that could be done was to develop a joint policy committee of hos-pital and community representatives. The discussion then wandered to the question of how much care the center should provide. While it was felt that an emergency room could probably not be supported twenty-four hours a day (which turned out not to be correct), a "drop-in clinic" was suggested where no appointments would be needed but emer-gency services would be limited.

On May 23, 1968, Dr. Bucove, the new head of the New York City Health Services Administration (HSA), addressed a Health Action Con-ference. He said the health center for East New York would be ready in three years and would serve 55,000 people. He also said there was a need to develop programs now and shift them later into their new home, specifically mentioning drug and alcohol programs. Dr. Bucove was asked whether the HSA would fund some of these interim services or pay for space to be rented, but he ducked such questions.

Dr. Henry Hicks was with the Interboro Hospital, which had been trying to get approval to treat mental health patients on an outpatient basis. Interboro was drowning in referrals from schools, numbering around 250 a week. Mothers were coming in on behalf of their children, and he saw a great need for family therapy, but his staff people were not trained in that area. But they were in the community and wanted to be involved.

At a meeting on June 25, there was considerable discussion about how to organize a new mental health committee. Model Cities staff wanted it to affiliate with Model Cities; Juliet Greene felt this would just hold things up. But the group voted for affiliation anyway, only to find out later that it wouldn't be independent and probably wouldn't get staff and support services, either.

On June 27, Dr. Bucove was given a tour of East New York and shown the routes people would have to take to get to the center. He promised to start work on the staffing and on interim facilities to get ahead of the game. He proposed a fifteen-member health planning commission with representatives of city, providers, and consumers and hoped to hold hearings shortly. There was a lot of discussion following his talk, centered mostly on career training and available monies for programs. Bucove promised to answer questions raised at the meeting in writing.

On the same day, Dr. Henry Hicks, acting as chairman of the Mental Health Committee of East New York, sent Dr. Bucove a letter asking that a full, comprehensive hospital be established in the center of East New York, that the health center already approved be constructed in twelve months, that the city provide funds for a halfway house for alcoholics, that it start a new bus line linking East New York with Brookdale and Kings County Hospitals, that the city give up on plans to put a 600-bed mental hospital in Spring Creek (and that it decentralize such a facility into twelve sub-units), that it utilize and train local people to build and operate such facilities and, finally, that it use existing hospital facilities such as Interboro, Pride of Judeah, Linden General, and Lutheran to meet the people's needs temporarily. It was a great letter, but it elicited no visible response.

On August 8, 1968, Juliet Greene again raised the question of interim facilities for the health center. The Committee also discussed training and job creation as important components of any health center activity. On August 18, the Model Cities health committee had a meeting, attended mostly by officials from a variety of agencies. Agencies were cautiously beginning to see the possibility of contributing staff for specific uses such as alcoholic rehabilitation. The U.S. Public Health Service (PHS) indicated that it would be willing to train someone to educate and advise the community on tuberculosis, venereal disease, immunization, and nutrition.

Planning for an East New York health center ultimately involved a huge cast of characters. In addition to half a dozen East New York community representatives, four nearby hospitals and up to a dozen government agencies might be represented at any of these meetings.

At the November 4, 1968, meeting of this group, the discussion revolved around the need for mental health services in East New York vis-à-vis the projected 600-bed mental health hospital slated for Spring Creek, at the southern end of East New York (see map 1). Local people spoke of specific needs. Some spoke of proposals dealing with sheltered workshops for the mentally retarded and the need for training in the schools with regard to mentally retarded children. Liz Bowers, of Model Cities, cited the chronic need for drug addiction treatment centers and halfway houses to which addicts could come for treatment and counseling. Child guidance services were sorely needed; Dr. Hicks reiterated that his center was averaging 250 outpatient referrals a week and was barely scratching the need. An extreme shortage of doctors and medical services in East New York was pointed out, and the requirements for obtaining funding and the kinds of programs available were briefly addressed. It was agreed that committee members would prepare their questions and proposals for a follow-up meeting.

At the follow-up meeting, on November 13, the discussion again revolved around identifying the size and type of mental retardation and mental health problems East New York was facing, and it was obvious that no one had any idea of how to find out.

Again, at a CBENY Mental Health Committee meeting on December 9, 1968, the emphasis was on identifying the needs for mental health services in East New York, but, this time, Cecil Seale indicated that the Community Mental Health Board would work with East New York to help determine need. It was also agreed to start a Saturday day-care center for six to ten children who were intellectually, vocationally, and/or socially unfit to attend school. Many East New York activists volunteered for the program, including Frank Rivera (who volunteered space at CBENY), Corinna Grant, George Goldsmith, and Clinton Patrick.

Model Cities did not send a representative to the meeting and was chastised for not doing so in a committee letter written by Frank Rivera.

The saga continued. In March 1969, a proposed program for a Planned Parenthood facility in East New York was presented and well received by the Health Committee. It contained health programs for women, men, children, and families, as well as social services consultation and referral and a community education component. PPNYC (Planned Parenthood of New York City) wanted to utilize three buildings on Site 23, scheduled to be condemned on or about May 15, 1969. PPNYC had set aside $360,000 in operating funds for three years. Two of the buildings would be rehabilitated for the service, and the third would be used for parking. A dozen tenants would have to be relocated.

The Neighborhood Family Care Center was scheduled to go before the Board of Estimate for final approval before the end of 1969.

All this time, my staff had been gradually collecting data on health needs. We had data on OPD (outpatient department) visits, data suggesting that 60 percent of Kings County Hospital emergency room visits were by East New York residents, and an analysis showing that, while Brooklyn probably had enough hospital beds, these were poorly distributed. By April 1970, the case for a new hospital in East New York appeared to be strong. Brookdale was not on a direct subway stop from East New York; bus service, irregular at best, was no substitute. Brookdale itself stated that a shuttle bus would be well utilized and was urgently needed by communities such as Brownsville and East New York. Further, Brookdale was still thought of as a "private hospital" and did not have a reputation for providing good service to poor patients. The smaller hospitals contributed some service to East New York but did not begin to fill the gap.

In a study by David Crane, a consultant for the City Planning Commission on Spring Creek, the suggestion was made that a new hospital in Spring Creek would be a welcome addition to the now-sparse coverage between Brookdale and Jamaica Hospital, nearly fifteen miles to the east. The new hospital could serve East New York and a significant portion of western Queens. The Crane analysis was somewhat simplistic, however, and could not be considered a serious attempt to satisfy hospital needs in the intervening area.[5]

A basic fact about East New York was that private physicians had left the area, leaving it unserved. If there were a hospital in East New York, physicians with hospital-oriented practices would open offices near the hospital, thus increasing coverage and service. We concluded that a small hospital of 300 beds would make a lot of sense. Such a hospital could provide about sixteen services. If the size were increased to 600 beds, only an additional four services could be added.

Central Brooklyn Model Cities put forward its own five-year plan, which called for a 500-bed hospital to replace Greenpoint Hospital, the establishment of three neighborhood family care centers, mobile medical teams, additional dental services, the provision of additional ambulance services, health education, training and programs for the mentally retarded, psychiatric services, drug addiction and alcoholism treatment, and residences for homeless youths, unwed pregnant women, and senior citizens. Not a bad shopping list.

Time passed. In June 1974, Martin J. Warmbrand, consultant to the East New York Development Corporation, called the need for a new medical center in East New York desperate.[6] The ratio of East New York doctors to the population was 27 per 100,000, compared with the city-wide average of 250. East New York had only a little more than half the number of hospital beds per 1,000 that was available in the rest of the city. None of these arguments, from our own analysis to Warmbrand's findings, ever impressed the powers that be.

By this time, the health center on Pitkin and Pennsylvania Avenues was under construction. It was completed in 1975, but it took two more years before it was fully equipped and open for business. During that interim period, the original group of fighters was still on the job. In June 1975, the Health Committee included Juliet Greene, Corinna Grant, Edward Griffith, Granville Payne, Marshall Stukes, and Frank Rivera, among others. Getting the project officially opened involved many more activists, including Lillie Martin, Corinna Grant and Catherine Priester, all of whom became chairwomen of the Center's advisory board. Lillie Martin chaired the advisory board for fifteen years; she finally resigned on August 31, 2001.

The plan to open the Pitkin Avenue site met with many delays, resulting in the temporary opening of the clinic at 560 Sutter Avenue (now occupied by the Housing Authority police). The Center moved to its present location at 2094 Pitkin Avenue in 1977. Since its inception, there has been a tremendous expansion of services and in the number of employees. It started with only a few of the services it now contains, namely pediatrics, medical, dental, and obstetrics clinics.

In 1993, the Center became a freestanding diagnostic and treatment center, fully certified under New York State Department of Health (NYDOH) Article 28. The center now offers a comprehensive set of primary-care services, including pediatrics, obstetrics, adult medicine, family practice, and specialty care services, including geriatrics, optometry, dentistry, podiatry, and behavioral health. Support services include breast health education and mammography, HIV counseling and treatment, laboratory services, nutritional counseling, radiology services, WIC (women and infant care), social work, sonography, electrocardiography, and transportation services. In addition, ENYDTC is a provider for several managed-care plans: MetroPlus, Center Care, Care Plus, P.C.A.P., Fidelis, and Neighborhood Health Providers. In September 1996, ENYDTC set up school-based health services at I.S. 166 and I.S. 302. The Center also supplies medical services to the William Avenue Women's Shelter and to the Forbell Men's Shelter and sponsors an annual street fair, a men's health forum, and many other outreach activities. In 2001, the Center served a patient population of 22,562 (60 percent African American, 36 percent Hispanic), who made 101,397 visits during fiscal year 2000. The Center is part of the Brooklyn/Staten Island Family Health Network of the New York City Health and Hospitals Corporation. Additionally, there is an East New York Diagnostic and Treatment Auxiliary, which raises funds to assist in patient care. It presented the Center with a new electrocardiogram machine on June 3, 1999.

Funding for the Center has been dwindling of late and has often been rocky in the past. In the early 1980s, for example, staff went as long as eight weeks without pay. More recently, the federal government, which used to provide 75 percent of the funding (the other 25 percent was made up by the city and the state), has steadily reduced its allocations, but the city and state have not increased theirs. Cost of services is met through Medicare, Medicaid, or other insurance or paid for on a sliding scale.

A glimpse into the enormous difference the health center has made in East New York is demonstrated by the unexpectedly low infant mortality rates in the area. In the ghetto areas of Bedford-Stuyvesant and the South Bronx, the infant mortality rate in 1996 exceeded 10.7 percent; in Brownsville it was 7.8 to 10.7 percent; in East New York, by contrast, it was only 5.8 to 7.7 percent.[7] This despite the fact that more than 8 percent of pregnant women in both East New York and Brownsville did not receive prenatal care.

Dr. Anthony Rajkumar, administrator of the Diagnostic Center at the time, explained the lower infant mortality rate by the growing success of the Center's outreach to teens and other women of childbearing age.[8] It pursues school-based programs as well as programs in Housing Authority projects and in other CBOs (community based organizations), and reaches significant numbers of pregnant women. On an average day, forty to forty-five women attend the maternity clinic. Over a recent ten-month period, some 800 women received prenatal care at the Diagnostic Center. Buoyed by the positive response to its efforts, the Center would welcome additional funding to further expand its outreach programs.

8

Vest Pocket Implementation

IN THE FALL of 1968, after the Vest Pocket plan was approved, the focus of intense activity was on the plan's implementation. Because we had an early start, we made steady progress despite local squabbling, processing bottlenecks, lack of experience, and mixed signals from the supervising agencies. Within twelve months, the first rehabilitated buildings were completed and the first new housing was under construction. Yet, it took seven years before the last project, the Remeeder Houses, was completed in 1975.

For many of the sponsors, the completion of their new or rehabilitated buildings was just the beginning. Troubles with tenants and vandalism, management inexperience and ineptness, and an unforgivable bout of greed and corruption involving nonprofit projects such as the Remeeder Houses of the Community Redemption Foundation all intervened to make some projects nightmares for hundreds of families.

While some local nonprofit sponsors were actively involved in looting their projects, the top echelons of city and federal agencies actively aided and abetted the looting process and profited from it. "Tenants be damned" aptly describes the approach of the renegade participants.

Not every nonprofit sponsor was ransacking its project. Most were straight arrows, following the rules and regulations to the best of their ability, fending off suggestions by politicians and others of ways to skim some cream off the top. On the other hand, I would be surprised if many of the project managers did not succumb to at least some of the temptations.

ORGANIZING FOR NONPROFIT HOUSING SPONSORSHIP

It all began at the Vest Pocket kick-off meeting with the community on November 8, 1966, when I asked whether any of the groups present were interested in becoming nonprofit housing sponsors of new and rehabilitated housing. Several churches and organizations responded favorably, and, after a good deal of organizing and spreading the word, a meeting on January 26, 1967, drew representatives of eight churches, six banks and several community organizations.[1] The interested organizations and churches were told to get permission from their membership or congregations to engage in housing sponsorship. To help this phase along, my office made special presentations to the governing bodies of churches and to groups of priests representing the Catholic churches.

On March 14, 1967, long before the plan was adopted, we showed potential sponsors the possible sites for rehabilitation in the Vest Pocket plan still being developed. We tentatively agreed that several groups of sponsors would jointly form mortgagor corporations and that each such corporation would develop its own project proposal. Shortly after the meeting, Daniel Himmel, an assistant to Congressman Frank Brascoe, expressed the interest of Local 485 of the International Union of Electrical Workers (IUE) in participating in the housing and rehabilitation program.

Once the plan was approved by the community and city officials, city officials and the nonprofit sponsors met to ensure that sponsorship was materializing in a substantial form. The officials were soon convinced; the City Planning Commission approved the Vest Pocket plan on August 9, 1967, and the Board of Estimate gave its approval on September 24, 1967.

At about the same time, a new organization called the Community Redemption Foundation (CRF), composed of ten black men, burst on the scene. Brought together by Harding Bowman, it found ready collaborators in Bill Wright, Marshall Stukes, and John Williams, all of whom were active in the Vest Pocket planning process and all of whom hoped to make some money out of the deal. The group filled out a ten-member board of directors by adding prestigious blacks, including Raymond Copeland, Ph.D., Julius Brown, Hume B. Smith (a bank vice president), the Reverend Jacob Underwood, Harry Dawkins Jr., and William Lewis. While most of the members knew nothing about housing, they signed up to take advantage of one of the few opportunities to participate in the mainstream action that had come their way. Harding Bowman was elected chairman.

The CRF announced its desire to sponsor a project; it quickly selected Sites 15 and 25 to rehabilitate and recruited high-profile professionals to develop their proposal. While the all-black membership of the CRF, with its obvious separatist overtones as well as its apparent swift progress, caused a certain amount of apprehension and suspicion, it also spurred the other groups to greater action.

Simultaneously, the East New York Savings Bank became more active in the effort, made meeting space available, and called a meeting of the various sponsors to consider further steps. Marshall Stukes, the bank's vice president for housing rehabilitation, acted as secretary to the group. In addition to those who had already agreed to become sponsors, half a dozen other churches and several banks sent representatives. At that meeting, the CRF and IUE sites were approved, and the other sponsors agreed to divide the remaining sites among the corporations to be formed.

From that point on, meetings were held weekly at the East New York Savings Bank. Sponsors gradually formed themselves into consortiums and accepted responsibility for portions of the project. One consortium consisted of CBENY, St. John Cantius R.C. Church, St. Michael's R.C. Church, St. John's Lutheran Church, and Grace Baptist.

Another consortium included St. Malachy R.C. Church, the Church of the Holy Redeemer, and the New Lots Reformed Church. The Long Island Baptist Societies became a third sole sponsor. At a meeting on May 24, 1967, the assembled sponsoring groups established themselves officially as the East New York Nonprofit Housing Coordinating Committee (N-PHCC) and elected Harding Bowman chairman.

Many, if not most, of the churches involved were members of CBENY and had been active in the community's struggle to survive the devastation that had accompanied the racial transition. The banks also had much at stake; despite having redlined the area, they still had major loan portfolios at risk.

The HUPC (Housing and Urban Planning Committee), creator of the Vest Pocket plan, continued to meet. One meeting included minority contractors, most of whom felt they could not bid on these projects because the contractors' businesses were small and could not put up the money for the needed contractor's bond. The best they could forsee was acting as subcontractors to a major firm. The meeting also discussed developing agreements with construction unions to use non-union labor and facilitating the entry of qualified blacks and Puerto Ricans into the unions as members.

A few of the CRF's members, having been an intimate part of the Vest Pocket planning process, played fast and loose with the approved plan. On August 9, 1967, the CRF presented an architectural sketch of its project, which proposed new housing instead of rehabilitation, displaced an additional 245 households, and closed a street, thereby negatively affecting traffic flow. I immediately wrote Harding Bowman, chairman of the CRF, indicating that the plan was unacceptable and not in the spirit of the Vest Pocket plan. I urged the CRF to withdraw it. The CRF ignored the letter.[2]

By November, the site selection process was still in flux. Many sponsors wanted sites other than those they had initially selected, many wanted to increase the size of their sites, and some fought over who had first claim on certain sites.

In a December 20, 1967, memo, the Buildings Department erred by not putting holds on buildings that were rated unsafe but that were to be rehabilitated. This resulted in their untimely demolition. The building at 556–558 Sutter Avenue was being demolished; the seventy-five-unit 408 Sheffield Avenue was hanging on by the thread of a temporary hold; and four buildings on the IUE site seemed to be in the demolition pipeline but should have been on hold. In January, two more buildings slated for rehabilitation were torn down.

By March 20, the site scramble had quieted down, with the assignment of Site 3 to the Long Island Baptist Societies and Site 32 to the Grace Baptist Church. IUE was awaiting city and FHA approvals, their architects poised to draw up final plans.

Alan Drezin, the attorney for CBENY, reported the formation of a fifteen-member board of directors for the East New York Nonprofit Housing Corporation, two from each church and three from CBENY. Marshall Stukes reported that the Long Island Baptists had selected a contractor, architect, and expediter. Again, the question of using local labor was raised; again, it was not resolved. Two churches, Calvary and St. Cyprians, opted out of sponsorship for sites 1 and 5, in April 1968. Inability to reach agreement with their Puerto Rican cosponsoring organizations prompted their withdrawal.

Early in 1968, sponsors who wanted to switch from rehabilitation to new construction took the stage. We had followed HDA guidelines in the selection of buildings and sites suitable for rehabilitation, but people experienced in rehabilitation techniques were essential to make such projects work, and the needed experience was missing. Some sites had more than one building type, requiring separate design and proforma financial analysis; this led to confusion among sponsors, architects, and their packagers. Bob Brodsky, head of rehabilitation at the New York City Housing and Development Administration, complained—even though the sites met HDA guidelines—that the sites were too narrow and too small, that some buildings were too small to rehabilitate, and that FHA had never set guidelines for consultants, thereby forcing architects to design and redesign their projects.[3] Many nonprofit sponsors and their professional teams were ill equipped to deal with the complexities; they needed an easier task. By contrast, Daniel Himmel's IUE rehabilitation project moved steadily forward and was rapidly completed.

Not all those wishing to switch had complicated site problems. The CRF wanted to demolish Sites 15 and 25, even though two of Site 15's buildings needed only cosmetic rehabilitation. My firm was ultimately pressured into approving most of these changes but did successfully prevent CRF's proposed project expansion and the closing of the street between Sites 15 and 25.

Discussion at the HUPC (Housing and Urban Planning Committee) meeting on July 15, 1968, revolved around the community facilities portions of the plan. As prospective sponsors of the development of Site 30, United Youth in Action, the Brooklyn Institute of Arts and Sciences, and the Brooklyn Public Library had been drafting a program for an arts-sciences-library center in the hope of enlisting funds for capital construction. Gerald Hayes, chairman of the committee, sent a letter to Donald Elliot, chairman of the City Planning Commission, requesting that $20,000 for center planning be included in the city's capital budget. The budget request was ignored.

Also on July 15, HUPC crossed wires with the Board of Education, which wanted to establish Head Start Center #1 on Site 29. The Board's architects expected to put a new building on the site, although the plan called for rehabilitation of what used to be the Hebrew Academy. The architects finally gained entrance to the building and found that it could be converted. The Board acceded, and, on October 21, the Board of Education announced that it was adapting the Hebrew Academy building for use as Head Start Center #1. Chalk up one for the community view.

In August, relocation issues dominated the HUPC meeting. Of those displaced, just over 25 percent were relocated into public housing. The 15 percent vacancy rate had vanished; many of the displaced site tenants had moved into other deteriorating buildings close to the project area; most had to search elsewhere for an apartment or a room in

someone else's flat. My firm's November 4 relocation report also complained about the mass relocation of the 1,359 on-site families.[4] The city
could and should have pursued relocation more slowly, carefully, and
sensitively. The report recommended a moratorium on relocation of 300
to 400 of the remaining site tenants over the winter months; those families were to be relocated to new or rehabilitated units in the spring. The
city ignored the report. Winter became a nightmare for hundreds of
families.

More discussions about community facilities took place at the
HUPC meetings. The question of who would pay for the acquisition,
development, and operation of community facilities was central, but
there were no quick answers. Possible options included Model Cities,
capital budget appropriations, and community facilities monies from
Federal Housing Administration (FHA) projects, all of which presented
major problems.

While HUPC was working away on thorny implementation issues,
the main topic at the November 6, 1968, meeting of the N-PHCC (East
New York Nonprofit Housing Coordinating Committee) was its desire
to phase out HUPC (which had prepared the Vest Pocket plan) and to
give its functions to the East New York Model Cities Physical Development Committee, which was responsible for Phase II planning (see
chapter 9). This group sought less demanding oversight of its activities
and was already beginning to flex its muscles.

At the N-PHCC meeting of June 18, 1969, I opposed the change
from rehabilitation to new construction on Sites 8, 10, and 13, but the
N-PHCC, taking matters into its own hands, approved the change, anyway. The IUE plans had been approved by the FHA; the group was now
awaiting builders' certification to begin work. Construction was also
scheduled to start on Brooklyn Church Extension Society sites (Long
Island Baptist Societies) on July 3, 1969.

THE CONSTRUCTION PHASE

Finally, a project was ready for construction. In the *New York Times* for
August 31, 1969, Mayor Lindsay was shown breaking ground on the
622-unit development at Miller and Pitkin Avenues, sponsored by the
Long Island Baptist Housing Development Fund Co., Inc. Lindsay
called it "the first living proof that a community can create housing in

record time." The project was a record-breaker, moving from City Planning Commission approval to construction in less than two years.

Harding Bowman, furious at how the mayor and representatives of city agencies ignored the locals at the ground breaking for the Baptist Society project, sent a letter to all the other sponsors indicating that they should take charge of any ceremonies such as ground breaking and make sure that the community input was fully reflected in the program.

Two rehabilitation projects were scheduled for completion by the end of 1969; the Long Island Baptist Societies' new construction project was scheduled for completion in October 1970; two other low-income projects were scheduled for completion in July 1970. In four of six projects, occupancy was expected before mid-1972.

During the first half of 1970, many groups evaluated the Vest Pocket plan and its implementation. Government officials found flaws in their own processing procedures; HDA supervision was considered lax, sometimes ineffective. HDA/FHA interaction was problematic; each interpreted requirements differently even within its own offices. With one exception, nonprofit-sponsored housing projects were moving slowly toward implementation, encountering numerous delays. All the projects had been underway for over two years, and most appeared at least a year away from completion.

Mr. Lapadula, chief underwriter for the FHA, felt that long-term entities like the Bedford-Stuyvesant Restoration Corporation made better sponsors than outside groups, which undertake a project, learn how to do it, then retire from the field, wasting their hard-won expertise.

According to Lapadula, the architects weren't familiar with FHA design and cost limits and had to resubmit their designs many times. Small builders had to be bonded by larger contractors; sponsors failed to submit FHA-mandated exhibits; some consultants who tried to do their own packaging were ill equipped for the job. The IUE was good at this, but most sponsors weren't. Lapadula also thought a combined nonprofit management structure should be developed to service all the projects.

According to my staff, the major hangups included (1) the prevailing system of complex and overlapping official approvals, and (2) the lack of assistance, follow-up, or checks on sponsor and consultant progress by relevant agencies or the community.[5] The report also noted the three-to-eight-month delays in obtaining state seed money. Paradoxically, to get seed money (a pittance, really), sponsors had to submit project documents that they needed the seed money to produce. It also would have made sense for the HDA to develop feasibility studies for the sites and then offer sponsorship opportunities to local groups.

Despite the problems, the East New York programs were generally believed to be working well; the overall speed of implementation compared favorably with past experience and with progress in other parts of the city.

The Long Island Baptist Society's Site 15 was ready for occupancy by December 1, 1970; other sites were scheduled for occupancy in January and February 1971. Grace Baptist Church's Site 32 anticipated a construction start in December 1970, with occupancy by April 1972.

By January 1, 1971, practically all relocation from the housing and community facilities sites had been completed. Also, as of that date, some 106 new and rehabilitated units had been completed, and another 1,095 dwelling units (including 622 public housing units) were under construction. Construction of two early childhood centers and a day-care center was also under way.

On February 17, 1971, the N-PHCC held a major discussion on IUE's Site 19. Due to burnouts and demolition, the IUE plan had to be changed from rehabilitation to the construction of ninety-four new units. Daniel Himmel stated that the IUE could no longer develop the site as a nonprofit but could do so as a limited-dividend project. The Reverend Underwood, speaking for Grace Baptist Church, said his group could develop the site as well as anyone else. Elaine Weiss, a consultant to the HDF (Long Island Baptist Housing Development Fund), also put in a bid to become the designated developer of the site. Basically, she said, the same plans used to develop Site 3 could be used on Site 19. It was decided to refer the matter to the Model Cities Physical Development Committee, but, before it got there, the HDF had somehow become the designated sponsor of Site 19.

POSTCOMPLETION BLUES

As projects were completed, unanticipated results and problems surfaced. By December 1970, estimated rents for new construction ranged from $102 to $132 for a one-bedroom apartment to $195 to $207 for a four-bedroom apartment. In rehabilitated dwellings, one-bedroom units went for $104, while five-bedroom units went for $157. These rents were a lot higher than anticipated; the nonprofit sponsors apologized, but the figures didn't change.

Rents continued their rise as projects were completed. By April 1971, tenants of newly rehabilitated six-story buildings on Wyona and Blake Avenues were faced with $190-a-month rent for five rooms and were told that DOSS (Department of Social Services) was unwilling to pay that much for a welfare rent allowance. Rents at other than New York City Housing Authority sites were coming in much higher than expected, and there didn't seem to be anything anyone could do about it.

In April, 1971 Daniel Himmel reported on the IUE's rehabilitation project, fully rented for about six months. Building entrance doors were constantly being broken, rent collection was a headache, and windows required protective gates. The IUE was looking for a major company to take over the management. The original management budget was entirely inadequate for anyone to do a satisfactory job.

At the September 8, 1971, meeting of N-PHCC, five months after his report on the IUE project, Daniel Himmel felt that things were going better. Locks were still being broken, but rent collection was better, and the tenants association was now operating.

At the same meeting, the Long Island Baptist Housing Development Fund Company, Inc. (HDF) revealed that rampant vandalism was affecting its buildings. If it put a lock on a door, the next day the lock was gone. The HDF had investigated hiring a protection company, but the estimated cost of about $1,000 a night was excessive. Tenant meetings were held, but the response was poor.

Corinthia Shaw of the Tenants Action Council (TAC), reported on a program that involved educating mothers. People who have lived in substandard housing all their lives and move into new housing do not respect locked doors and increased security, she said. When these things were explained, Shaw went on, they learned to respect other people's property and to respect themselves and their community. This approach was only partly successful in East New York; a more thorough approach was needed.

At the May 31, 1972, meeting of the N-PHCC, the East New York Nonprofit Housing Corporation said it was looking for a capable and dependable management company, since their project would be ready for occupancy in August. It was preparing to screen tenants and to require tenant orientation along the lines to be described by Enoch

Williams, executive director of the Council of Churches. Williams described the program at the meeting. Tenants were screened and their apartments inspected for cleanliness; tenants were then given a federal application form. They were then required to attend a tenant orientation class, consisting of eighteen hours of instruction over nine nights. Prospective tenants needed a certificate stating they had completed the course before they could sign a lease. Classes were on the following topics:

- History of sponsoring group and community
- What tenants could expect from management
- Maintenance of apartment equipment (e.g., stoves)
- Decorating the apartments
- Pest control
- Moving-in process, leases
- Upkeep of the exterior of the building
- Security
- Facilities maintenance

The East New York Nonprofit Housing Corporation announced, in November 1972, that it had entered into an agreement with Urbanco, a management company, to provide management services to its project. It was also working closely with Lillie Martin, of East New York Housing Services, on the screening of tenants.

The Brooklyn Hispanic project on Sites 1 and 5 was scheduled for completion in June 1973. The neighborhood Health Center, site 41, was under construction. The Early Childhood Center on Site 29 had been completed. The plan had taken almost seven years to implement, but it had produced some 2,300 units of new and rehabilitated housing, as well as many community facilities. The CRF estimated that its Remeeder Houses project would be completed by April 1973 (it finally had its mortgage closing in 1975). All in all, a pretty impressive result.

THE REMEEDER HOUSES

The seedy side of the nonprofit housing effort is little known. Despite a lack of experience in housing, the CRF (Community Redemption Foundation) managed to get a contract from the NYCHA (New York City

Housing Authority) to build a turnkey housing project for the Housing Authority in East New York. Joseph Colon, who was able to get CRF appointed as the developer by pulling strings with city and federal officials and others on the take, arranged this. To undertake this project and its own Vest Pocket project, the CRF created the Remeeder Housing Development Fund Company, Inc. (RHDFC). This first project, consisting of three six-story buildings containing 167 apartments, was completed and turned over to the Housing Authority on November 30, 1973. Working through Winsco Construction Corporation, a builder that was part of the deal, the construction budget was shaved and the siphoned-off monies distributed to those who made the deal possible—including the Remeeder board members. When Marshall Stukes, the elected secretary–treasurer of Remeeder, refused to approve checks unsubstantiated by Winsco vouchers or change orders, he was summarily (and illegally) replaced with a board member, Ray Copeland, who did approve the withdrawals.

Eight years later, just before the final closing on the project, Joseph Colon threatened to expose the wrongdoing unless he was compensated for his work. He claimed that he was owed $300,000 in commissions. A settlement was reached with Remeeder in which Colon agreed to accept a small percentage of the project mortgage (amounting to about $150,000) as his commission; in return, he promised not to mention the matter further to the principals or to the agencies involved.[6]

In July 1975, Remeeder completed its own Vest Pocket project, the Remeeder Houses, consisting of four six-story buildings containing 260 moderate-income apartments. Some $600,000 was skimmed off the construction budget by the same builder and distributed to everyone in on the deal—including most Remeeder board members. The Reverend Underwood and Hume Smith both resigned from the CRF board, refusing to have anything to do with the payoffs. On the HUD (U.S. Dept. of Housing and Urban Development) project certification punch list, the following was noted: "there was a flood in all buildings with water coming up two feet, inundating the electrical controls on the boilers."[7] The fault lay with the undersize waste pipes. Despite efforts by Bill Wright to raise serious questions, Winsco stood in the way of any effective oversight of construction by the Remeeder board, and no corrective action was taken by HUD officials. Both were sharing the cream. Tenants were the losers, having to live in a shoddily built project.

After a 1989 HUD inspection showed the project to be in terrible shape and in default on its mortgage payments, HUD threatened fore-closure. This precipitated the early April 1989 resignations of John Williams, president of the Remeeder HDFC, and of two board members, Julius Brown and Raymond Copeland, all of whom had probably been helping to loot the project.Harding Bowman was elected to serve in Williams's place, and Bill Wright, Harry Dawkins Jr., and William Lewis, all members of the board of the CRF, were elected to replace those who had resigned from the Remeeder board.

The politically connected managing agent, BPC Management Corporation, had totally neglected the project since its appointment in the mid-1980s. If the Remeeder board was to stand a chance of retaining control of the project, it had to terminate BPC as managing agent. It did so, effective September 1, 1989, though BPC was continued as managing agent on a temporary basis, until a successor could be found.

While BPC was still acting as temporary agent, Bill Wright spent some time visiting the project, after which he wrote a critique to Remeeder board members and to federal officials. He accused BPC of failing to get a good day's work out of its maintenance men and failing to supervise the development or to keep adequate records.[8] Wright also charged that there had been improprieties and irregularities on the part of all the previous directors (John Williams, Raymond Copeland, Julius Brown, Marshall Stukes, and Frances McGrath, of the East New York Savings Bank). He called for a full meeting of the Remeeder board with a federal official present. There was no response to his letter.

Bowman, meanwhile, had been trying unsuccessfully to satisfy HUD's concerns. On May 6, 1991, HUD informed Bowman that he had not met their conditions for a modification of the contract or for correcting the unsatisfactory conditions and that foreclosure was still being considered. HUD again asked Bowman to submit a Management Improvement Plan, which would provide details on how and when deficiencies were to be corrected. It also noted that any fees paid to the nonprofit board must be returned to the project.

On March 1, 1992, Giscombe-Henderson, Inc., the new managing agent, filled out a HUD form listing the physical repairs needed at Remeeder Houses, as well as a schedule for their completion. The project was in dreadful shape. The plan called for replacing the intercom systems, modernizing the elevators, replacing the oil burners and controls, painting the exterior walls, and replacing the precast window sills in all four buildings. Mailbox replacement was needed in three buildings.

Many repairs were needed in the basements, apartment interiors, roofs, and exterior grounds.

Bill Wright, in a letter to Harding Bowman dated June 25, 1992, asked for an accounting and explanation of (1) an $8,000 check made out to Harding Bowman, (2) a $32,000 retainer paid to Fred Wallace, a Remeeder attorney, (3) an $83,000 expenditure for unexplained computer systems, and (4) a mysterious $9,000 staff line that could not be located in the audit. The letter accused Bowman of unilaterally terminating the new management company, Giscombe-Henderson.

In response to these accusations, Harding Bowman moved to take complete control of Remeeder. He refused to call a meeting to discuss Wright's charges. He also refused to hold the required annual meeting, scheduled for June 18, 1992.[9] What Bowman did do was to call an illegal Remeeder board meeting on July 31 at which he elected three members of his family to be directors. The new board then voted to remove Bill Wright and Harry Dawkins Jr. as directors.[10]

On August 17, 1992, Nasher Realty Associates, the new managing agent, reported problems similar to those listed by Giscombe-Henderson. In addition, Nasher found roofs that leaked profusely even though they were new, roof doors that were off the hinges or lying on the roof, many broken window panes and rotten wood frames, undersized main waste lines that resulted in continuous backups, and many apartments in a state of disrepair.

Nasher discovered that tenant payment records were inaccurate, that the cash position was unclear, that the bank security account was insufficiently funded, that apartments were omitted from rent rolls, and that vacancies went unreported. They also found more than $350,000 in rent arrears and a mortgage delinquency amounting to $1,022,540. Workmen's compensation had been canceled for nonpayment. Because of these deficiencies, stated Nasher, HUD was proceeding with foreclosure.

On October 26, 1992, Bowman wrote to HUD that Remeeder's attorney, Fred Wallace, had told him that the questionable disbursements were legal and appropriate. On January 24, 1993, Nasher reported that HUD was not buying Bowman's explanation for the questionable disbursements and, in addition, wanted a return to the project of some $29,254 in excess fees and other overages incurred in 1991. Without accomplishing these tasks, Nasher did not believe that it could resolve the mortgage issue with HUD.

On March 30, 1993, Nasher informed the Remeeder board about steps it had taken during February and March. These included identifying vandals and sending letters to their families threatening eviction unless the vandalism stopped, starting a tenant patrol, instituting an aggressive rent collection policy, and continuing work in occupied apartments to bring them up to standard.

The record for April 8, 1993, contains a letter to Henry Cisneros, secretary of HUD, asking that HUD reach a negotiated settlement with Remeeder. The letter was signed by Congressman Edolphus "Ed" Towns.

According to the April 30 report of Nasher Realty Associates, entrances had been made wheelchair accessible, and the 1992 audit was almost complete. When it was complete, Nasher would ask for a rent increase (which would increase Section 8 payments, not tenant rents) and seek funds for new windows, roofs, roof fans, waterproofing, oil burners, boiler repair, sidewalks repair, and twenty-four-hour security.

Despite Nasher's reports of progress to the Remeeder board, tenants were not happy. On December 22, 1993, tenants circulated flyers complaining about the condition of buildings and grounds, the need for locks and intercoms on all entrance doors, the lack of twenty-four-hour security, and the dearth of on-site personnel to respond to complaints. It ended with an underlined threat *"TO TAKE MATTERS INTO OUR OWN HANDS AND HAVE A MAJOR RENT STRIKE."*

This was the general situation at the end of 1993. For almost five years, HUD had been threatening foreclosure, but it never did foreclose. Why? Probably because the project was a cash cow. The nonprofit sponsors and their agents had already shown themselves ready and willing to deal. And many HUD political appointees (and possibly career officials, as well) seemed open to opportunities to profit. If there was a tenant outcry, moreover, it would never be heard outside the ghetto.

The last item in the file made available to me is the May 24, 1996, letter written to HUD by Bill Wright. Either through a foreclosure and resale or by some other maneuver, HUD had transferred the Remeeder Houses from Remeeder HDFC to a new entity, National Realty, under the leadership of Harding Bowman. Wright complained about the many improprieties in the property transfer, and questioned HUD's acceptance of Bowman as a project leader—Bowman, the man who had illegally reconstituted the Remeeder board and who had been deeply involved in the project's illegal disbursements. Wright asked HUD to return the project to the old Remeeder board or, failing that, to list the actions it took that had resulted in the property transfer. He never received an answer to his charges or his query.

This was a ghastly experience with management. It was probably not typical of the sponsorship experience in East New York, though it is unlikely that many projects escaped problems with managing agents, kickbacks, and serious lapses in dealing with tenants. In the Remeeder case, members of the board of directors prior to 1989 were looting the project in cahoots with the managing agent. Following his becoming president of Remeeder, Harding Bowman concentrated on covering up his own and others' misdeeds and on gaining complete control of the project, freezing everyone else out.[11] In this, he was successful.

None of the actors in this play, including Bill Wright, who tried to blow the whistle on Bowman, were guiltless. With the possible exception of the Reverend Underwood and Hume Smith, all the directors of the CRF fed at the trough at one time or another. While Bill Wright didn't hesitate to accept his share of the cream, he also felt strongly that the Remeeder Houses tenants deserved a decent place to live. If he could have dislodged Harding Bowman, moreover, Wright would have happily taken control of Remeeder.

For all these men, the severe restrictions placed on nonprofit operations has proved to be counterproductive. While a nonprofit organization is required to organize, supervise, and be accountable for operations under its aegis, it is not allowed to recover a single dollar in costs or fees for its efforts. Also, a person cannot be on the board of directors of a nonprofit corporation and be on staff at the same time. Nonprofit organizations are hobbled by this restriction; their best people are often ineligible to direct operations.

Compare this with real life. In a for-profit operation, the CEO can also be chairman of the board. He can hire his wife or husband, his sister or a bunch of nephews, and not a single eyebrow is raised. Why is it different for nonprofits? The government's idea was to keep "poverty pimps" honest, but all government has done is to shackle nonprofit operations and to tempt sponsors to repay themselves for their time and energy illicitly. Better to pay them licitly!

I'm not suggesting that the Remeeder excesses would not have occurred under different circumstances, but I do think that more straight arrows would have been produced if the nonprofit sponsors had felt they were appreciated and were paid to see that an adequate job was being done and if their performance had been closely monitored by the funding agencies. The supervising agencies such as HUD were almost criminally negligent in the Remeeder case. They did not keep a sharp eye out for wrongdoing or inadequate maintenance; perhaps even more important, they did not take swift corrective action when they did see things go wrong.

The possibilities for corruption in housing management are legendary and are as plentiful in the for-profit as in the nonprofit sector. Of course, the for-profit owner has much to lose if his project goes to pot. But, as Bowman has taught us, the nonprofit owner also has much to lose. The major difference is that the for-profit owner is entitled to a profit, while the nonprofit sponsor is not allowed to charge a reasonable fee for his services. As a result, kickbacks and skimming have become the norm. In addition to easing the restrictions on nonprofit employment, closer monitoring of management operations is certainly indicated.

It is noteworthy that several Remeeder board members and other East New York black men attended Louis Farrakhan's Million Man March on Washington, D.C., which embraced the values of separatism. They were publicly proclaiming their right to a share of the pie as well as proudly asserting their blackness. They may also have been expressing the rage that grew within them as they aged and came to fully appreciate the depths and ruthlessness of white prejudice.

A tenant coalition covering Vest Pocket and other projects would be the way to go. Whether or not fee-for-service is instituted and whatever the reasons used to justify illegal gains, the community goal must be to bring effective management to all the projects, to root out and expose corruption, to ensure satisfactory maintenance throughout the Vest Pocket project areas, and to make tenants satisfied with and proud of their housing. If some projects are lagging, a coalition could exert pressure on the supervising agencies for more active agency monitoring and enforcement. A tenant coalition could also seek legal access to project records, recover damages in cases of management abuse, and press for tenant representation on the board of directors. It will never be easy, but a barking watchdog should help to curb the excesses of sponsors and their managing agents.

9

The Model Cities Fiasco

ON NOVEMBER 2, 1967, Mayor John Lindsay established the Model Cities Committee by Executive Order No. 55. A sham from the word *go*, the Model Cities program was just another cruel hoax played on minority and other poor communities. Funding for the program was one-twentieth of what was needed to make it effective. Smaller cities did better than larger ones by zeroing in on doable projects; New York City's program of some 300 discrete projects foundered on the complexities of developing and processing them through totally unprepared local communities and city bureaucracies. Nor were city agencies about to give up power to Model Cities agencies or groups. Housing improvement, a basic thrust of the program, proved almost impossible to plan with sufficient community input and was sabotaged by the ending of nonprofit housing sponsorship in 1970 and by President Richard Nixon's housing moratorium in 1972. Real impacts were made only in isolated components such as day care, legal aid, and job training. Most of the money was wasted in administrative costs and overly ambitious programs.

The city, hoping to move on a fast track following the Vest Pocket program, awarded my firm the East New York Model Cities Physical Development planning contract in December 1967. For this Phase II program (as it was locally called), the city made an allocation of 3,200 additional new and rehabilitated units, half of which were to be public housing units. The city also asked that half the units be designated in an Early Action plan, sort of a follow-up to the Vest Pocket program. A capital improvements program that included schools, day-care centers, parks, and other facilities was also to be planned. No funding was in place for any of the nonhousing plans, and, as it turned out, the housing funds dried up before they could be used, as well. Equally bad, the city (and its consultants) totally miscalculated the effort required to do this planning work. The smoothness with which the Vest Pocket program progressed blinded everyone to the pitfalls ahead.

ORGANIZING FOR MODEL CITIES

Progress in organizing for Phase II planning was slow for a variety of reasons. First, the multiple objectives of the overall program and the creation of an umbrella organization, the Central Brooklyn Model Cities Committee, established to cover the three Brooklyn areas (Bedford-Stuyvesant, East New York, and Brownsville) resulted in an unwieldy, confusing, and contentious group of committees, all competing for some attention and funding available only through the Central Brooklyn Model Cities office, directed by Horace Morancie, who proved to be miserly with funds and staff support for most activities. Local activists felt that the Central Brooklyn office saw itself as a new power base in the community, rather than as a community service organization. Horace Morancie indicated that his office would review East New York nonprofit sponsorship plans, for example, clearly a function of the East New York Housing and Urban Planning Committee (HUPC). It was also decided that each of the five subject committees (Sanitation and Safety, Physical Development, Multi-Service Systems, Economic Development, and Education) in each of the three local areas would have five members—a disastrous idea that never worked in practice. At best, two or three committee members would show up at a meeting. With little local participation and no technical assistance, few viable programs were produced.

The difficulties began to surface immediately. It took months to structure the Model Cities Policy Committee. A whole new cast of characters who had not been involved in the Vest Pocket planning program were now involved in the Model Cities effort, and they wanted to restructure the ballgame. Everyone was out to get a piece of the action, if necessary at someone else's expense. At a meeting of the Central Brooklyn Policy Committee to which I was not invited, the idea of my being Model Cities consultant came under attack from people who didn't even know me.

A little later, I came under attack again, this time in Brownsville. I had also been made supervising consultant to the Brownsville Model Cities program to assist a new black consulting firm, Lucas and Edwards, which was to do the actual work. "Wasn't your brother responsible for building a school that collapsed and hurt dozens of children a few years ago?" was tossed at me by the black militant Sonny Carson. I figured this was a joke and, along with many others at the meeting, laughed it off, but other people took it seriously, and the following week I was forced to answer the question at another Brownsville standing-room-only meeting, responding that my brother was a lawyer, not an architect or builder, and had nothing to do with schools.

Recognizing the danger in these attacks, I wrote Leo Lillard, as chairman of HUPC, and asked him to use his influence to end these attacks or to call a meeting of East New York leadership where I could face whatever charges people wanted to make and answer them. I thought the attacks were divisive and would weaken my relationship with both the community and the city. I asked HUPC to tell the Model Cities Policy Committee and Eugenia Flatow that it fully supported my efforts and that the Policy Committee should quickly establish a Model Cities Physical Development Committee so that we could start serious work on the Phase II plan. Already, three months had gone by without a working Physical Development Committee in place.

It took time, but HUPC did respond as I'd hoped. At HUPC meetings in March there was continuing discussion about supporting me as planning consultant for Model Cities. Finally, on April 7, 1969, HUPC passed a resolution stating that, since I had been instrumental in guiding the preparation of Phase I of the Vest Pocket plan and since HUPC had been implementing that plan and did engage the full participation of the community, and since HUPC desired the full participation of the community in Phase II, it was resolved that the community continue to participate and control the planning process, that Walter Thabit be continued as consultant, and that copies of the resolution be sent to Mayor Lindsay, Donald Elliot, Eugenia Flatow, and Horace Morancie. In addition to Leo Lillard, Renee Ossit, Juliet Greene, Onofrio Fiorentino, Lena Goldstein, Granville Payne, and Sara Ross, all vest pocket regulars, were among those in attendance. There were only occasional attacks after that.

Around March 15, 1968, the final selection of twenty-five East New York Policy Committee members and the selection of the five subcommittees, one of which was the Physical Development Committee, was completed. By early April, the Model Cities Physical Development Committee was holding meetings, but few people attended. Meeting notices were not being sent out; the community was not being informed of the progress of our housing surveys and had not had a chance to respond or react to them.

My staff had already completed a vacant building survey, which showed a total of 500 vacant buildings, 150 more than in the most recent survey, and many of which had already been torn down. Responding to the city's pressure for quick results, we had also begun a detailed survey of building conditions in the Model Cities area. East of Pennsylvania Avenue, a new area of deteriorated, vacant, and burned-out housing surfaced, and the area surrounding the Vest Pocket project sites were also on their way to further destruction. Abandonments, foreclosures, and vandalism had increased.

Though meetings of the Physical Development Committee at this stage were marked by poor attendance, the survey results provoked a good deal of discussion about how many of the 3,200 housing units to be built should go east of Pennsylvania and how many should be located around the current Vest Pocket sites. The schools situation, recreation, day care, and health needs were also mentioned, but discussion was deferred pending the needed studies and analysis.

While Phase II planning was my firm's main responsibility, we spent a lot of time in HUPC meetings catching up with day-to-day affairs, including the desire of many nonprofit sponsors to switch from rehabilitation to new construction, the future of the Waterworks site, the fate of the promised swimming pool, the location of the police precinct, and Jaffee-proposed rehabilitation, as well as the continuing interest in school planning and community facilities proposals.

Letters were sent to Eugenia Flatow, the mayor's executive assistant for Model Cities, complaining that Morancie had made a shambles of our planning efforts, as a result of which we were not getting community participation. Meeting notices were arriving late if they came at all; none had gone out in the previous month. When he did send mailings out, Morancie sent them only to the twenty-five people on the East New York Model Cities Policy Committee, most of whom couldn't care less about the Physical Development Committee. He refused to provide secretarial services to the committee so that it could send out its own mailings. He was also beginning to make unilateral planning decisions, an arrogant seizure of power.

At a meeting on May 28, 1968, East New York's Model City Policy Committee was finally formalized. During the meeting, attacks were made against Morancie, Tom Quick (an East New York activist), and myself. A total of twenty-six East New Yorkers ended up on the East New York Model Cities Policy Committee, ten of whom had been active during the Vest Pocket planning process. The rest had never heard of me or of HUPC. Respect and confidence had to be earned all over again.

THE MODEL CITIES PLANNING EFFORT

Judy Stoloff, of my staff, headed one of her reports "Muddled Cities Committee, 5/4/68." That meeting started with a discussion of who should oversee the Vest Pocket plan through the implementation phase. Then the question of whether planning had already been done on Phase II was brought up. Gerald Hayes, a Vinnie Jones protégé and chairman of the East New York Model Cities Policy Committee, was convinced that we already had a plan and were not showing it to the community. If you've read this far, you know we did not have a plan; but, for the still-doubting Thomases in Brownsville, I assure you that we did not.

By mid-June, we had done about 30 percent of the work and spent 50 percent of the money.[1] By the end of July, the survey work for housing type and condition had been completed, and work was started on the analysis and mapping of various planning components. Conditions had measurably worsened near the Vest Pocket sites and between Dumont and Riverdale Avenues, south of the Target Area. In the newly deteriorated area east of Pennsylvania Avenue, a large number of vacant buildings had surfaced; two-thirds of the buildings required extensive repair or replacement.

Homeowners or prospective homeowners had special problems. Many of the newly vacant buildings represented foreclosures for nonpayment of interest and principal. People had had to pay excessive prices for their homes and were saddled with hefty monthly mortgage payments. To get at some of these problems, a special survey of homeowners, brokers, banks, agents, the FHA, and others was undertaken.

Altogether, twenty-two owners were surveyed in the areas where a third of the buildings were owner occupied. In two-thirds of the cases, part of the building was rented out. Three-quarters of the owners were black; all but one of the remainder were Hispanic. Only four of the owners had incomes above $7,000.

Most purchase prices of the homes were between $15,000 and $20,000, only four were higher. Half of the owners had bank mortgages. Most owners had FHA-insured mortgages; half the homes carried second mortgages, with some carrying home improvement loans, as well.

The picture that emerged was clearly one of hardship both in attaining and sustaining ownership.

Four real estate brokers, two black and two white, were interviewed by my staff.[2] Black brokers felt that banks and mortgage companies would no longer lend money without FHA insurance, that speculators had entered the arena, that buyers with limited mobility and resources were running into many financial difficulties. The white brokers looked for urban renewal to salvage the area and to rescue their speculative purchases. All agreed that buying and selling were slow and that insurance cancelation was a major problem. All felt that owner occupancy was on the decline.

One broker claimed that the FHA failed to investigate buyers' true ability to finance their purchases. Two brokers reported between 150 and 160 FHA foreclosures in the past year in East New York and Brownsville, mostly because overextended buyers had purchase-plus-home-improvement loan packages that increased monthly costs beyond a buyer's ability to pay. Properties taken back by foreclosure were reportedly "warehoused" and sold in packages of 100 or so to banks at a discount. Many buyers made a $1,000 down payment that was simply applied by the seller to a second or even third mortgage, with the buyer closing the deal without ever knowing the terms or the price he was paying for the property. Brokers using unsavory practices duped prospective homeowners into buying homes at outrageous prices and on onerous terms, and there was no one looking out for buyers' interests.

Out of this investigation, we prepared a Home Maintenance and Improvement Program designed to correct and prevent the continued deterioration of small home properties in East New York as part of the Phase II plan. It contained two parts: (1) a program to repair vacant buildings and return them to residential use, and (2) a program to provide assistance to homeowners to keep and maintain their properties. Along with many other Phase II recommendations, the proposal was completely ignored.

Housing was only one of the many sectors we were responsible for. The inability of the Parks Department to satisfy the needs of the community had caused grave concern, and the committee agreed to make recreation one of the plan's biggest thrusts. We prepared a parks and recreation plan that gave the community a substantive role in the operation and maintenance of recreation and park facilities. Radical changes in programs, administration, and funding of park and recreation efforts were proposed. Both indoor and outdoor facilities were projected. A site for a major recreational facility was included in the Vest Pocket program, but community people also envisioned a center such as the Brownsville Boys Club or the St. Johns Community Center in Bedford-Stuyvesant; provision for just such a center was made in the plan.

We recommended the rehabilitation of existing parks and playgrounds, including Linton Park, Sperandeo Brothers playground, and two other playgrounds (one of which was used to park police cars), greatly expanded community use of Jefferson Field, and an expanded use of play streets, as well as the establishment of an East New York Park Headquarters, out of which all outdoor recreation programs and park maintenance and repair activities would be undertaken.

In late summer, the Central Brooklyn Model Cities office distributed a memo noting the mass cancelation of fire insurance coverage by numerous insurance companies and listing ten companies that were still writing insurance in the area. A petition to the governor and the state legislature to enjoin such cancelations was prepared and circulated locally, but nothing came of it. Policies continued to be canceled or not renewed.

The August 28, 1968, meeting produced an unusual discussion on the need for day care. Men thought more day care might encourage delinquency among mothers (demonstrating their ignorance of the problems women face in bringing up children, as well as the poor regard in which men held women); women thought it was a good idea. Morancie was again criticized for his continuing failure to supply the Model Cities committee with staff support.

On October 4, the Central Brooklyn Model Cities office informed the East New York Model Cities Committee that DOSS (Department of Social Services) intended to construct a group day-care center at 452 Pennsylvania Avenue. Leo Lillard, responding for HUPC, reminded Morancie that HUPC was on record opposing the center because (1) it was too close to Site 21, which was also planned as a day-care center, and (2) no discussion had been held with the community on this proposal. Lillard thought that DOSS was trying to avoid its commitment to build a day-care center on Site 21.

The Physical Development Committee then discussed community college needs, and school seat needs, and it was agreed to oppose the building of P.S. 13 on Jefferson Field and to support locating the school further east. Horace Morancie was informed and asked to send copies of the Committee's position letter to the Board of Education and other city officials. Morancie failed to do this, undercutting the Physical Development Committee's efforts to influence school planning.

Finally, on November 1, 1968, ten months after starting work, the Model Cities East New York office was officially opened at 2095 Pitkin Avenue, with Amos Gaillard as program manager. He quickly informed us that he had to get Morancie's personal approval to send out meeting notices. Gaillard rarely if ever got that approval, so the office never did help involve the community in the planning effort.

On December 18, 1968, I wrote to Morancie, saying that the committee needed to have meeting notices sent out and that HUPC also needed staff support or its load might be transferred to the Physical Development Committee, as well, holding up progress on the plan. There was no response to the letter, but every slight by Morancie simply increased local opposition to his chokehold on policies, programs, staffing, and funding.

As we approached the site selection phase, I briefed the committee on rehabilitation programs and on new housing options. In the vest pocket program, I reported, new housing rents were coming in higher than expected. Attendees wanted more planning for relocation from Model Cities sites, since there might be a lot of it. It was agreed to include more on relocation in the Phase II plan.

Among the main attendees at these Model Cities meetings (not all of whom showed up at every meeting) were Vincent Jones, Gerald Hayes, Amos Gaillard, Gilberto Matos, Lena Goldstein, Marshall Stukes, Granville Payne, Leo Lillard, Evelyn Downing, Father Galuska, the Reverend Pangborn, Alan Drezin, Harding Bowman, Rockman (from Rosen Associates), Herbert Wright (coordinator for CRF), Legendre (turnkey architect for the CRF), Don Haymes, Sol Stevens, Daniel Himmel, Leo Fiorentino, Renee Ossit, Evelyn Millman and Morris Eisenstein—largely a mix of the Vest Pocket planning group plus some of the nonprofit sponsors.

It was comforting that many of the most dedicated members of the Physical Development Committee turned out to be old hands from the Vest Pocket program. My Vest Pocket relocation report was presented and discussed.[3]

Model Cities planning, which should have been finished in six to nine months, had already taken fourteen months and was not nearly complete. As a result, many ad hoc decisions had been made, threatening the planning process and community unity. Among the most difficult to swallow was the Central Brooklyn Model Cities' decision to displace 1,200 families in the northwest quadrant, designating the area exclusively for industrial use. We had no input into that discussion. Much as we disliked it, we did have to include the P.S. 13 site on Jefferson Field in the Phase II plan. We also had to respect the community decision to locate the East Brooklyn High School site in the center of the community and to make it part of the Phase II plan.

On March 6, 1969, I wrote to Eugenia Flatow, saying I was "shocked and outraged" by Morancie's threat to present his own first-year housing and community facilities plan to the East New York Physical Development Committee, to be followed the next week by a presentation to a mass meeting of the Central Brooklyn Model Cities Policy Committee. Considering the almost total lack of staff support given by Morancie to the East New York Physical Development Committee, and the failure of the city to arrange needed meetings with housing officials, the imposition of this top-down planning on the community was the worst sort of insult. I urged that the threatened presentation be withdrawn and that the city, Morancie, and the East New York community representatives sit down and work out a schedule that would allow the community to complete its own first-year plan.

THE PHASE II PLAN

Starting before the pull-back of the Morancie plan, regular meetings of the Physical Development Committee were finally being held; they took place on January 27, February 20, and March 25, 1969. As of then, my consulting firm had gone nine months without receiving city funds; I was now supporting my firm's planning effort with my own money.

In April, the East New York Model Cities Physical Development Committee began preparations for a full-scale community meeting on the Phase II plan. At my initial presentation, on May 6, I accompanied my talk with more than twenty-eight maps, including five housing maps, three community facilities maps, a retail analysis, traffic and bus route maps, and various planning maps including one showing changes in the Vest Pocket plan to date. The presentation culminated in the proposed Phase II plan, which called for 1,500 new and rehabilitated units in the tenement area and another 1,600 units of housing in devastated areas east of Pennsylvania Avenue. In addition to housing, the Model Cities plan called for a modest educational park (five 300-seat minischools, plus five new elementary and middle schools), the East Brooklyn High School, four day-care and early childhood centers, a 70,000-square-foot shopping center, two multiservice centers, two recreation centers (in one of which was an Olympic-sized pool), three acres of park and play space, an added bus route, and a sensible approach to relocation. It also proposed serious study of the feasibility of a new hospital.

The plan was well received, and a number of sensible changes were suggested. After two revisions and more meetings, the final plan was published by the Central Brooklyn Model Cities Committee in June 1969. Months later, on February 9, 1970, the East New York Model Cities Phase II plan was officially presented to city officials. It is sad to report that none of the proposed housing units or other facilities were ever built.

At a September 2, 1969, meeting of the Physical Development Committee, Evelyn Millman, of the United Community Centers (UCC), said she was not pleased with the Thabit plan for an educational park, insisting hers was the one the community wanted. Priscilla Wooten said that the community was not involved in Thabit's schools planning. Bill Wright asked her where her input was, and she said that the Education Committee had never met. The compromises forced on us by the Board of Education negatively affected the results; my office's school planning efforts were no match for the Board of Education's ruthless exercise of power.[4]

At about this time, a flyer asking people to come to a rally in opposition to the Phase II plan to demolish a row of houses on Barbey Street was being distributed. The organizer of the rally was Harding Bowman, chairman of both the CRF and the N-PHCC, who owned a house on that street. Some of his neighbors were up in arms at the idea that their houses were being taken.

Many of these and other issues raised around the Phase II plan may have had some merit. The planning had been conducted in a somewhat constricted fashion, much of the time without widespread community participation. The larger community had not been fully involved; it was a wonder that more opposition did not surface.

At the meeting, also, a few disgruntled people began raising questions about holding new Model Cities elections. They were just getting into it when Gerald Hayes walked in. He told the people who wanted new elections to get lost, and the meeting staggered toward a conclusion, with accusations and counteraccusations, threats and counterthreats hurled back and forth as the meeting room emptied out.

But the bubble was about to burst, anyway. A change in HUD regulations was proposed that would require nonprofit sponsors to put up 5 percent of project equity and to finance social services in the projects they built; they were currently eligible for 100 percent loan guarantees.[5] Roy Wilkins, then president of the NAACP, wrote to George Romney, Secretary of HUD (Department of Housing and Urban Development), saying that "nearly all nonprofit efforts by Negro organizations, community groups and religious bodies will quickly grind to a halt" if the proposed regulations were approved. Mr. Gullidge, owner of a construction company in North Carolina and a former president of the National Association of Home Builders, said, "The non profit sponsor does not belong in housing production except under a very limited set of circumstances." Like riots? The new regulations were soon approved; nonprofit sponsorship did grind to a halt. Within a year or two, except for projects already in the pipeline, the housing programs themselves were dismantled or so restricted that progress became impossible.

On July 27, 1970, a status report on DOSS day-care centers was put together by my staff. It showed nine potential sites for day-care centers, to be sponsored by a variety of church and community organizations, that had received varying percentages of the needed approvals. Five of the proposals had been approved by the Model Cities Committee. One center was under construction; several others were on hold pending lease negotiations.

Model Cities meetings continued to be held in desultory fashion for the next year.

In November 1970, Amos Gaillard, project manager for the East New York Model Cities office, was terminated. A strong letter disapproving this action was sent to Judge Williams, the new citywide head of Model Cities, but brought no response. Then, on Tuesday, December 8, Frank Rivera, now chairman of the Physical Development Committee, reported that Judge Williams had turned down East New York's appeal for a new contract, and suggested that we approach Central

Brooklyn Model Cities for money. Frank called a meeting to discuss my report on planning progress and to see where we should go from there.[6] The report called attention to the good start made on implementing the Vest Pocket plan, the completion of the Phase II plan as of February 1970, and the lack of any substantive action since. It also summarized the magnitude of the housing abandonment problem and reviewed the basically unsuccessful attempts being made to do something about it.

My own meeting with Judge Williams was the most hostile session I have ever attended. I told him we were some $14,900 out-of-pocket on our Model Cities contract and asked for a contract extension and additional monies to continue services to the community, as well as to publish the final report on the Phase II plan. His answer was an abrupt no, and that was the end of that.

At the end of August 1971, I saw a copy of the HUD fiscal year 1972 appropriations for Model Cities as hammered out by a joint Senate-House conference committee. Rioting was now in the distant past; Model Cities was a growing embarrassment; cities not originally funded wanted to be included. The inclination of Congress was to terminate the program. As a result, the conference committee agreed to fund Model Cities at a national figure of $175 million, compared with $575 million the previous year. The funding was an obituary notice.

Without much hope, the New York City HDA (Housing and Development Administration) applied to HUD for approval of two large urban renewal areas, one in Brownsville and one in East New York, but it was soon informed by HUD that the federal government was deferring all new projects pending resolution of the debate over revenue sharing. The new project areas were never approved; the urban renewal program was dead.

The final blow to the Model Cities fiasco was the 1972 elections for membership on the Central Brooklyn Model Cities Policy Committee. Out of this community of several hundred thousand people, fewer than 100 persons voted in the election. Community participation had been effectively stifled.

10

School Planning

WE NOW REVIEW the travesty that was called school planning in East New York.[1] From 1965 to 1974, not only did the Board of Education fail to supply thousands of East New York children with a full school day for years on end, but it also pursued school planning as if it were an interactive game called "Fool the Community." The school bureaucracy made proposals and took forward-looking steps but produced nothing. Outcries against the lack of action inspired fresh initiatives, which inevitably ended in fatal delays or abject failure.

The Board's failure to produce a single new facility in East New York in eight critical years is remarkable. Needed elementary, intermediate, and high schools were sabotaged; educational parks were trifled with and sabotaged. If anything can explain the Board's almost glacial progress, it is its frenetic dance-in-place as it postured shamelessly in front of the black and white communities, ultimately favoring the latter.

THE SCHOOL PLANNING PLAYERS

As a Model Cities planning consultant, my firm was hired to prepare a housing and school facilities plan acceptable to the East New York community. The school planning part proved especially difficult. There were many players, often with conflicting agendas, and little or no direction (or encouragement) from the Board of Education. Clearly defined policies on smaller schools, on 4-4-4 systems (K–grade 4, grades 5–8, grades 9–12), on resources, and on educational parks were never forthcoming. Anything resembling a specific goal for racial integration was avoided.

Many agencies and community organizations were involved in school planning, including the School Planning and Research Division

of the Board of Education, the District 19 office of the Board, the Site Selection Board, the Bureau of the Budget, the mayor's office, the School
Planning section and the Brooklyn Local Area Planning Office of the
Department of City Planning, consultants to the City Planning Commission and the Board of Education, and the Linear City/Cross-Brook-
lyn Expressway agency sponsors.

Locally, up to a couple of hundred people might turn out for an important school meeting. Local organizations included United Youth in
Action, which held meetings on school issues affecting its immediate
area; the multiracial United Community Centers, involved for years in
school issues and strongly committed to integration; the East New York
Community Corporation (the local antipoverty agency), previously
committed to integration, then, later, committed to black control; and
CBENY (Council for a Better East New York), a leaky umbrella organization. Many churches, the local school board, and agitated parents
were also active. Central Brooklyn Model Cities (which covered Bedford-Stuyvesant, Ocean Hill/Brownsville, and East New York) played
its own educational power games—ineffectively, for the most part.
And, of course, the East New York Model Cities Committee, for which
my planning firm worked, had its own Education Committee.

In East New York, community organizations in existence for more
than a few years were a rarity. Most were single-purpose groups, recently organized. One group concentrated on housing, another on operating a credit union, a third on antipoverty programs, still another on
youth. Communitywide councils like CBENY were weakened by internal conflict; cohesion and unified direction were difficult to attain.
Responses to government ranged from long-suffering searches for sympathetic response to angry demonstrations and fiery public hearings.

What I did not know, but gradually learned and am still coming to
terms with, was the ruthlessness, the deceitfulness, and the racism of
the school bureaucracy. In this chapter, I describe how Adrian Blumenfeld, the administrator of the School Planning and Research Division of
the Board of Education, held the school planning and construction reins
in his iron and unyielding grip. His modus operandi was to deceive, divide, conquer, and, if necessary, ignore the community and its needs.
None of the other players, even taken together, mattered to any significant degree. Considering how many agencies were involved, and how
much local interest and activity in school planning there was, that is a
frightening fact.

SCHOOL PLANNING

The Board's School Planning and Research Division established its own "demographic section" in 1960 and began estimating pupil projections and seat needs, taking over this task from the City Planning Commission. Yet, as of 1968, there was not a single demographer on staff. In its assessment of East New York's school needs, it gave no consideration to the continued in-migration of large families with school-age children, nor did its plans incorporate the elimination of portable (toiletless) classrooms in five of the community's schools. The extra needs of children reading below grade level were simply ignored, as was the need for preschool facilities.

The Board acknowledged that nine schools needed replacement in its 1970–1975 capital program; many schools were more than fifty years old and lacked hot-lunch facilities, gymnasiums, science labs, and other facilities. Nevertheless, only two elementary schools (P.S. 13 and P.S. 72) and one intermediate school (I.S. 381) were scheduled for construction in or near the Model Cities area in the Board's 1969–1970 building program. The elementary schools had "a" status for site selection and design; the intermediate school was included in a dubious educational park.

In contrast to the Board's building program, my office published its assessment of needs in March 1969.[2] Just to eliminate split sessions in thirteen schools and the busing of 674 children would require, a minimum of 6,023 seats. This tremendous shortage was precipitated at least in part by the gradual closing of three Roman Catholic schools in the 1960s, to which most Irish and Italian parents had sent their children.[3] Our estimate did not call for the removal of the forty-seven portable classrooms in use on five school playgrounds, though it could have. It did call for the immediate construction of four elementary and four intermediate schools, including the replacement of the very old and obsolete P.S. 63.

More than 2,200 seats in prekindergarten programs were also needed but were not included in our estimates. They should have been. Mayor Lindsay, against the recommendations of the City Planning Commission, had budgeted more money for early childhood centers, but East New York was not one of the recipients. True, money wasn't there even for kindergarten seats, but the needs certainly were.

The failure to provide adequate physical facilities was more than matched by inadequacies in the instructional program. Researchers at the University of Wisconsin tracked 1,500 Chicago children from age five to age twenty and found that poor children who had attended programs like Head Start, with the active involvement of parents, committed fewer juvenile crimes. The idea hadn't yet penetrated the city's educational bureaucracy. Reading scores in East New York were among the lowest in the City of New York.

A case can be made for not supplying permanent seats for peak pupil enrollments in areas such as East New York, where enrollment can be expected to peak and then fall off by 20 percent or more as the population ages. But that doesn't mean that it's all right to let thousands of children go without seats or to put them on short sessions. Permanent seating should be provided to cover peak pupil enrollment; overage and obsolete schools can gradually be phased out as enrollments fall to long-term projected levels. Temporary space can be leased or constructed to fill in the gaps caused by construction delays but is not a long-term solution. Even the closed Catholic schools could have been used creatively to reduce the seat shortages.

Temporary classroom space was not much of an option in East New York, however. Elizabeth O'Daly, the district superintendent, had previously conducted searches for such space but managed to find only one or two sites, one of which took five years to bring on line. In February 1968, my office undertook a similar survey, checking out vacated synagogues, vacant industrial properties, and other possible spaces. All but one out of nineteen prospects had been vandalized or burned out or were otherwise unusable. One obvious solution was the immediate construction of *new* school space, but neither the Board nor the city was responsive to the urgent needs.

City and state administrations were as much to blame as the Board of Education for the failure to build enough new schools. Funding, controlled by the Bureau of the Budget, was always limited. If the Board needed ten new schools, it was lucky to get three. The Board played along, typically understating the needs, especially in minority communities.[4]

From 1967 through 1974, though new schools were high on the community's agenda and vigorously fought for, the schools bureaucracy fought just as vigorously against them. The result: not a single new school was built in East New York for eight years.

P.S. 13 SITE SELECTION

The P.S. 13 site selection process is a classic example of the Board's dishonesty in its dealings with East New York. In April 1967, top priority for new schools went to Flatbush-East Flatbush and to Midwood-Flatlands in Brooklyn, mostly white communities where needs were not nearly as great as those in East New York.

East New York parents were outraged and let the Board know how they felt. In response, Adrian Blumenfeld seemed to put P.S. 13, one of the two elementary schools the Board had earmarked for construction in the 1969–1970 building program, on a fast track, moving rapidly toward site selection and construction. He first proposed to build an expansion for Jefferson Field (a one-square-block playing field located down the street from East New York's Jefferson High School) in the proposed Spring Creek Educational Park in Canarsie, a couple of miles away. He included I.S. 381 (the intermediate school scheduled for early construction) in the Spring Creek Educational Park, as well. He then proposed to locate P.S. 13 on the current Jefferson Field site because there would be no relocation load and construction could proceed rapidly.

In Machiavellian terms, it was a master stroke. The whole idea was a fraud, and not just a rob-Peter-to-pay-Paul scam either. Yes, it would rob East New York of scarce open space, but that was the least of it. It was a terrible proposal because P.S. 13 could not be built until the Jefferson Field expansion, as part of the Spring Creek Educational Park, was completed, and, as I explain later, that itself was pie in the sky. The Spring Creek Educational Park was a wholly unproven and complex undertaking that had won the approval of neither the school bureaucracy, the black community, nor the white community. It would have been a miracle if it had ever been built.

Adrian Blumenfeld was pressed to choose an alternate site by East New York Model Cities, as well as my office and by others, but Blumenfeld was adamant about using the Jefferson Field site. After many meetings and an exchange of several letters, he bluntly told the Model Cities Committee to plan the needed open space somewhere else.

Blumenfeld also managed to get local support for the Jefferson Field site. His staff claimed that the local school board had submitted a dozen sites for P.S. 13 to the Board of Ed, including Jefferson Field. This proved to be false, but the rumor did much to neutralize local opposition. Blumenfeld also proposed to place P.S. 72, the other elementary school proposed by the Board of Ed, to the east to quiet more of the opposition. Ultimately, the local school board agreed with Blumenfeld, and the Jefferson Field site was approved and sent to the Site Selection Board on October 28, 1968. In his presentation to the Board, Blumenfeld never mentioned that the site was the athletic field of Jefferson High.

In 1967, the Spring Creek Educational Park became part of Linear City (a grandiose scheme for a 5.5-mile expressway combined with community facilities, schools, and housing)—a death warrant, as it turned out. When the Linear City initiative bit the dust in 1969, as it richly deserved to do (see later discussion), the Spring Creek Educational Park (including the Jefferson Field expansion and I.S. 381) was canceled, as well. P.S. 13 could not be built on the old Jefferson Field site until the new Jefferson Field, ultimately located on Flatlands Avenue, was finally completed in 1974. P.S. 13 was finally built on the old Jefferson Field site in 1975. At least six years had been wasted.

Also in 1975, P.S. 72 was completed, finally ending the seat shortage. By then, East New York had lost 12 percent of its population in just a few short years. The drop was caused by FHA foreclosures and by the emptying of hundreds of buildings, HPD's (New York City Department of Housing Preservation and Development) demolition of vacant and abandoned residential buildings, and the Board of Education's site clearance for P.S. 72 and the East Brooklyn High School (which was never built).

HIGH SCHOOL PLANNING

Planning for new high schools was perhaps the most volatile and emotionally charged issue in school planning. Blacks generally wanted new high schools in the ghetto; whites were passionately against it.

Capital budget funds had been set aside for fourteen high schools, but the Board of Education was pushing for renovations and additions instead of new facilities, hoping at least in part to defuse the racial issue.

At a meeting with Martha Davis, in charge of high school planning for the CPC (City Planning Commission), we were at first told that only nine of the fourteen high schools were presently budgeted.[5] Then she checked again. Oops! It turned out that several of those were being held up because of Linear City. Only six were currently budgeted. At the time, an unreleased CPC report estimated it would take twenty-two years to pay for all the needed high schools at the then-current rate of financing.

Also, much of the money previously allocated for high school construction remained unspent. Changes in policy and in school design, unforeseen site problems, strikes and other labor troubles, "holds" by the City Planning Commission (to find better sites), the need for Art Commission approvals, the complexities of proposals like Linear City or Spring Creek, which involve many agencies and are all but impossible to work out—all caused the delays. The situation was worsened by the Board of Ed's desire to convert all high schools into comprehensive high schools, offering both academic and general diplomas. Needless to say, the reactions of black and white communities also slowed or halted progress.

That East New York was in crisis had no bearing on results. By January 1968, high schools in East New York were severely overcrowded, with enrollment almost double capacity at both Jefferson High and Maxwell Vocational, despite their high drop-out rates. One might expect that the City Planning Commission, which also decides which schools get capital budget priority, would push the Board of Ed to satisfy the critical needs in minority communities, but there is no evidence that it did.

A few incidents serve to illustrate what high school administration in that part of Brooklyn was like. In spring 1967, the Jefferson High principal accused the United Community Centers of "encouraging juvenile delinquency." He was incensed because a handful of students had organized a boycott of the deficient school lunchroom, about which he and his staff had done nothing. Almost 99 percent of the student body joined the peaceful demonstrations for three days, after which the menu was significantly improved. The triumph lay not only in winning a better menu but also in proving that it was possible to create an atmosphere where all students—black, white and Puerto Rican—could work together in a school.

In late October 1968, the East New York Alliance, an organization of students, parents, community residents, and teachers, drew up a list of fifteen reforms that were needed right away at Jefferson High. Among the demands were the assignment of a permanent reading specialist to the school, the provision, in writing, to each student of the correct requirements for both general and academic diplomas ("confusing, vague, and incorrect" information had been handed out for years), and the involvement of students in planning assembly programs. Students also wanted to be allowed to have dances and to be permitted to plan lunch menus.

Overcrowding in the high schools resulted in serious disciplinary and administrative problems, often solved at the expense of students. In the 1966–1967 school year, Franklin K. Lane High School, which had become 80 percent minority and 20 percent white, was confronted with racial issues, including segregated entrances, segregated tables in the cafeteria, and segregated teams and clubs.[6]

In April 1969, Kenneth Clark, president of the Metropolitan Applied Research Center, Inc., sent a telegram to John Doar, then president of the Board of Education, describing the unlawful transfer and discharge of 674 mainly black and Puerto Rican students from Franklin K. Lane, in the northeast corner of the district, over a two-month period. Educational and human rights had been flagrantly violated. More than 400 "discharged" kids were wandering the streets. More than 200 "transferred" students had not been transferred to any other school. Another 125 had been referred to the Board of Ed for "counseling."

Clark also sent Doar a fact sheet detailing the treatment of blacks at Canarsie High since its opening in 1964. The white community had been physically resisting its integration ever since, reported Clark. Black students from Brownsville were attending Canarsie High, and they were often chased and beaten by white youths while police stood idly by and did nothing. Signs reading "NIGGER GO HOME" or other racist slogans were paraded by white youths; chair-throwing melees in the cafeteria and many incidents elsewhere in the school had been reported over the years.

In response to pervasive community pressures, seconded by the high school principals, a proposed East Brooklyn High School was finally given priority and approved for site selection by the School Planning and Research Division of the Board. At first, the Board of Education approved a site north of Atlantic Avenue for the school, but it was forced to reconsider because of an immediate community outcry. Adrian Blumenfeld, already unhappy with my planning office's involvement in school planning, reopened the site question but restricted the community's options to a site east of the Model Cities boundary, effectively silencing our input. This stricture also reflected a growing dissatisfaction with Central Brooklyn Model Cities and its proprietary approach to community development.

Many meetings were held on the issue during August 1968, and at the penultimate meeting in September, 170 of the 193 persons present voted in favor of Site 3, smack dab in the middle of East New York. A demonstration was then called for September 18 at 110 Livingston Street, the headquarters of the Board of Education, to demand that the Board approve the community's East Brooklyn High School site. Giving in grudgingly to the enormous community pressure, the Board of Education submitted Site 3 for the East Brooklyn High School to the Site Selection Board on March 11, 1969. The five-block site was bounded by Belmont Avenue, Jerome Street, Sutter Avenue, Blake Avenue, and Hendrix Street. It contained 308 units in one- and two-family houses in good condition, plus forty-five small commercial establishments.[7] The Site Selection Board approved the site on May 19, 1969.

Although the East Brooklyn High School was given "a" status, the East Kings High School (in a nearby white district) had "b" status and was to be built first.

In July 1970, the Board awarded a design contract for final design and construction documents for the East Brooklyn High School at a cost of $742,775. The site was subsequently cleared. All systems appeared to be go. But wait!

While plans for the East Brooklyn High School were being prepared —surprise! The Board of Education approved the East New York Charrette, encouraging the East New York community to develop its own Educational Park plan (described in more detail later). The community did so, creating a plan for an East New York Educational Complex that would contain the South Central High School and three intermediate schools only a few blocks away from the East Brooklyn High School site. Suddenly realizing that the high schools would be close to each other, the Board of Education terminated the East Brooklyn High School design contract on June 5, 1974. The East Brooklyn High School was dead.

The hidden reason for approving the Charrette and the East New York Educational Complex now emerged—so that the East Brooklyn High School could be knocked out of the construction budget. And, once it had served its purpose, the East New York Educational Complex was also sacrificed on the bureaucratic altar. Instead of a magnificent, new Educational Complex, the pittance ultimately passed on to East New York was a 250-seat addition to the Maxwell Vocational High School.

I am convinced that the pressure brought on the Board of Education by the surrounding white community played a prominent role in killing the East Brooklyn High School. No new comprehensive high school has ever been built in a solidly minority area, not in Harlem, not on the Lower East Side, not in Brownsville, certainly not in East New York.[8] None is likely to be, as long as the Board's and the white community's racial bias remains at its current punitive level.

THE EDUCATIONAL PARK

In one of the more dramatic challenges to the centralized bureaucracy, Dr. Max Wolff, director of research in the Migration Division, Department of Labor, Commonwealth of Puerto Rico, set forth his specific educational park proposal in 1964. Noting that 85 percent of Harlem's eighth graders were reading at or below the fifth-grade level, Dr. Wolff advanced the thesis that separate but equal schools cannot exist. In minority schools, Wolff argued, teachers expect low pupil achievement and do not work hard to teach black children reading and other skills; as a result, students become discouraged, don't learn to read, and drop out. Though the goal should be to help the children overcome whatever barriers exist to their progress, wrote Dr. Wolff, teachers too often conceive their professional obligation to be the protection of the status quo, inevitably resulting in poor educational achievement.

Dr. Wolff's solution was the educational park, a complex that would include elementary, junior high, and high schools in one location to serve combined black and white communities. Dr. Wolff even considered linking the park to a community college. Economies would result from the full-time use of auditoriums, gymnasiums, and art and music facilities. The educational park's libraries, music rooms, language laboratories, remedial centers, science labs, and athletic fields would incorporate modern scientific advances.

Brownsville would be an excellent place to start building educational parks, said Dr. Wolff.[9] Faced with severe seat shortages and scheduled to receive fourteen new schools in the next five years, the

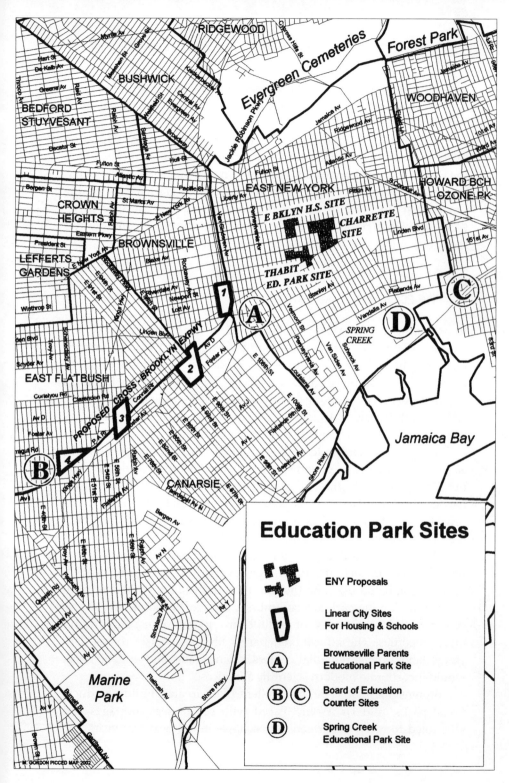

MAP 2

district could see the park developed over time, with new schools added to it as old schools were retired.

Brownsville school activists and citywide supporters bought Dr. Wolff's solution. The parents felt that if the park was adjacent to Brownsville, was big enough, and offered quality education, whites would be drawn to it. They proposed an educational park to be built in the Flatlands (between the black and the white communities) for 15,000 intermediate pupils (see map 2).

In September 1965, the Board of Education responded with its own educational park plan calling for two educational parks. One would be located in Flatbush-East Flatbush, and the other would be at the eastern end of East New York. Both would include three intermediate schools and a high school; both were far from Brownsville (sites B and C, map 2). The Board's planning staff felt that if the parks were in or near white areas, they would have a better chance of being integrated. And, needless to say, they would not be controlled by blacks.

Furious at the Board of Ed's response, on May 20, 1966, Milton A. Galamison, Thelma Hamilton, Helen Efthim, and Curtis Grace, the top Brownsville activists and organizers, among others, presented State Commissioner of Education James E. Allen Jr., with a petition calling for a stay on construction of the proposed elementary and intermediate schools. They asked that the New York City Board of Education be instructed to develop an educational park in Brownsville to meet the community's school needs. Commissioner Allen granted a temporary stay on June 24, 1966.

As if nothing had happened, on June 6, 1966, Adrian Blumenfeld sent his Spring Creek Educational Park proposal to the Site Selection Board. The 42.5-acre park (Site D, map 2) was to contain three intermediate schools (two of which were included in the stay order) and a high school, as well as the expansion of the Jefferson High athletic field.

The Spring Creek area was being developed as a "New Town in Town." Projected developments included Twin Pines Village, a 6,000-unit cooperative housing development on 160 acres, a 300-acre landfill project, a 60-acre, 1,500-bed pair of hospital facilities, a couple of public housing projects, a storm water pollution control plant, the Cross-Brooklyn Expressway, and the Spring Creek Educational Park. On the as yet uncommitted acreage, preliminary estimates anticipated another 6,000 to 10,000 new dwelling units, 110 to 130 acres of industrial use, creating up to 10,000 jobs, a new regional park of nearly 1,000 acres, and many other facilities. An elementary school in conjunction with Twin Pines was also scheduled, along with several small kindergarten classrooms and preschool seats in the public housing projects.

The situation became ever more complex. On February 26, 1967, Mayor John Lindsay announced a plan to develop a Linear City containing schools, housing, and community facilities astride a double-deck Cross-Brooklyn Expressway. The expressway was to run 5.5 miles, using the unused rail line from Bay Ridge, then running through East Flatbush and Canarsie, finally linking up with the Interboro Parkway (since renamed Jackie Robinson Parkway) along the Brownsville/East New York border. The announcement of this scheme was made jointly with Lloyd K. Garrison, then president of the Board of Education.

Making matters worse, on August 24, 1967, Commissioner Allen approved the Board of Ed's Spring Creek Educational Park as part of the Linear City development and as a positive response to Brownsville's demand for an educational park. He therefore lifted the temporary stay on two intermediate schools that would be built as part of the Spring Creek Educational Park.

While the Board of Education was presenting the Spring Creek Educational Park as an answer to the Brownsville parents' demand for an integrated educational park, the David A. Crane consulting firm, employed by the City Planning Commission to review the Spring Creek development proposal, came to a far different conclusion. In a report dated July 24, 1968, Crane made it clear that, as the Spring Creek area fully developed, the educational park would do no more than serve Spring Creek's own population. Students coming to it from Brownsville and East New York would gradually be phased out, leaving it a mostly white complex.

There are certainly difficulties with achieving an integrated (better) educational system via the educational park. Among these is the probability that tracking systems (built into the United Federation of Teachers' contract) will be established one way or another, frustrating the entire idea of an equal education. Also, unless teachers believe in the educability of the children (see chapter 13), students can not make great strides in reading scores or other evidence of learning. Much also depends on the quality and experience of teachers and on the size of school budgets.

The Linear City initiative outraged black communities (which were denied a substantial role in its planning), as well as white communities in the expressway's path (who suspected that the schools would be integrated and the housing predominantly low income). After several ill-fated attempts to gain community acceptance, city agency enthusiasm turned to dejection. The coup de grace came early in March 1969, when the Bureau of Public Roads rejected the city's application to add the Cross-Brooklyn Expressway to the federal Interstate Highway System, ending the fiasco.

THE EAST NEW YORK CHARRETTE

Despite the demise of Linear City, there was enormous interest in the educational park concept, promising as it did modern facilities, high-tech equipment and programs, and local control of a group of schools. Under urging by the East New York Model Cities Planning Committee, my office developed plans for an East New York Educational Park in March 1969. With the help of the innovative architects Bernard Rothzeid and Tunney Lee, our plan called for two intermediate schools and several elementary schools to house upward of 7,000 pupils along the southern border of East New York. A high school was not included, since the East Brooklyn High School site was only a few blocks away. To reduce relocation burdens, we proposed small academic clusters at the lower grades, 200- to 300-seat "academic" schools that would be built on as little as half-acre sites or even on the ground floors of new residential buildings. Community cores (e.g., auditoriums, libraries, art and music rooms) and specialized spaces (e.g., labs, computer rooms, administrative offices) would be in separate buildings, supplementing the limited facilities at the lower grades. The proposal was well received but short lived.

Enter the East New York Charrette![10] Totally out of character, on July 30, 1969, the Board of Education approved the East New York Charrette, which invited the community to plan its own educational park and funded it.[11] Jointly sponsored by the U.S. Office of Education (which contributed $20,000) and the Board of Education (which contributed $52,000), the charrette had as its mission to locate an educational park within the area bounded by Crescent Street, Linden Boulevard, Ashford Street, and Atlantic Avenue.

This was another Machiavellian gambit. It superceded our Model Cities educational park plan, promised to satisfy East New York's unmet school needs, and demolished the Board's racist educational park image all at the same time.

The western boundary was deliberately set just east of the Model Cities area. Both the City Planning Commission and the Board of Education were now furious at Central Brooklyn Model Cities for its attacks on the Linear City plan, its empire building, and other perceived shortcomings. As was also to be expected, my office was excluded from participation in the Charrette, except as an observer.

The community was pleasantly shocked and excited by this unexpected opportunity. The charrette was kicked off at a major community meeting on November 25, 1969, which attracted some 293 persons, 197 of whom were organizationally connected.[12] The East New York Community Corporation and its delegate agencies were heavily represented, as were the regular schools establishment (principals, paraprofessionals, school board members, staff) and the UCC, among other organizations. Priscilla Wooten, of the local school board, was elected chairman; Frank Rivera, Leo Lillard, and Paul J. Gallagher, also nominated, were made co-chairs. At Leo's suggestion, everyone interested was invited to join the steering committee, so 180 people signed up. The next meeting was set for December 11 at I.S. 292, where preparations were to be made for a two-week charrette in January 1970.

The community was now expected to retain an architect, provide a twenty-four-hour space and materials for the charrette, get expert help, set up expense controls, put out public notices of events and results, organize the charrette itself, set up community meetings to discuss issues and approve results, and follow up on implementation. A tough job for even a stable, well-organized group, and this one wasn't. Nor was the program staffed by experienced professionals who could guide the effort through turbulent waters. Officials from the U.S. Office of Education were not used to the rough-and-tumble of East New York activism; Board of Education staff kept a low profile.

The question that dominated the early meetings was whether to plan for an integrated educational park or one that was all black and locally controlled. The East New York Alliance for Better Education, which came into existence during the teachers' strike of 1968 (see chapter 13), saw control of the schools by blacks and Puerto Ricans as a life and death struggle. The Alliance led the protest against the expulsion of the 600 black students from Franklin K. Lane. It was militantly committed to community control of the institutions in black and Puerto Rican communities. The organization's most articulate leaders were Olivia Taylor and Leo Lillard, both of whom are black, and Don Haymes, who is white.

After the first few meetings, the average number of persons who attended charrette meetings dropped to around thirty-five. The atmosphere was tense, often filled with epithets like "honky" and "whitey." Names like "nigger" and "Uncle Tom" were often shouted at blacks who supported integration or who appeared to side with a UCC position.[13] The atmosphere drove out independent community residents, both white and black, leaving the field to employees of the Board, the ENYCC, the East New York Alliance, the UCC, and a few other groups. Toward the end of April 1970, the UCC resigned from the charrette when a meeting was scheduled for the first night of Passover despite an earlier agreement not to hold it on that night. The resignation was greeted with a barrage of anti-Semitic remarks.[14]

Finally, on Monday, April 27, 1970, the first week's schedule of the two-week charrette was ready. Sessions were scheduled throughout the week—mornings, afternoons, and evenings. They included meetings on site selection and development, educational park design, relocation problems, selection of an architect, curriculum development, social services, narcotics, special education, and so on. The Steering Committee was to hold meetings on the overall development, on fiscal matters, and on the resolutions adopted by the various individual sessions. Not many such resolutions materialized.

On May 18, the second week's charrette schedule was distributed. The schedule included many of the first week's topics and a few new ones. An impressive group of consultants, both governmental and non-governmental, were also invited to the various meetings. Many of them were from the Board of Education, including the Harlem activist Isaiah Robinson, then a member of the Board of Education, and Adrian Blumenfeld, chief site selector for the Board. Also invited were Max Wolff and Annie Stein, from the Center for Urban Education, Stanley Aronowitz, from Mobilization for Youth, Luis Fuentes, principal of P.S. 155, Jim Haughton of Fight Back, and many other well-known and outspoken community advocates.

While many of the invited consultants came to a meeting or two, most did not. Most Board of Education and other agency personnel failed to appear, though they were invited in writing by Herb Gottlieb, of the U.S. Office of Education. Many of these agency staffers didn't want to come because they would be asked to commit their agencies and they were not authorized to do so. Others, including many city-wide activists, could not attend on such short notice or wouldn't dream of taking a subway to the outlying sections of Brooklyn.

Though three site options were placed before the charrette committee during the second charrette week, Leo Lillard's favored Site 1 clearly dominated the discussion. It lay within East New York but was close to the border between black and Puerto Rican East New York and white Canarsie. It was sited just two blocks east of our proposed Model Cities educational park. Despite the huge fight over whether to have an integrated or a segregated educational park, Site 1, and the school structure it contained, was in line with integration objectives. There was general agreement to concentrate on that site.

A week later, most of the community's active citizen planners (including Leo Lillard) were joined by officials from the Department of Health Education and Welfare (HEW), the U.S. Office of Education, and people from the upper echelons of the New York City Board of Education. A long discussion of the site and associated problems took place, mostly related to the quality of existing housing, relocation loads, and educational park space needs. The following week, Don Haymes proposed a Charrette Housing Resources Corporation that would rehabilitate vacant buildings as a relocation resource, relocate families being displaced, and manage housing taken over by the city for the charrette complex, the Model Cities housing program, and the East Brooklyn High School site.

Toward the end of the second week, the charrette took on a more positive, focused tone, with many community people (mostly women) and high school and college students filling up the large room. While most of the work was being done by the consultants and students, few of whom lived in East New York, their involvement raised the spirit of the project, giving it new life.

The charrette was scheduled to come to an end on June 30, but the committee was a long way from being specific enough to complete its plans. Even whether to go to a 4-4-4 system had not been decided. Meetings on day care and on bilingual education were among the most productive, but much more work remained to be done. Professional help was employed by the Board of Education to flesh out the charrette committee's report.

On December 16, 1970, the East New York Educational Complex

was adopted by the Board of Education as the replacement for the Spring Creek Educational Park. It was to contain the South Central High School, I.S. 361, I.S. 366, and East New York's I.S. 381 (its last hurrah) on a site bounded by Sutter, Berriman, New Lots, Elton, Blake, and Ashford, as well as the intervening street beds. The resolution adopted by the Board corroborated the agreement among the Board of Education, Community School Board, and the Charrette Committee on the plan and the site.

What followed was a quiet year or two during which Pricilla Wooten, representing the community, worked with the Board of Education and the City Planning Commission to develop and implement the plan. Relocation of the 1,000-plus families to be displaced was a major issue, leading to a decision to implement the plan in phases. Dr. Max Wolff was employed to put together a final version of the report. A major architectural firm was appointed to design the project; the minority architects selected by the charrette committee were named as consultants.

One of the last items in my file is a New York Post story dated March 22, 1973. A 120-page report was finally issued by the Board of Education proposing a 4,000-pupil high school and three intermediate schools for 5,400 children on Leo Lillard's site. It was to include an ice-skating amphitheater, a swimming pool, stores, and a large community gym. Pupils would attend the schools in "houses" of 500 pupils each. None of the buildings was to be more than three stories high.

Once the public announcement was made and the Board seemed committed to the educational complex containing the South Central High School, the design contract for the East Brooklyn High School could be canceled. Once this was done, on June 5, 1974, the plan for the educational complex was allowed to gather some well-earned dust.

Priscilla Wooten blamed the community's failure to get the educational complex on the fact that East New York stood alone; it had no friends among the city's power brokers.

END STATE

The shameful and almost unbelievable conclusion—from 1967 through 1974, no elementary schools were built, no intermediate schools were built, no high school was built, no educational park materialized—all this in the face of enormous seat shortages, split sessions, and the use of buses and portables. At its worst, almost a third of East New York children were receiving less than a full day's schooling. Especially in the face of the area's critical needs and the community's unwavering involvement and activity, the school planning process was one of the darker sides of community politics in New York City.

The East New York experience also illustrates the depth and strength of the Board's bureaucracy and its long-range power to frustrate any action with which it does not agree. The school bureaucracy is impregnable. No city or state agency, no actively involved local community, not even the appointed Board of Education can force the bureaucracy out of its chosen path. Our educational system is under an administrative despotism, hard at work taking care of itself.

11

East New York under Siege

ANYONE WHO THOUGHT that the housing deterioration in East New York would end with the change to black and Puerto Rican occupancy was in for a shock. If anything, the rate of deterioration, and its extent, radically increased over the next decade. During that period, the racist policies of real estate brokers and speculators, the redlining by the banks, and the almost total neglect of the situation by the city and its agencies brought the area to almost total collapse. Through its new federal mortgage insurance program, adopted in 1968, the FHA contributed mightily to the result.

As early as 1967, when East New York had lost its attractiveness to middle-income blacks, houses were being sold to lower-income families. Whites were paid less for their houses than they were a few years earlier, and blacks were charged more. Smaller down payments were made possible by the use of purchase money mortgages (a contract to buy a house, rather than an actual purchase). Home improvement loan scams often added to the burdens of home ownership. Because of the increased cost of owning and the low incomes of owners, the default rate rose rapidly, reaching an estimated 15 percent in 1967–1968.[1] An exodus of higher-income blacks and rising foreclosure rates kept the rate of home ownership well below 25 percent.

THE VACANT BUILDING EXPLOSION

In late 1966, my firm undertook its first vacant building survey. We identified 167 vacant buildings in the Model Cities area (117 outside Vest Pocket and 50 inside Vest Pocket plan areas). The FHA owned only ten to twenty of these vacant buildings as of June 1967; the number rose to fifty-seven by June 1968.[2] While these were mostly buildings that met the strict FHA standards for insurance, corruption in the program was already pushing up the foreclosure rate. In the overwhelming majority of cases, vacancies in the one- to four-family area resulted from the inflated building prices and onerous mortgage terms imposed by brokers, mortgage companies, and speculators. A high default rate was inevitable.

The opportunity to make even greater profits without risk got a major boost in 1968, when an amendment to the Federal Housing Act was passed that permitted the FHA to insure mortgages in ghetto areas without some of the usual restrictions. Physical housing standards were eased; income requirements were relaxed; programs providing interest subsidies and allowing low down payments were adopted.[3] Thousands of houses in East New York became eligible for FHA mortgage insurance.

To this point, lenders had paid some (little though it was) attention to whether a buyer could pay off a mortgage, since it was the lender's own money at risk. They were now potentially freed from this restraint. Mortgagees could get FHA insurance, discount their mortgages, and sell them to government mortgage agencies. The lender's money was then in his pocket. If a mortgage was foreclosed, the federal government absorbed the loss.

Corrupt brokers, mortgage lenders, bankers, and FHA officials were quick to exploit this newly created opportunity. They ultimately sold buildings to anyone who would sign the mortgage commitment, fraudulently certifying sufficient income when necessary. When the owner defaulted, the building was foreclosed, tenants were evicted, and another vacant building ended up in the FHA portfolio. By March 1969, the FHA owned 132 vacant buildings in East New York and was acquiring more at the rate of ten to fifteen a month. The vacant buildings were targets for vandalism and fires, prompting a number of insurance companies to cancel or refuse to renew fire insurance policies.[4]

While the FHA normally repaired and resold foreclosed properties, it did not do so in East New York. As soon as a building became vacant, it was boarded up, followed almost immediately by vandalism. According to Mr. Hayner of the FHA, vandalism put the building into an entirely different repair level, and it would attract no buyers at the higher price. Hayner estimated that it would cost an average of $10,000 to bring such buildings to an insurable condition. Also, the FHA had difficulty finding contractors willing to work in East New York, except for minority contractors (of whom the FHA didn't seem to think much).[5]

The city had bought FHA-rehabilitated buildings in other areas under the lease-purchase program to house displaced, homeless families, but it did not do so in East New York or Brownsville. Private homeowners, speculators, and investors were also buying few East New York vacant properties at the monthly FHA as-is property sales. FHA couldn't solve the problem, Hayner said, and hoped the city or Model Cities would come up with an answer.

Deterioration spread like a conflagration. By mid-1969, a new housing condition survey showed that two-thirds of the housing in the Model Cities area required extensive repair or replacement. On some blocks, as many as 30 percent of the buildings had been burned out and destroyed. Only a third of the buildings in the Model Cities area were in fair to good shape, with the owner-occupied buildings in generally better condition.

This radical change in housing conditions occurred in just over two years. As I was giving a talk on my experience in East New York to a group of architecture and planning faculty members and students at Pratt Institute in 1996, I came to a slide showing the 1969 housing conditions in the Model Cities area, which followed by a few moments another slide showing housing conditions in 1967. I was struck by the difference. I was faced with the picture of much poorer housing quality in the tiny space of two years! I didn't remember this ever happening in my long experience, and I stammered my way past that map, unbelieving, and unable to explain it.

It wasn't until I began writing this chapter that I had sufficient documentation before me to accept the reality of those changes. I saw that we had not changed the rating system; our rating staff had gone through a two-week training period as usual and the results were true. In the short space of two years, the one- to four- family area had changed from a pleasant, fairly well-kept-up community to a collection of blocks in a serious state of disrepair, liberally punctuated with vacant buildings. The sharply lower housing quality could be traced to the abundance of FHA-insured houses occupied by families that could not afford to make payments, much less maintain their houses properly. It was also traceable to absentee landlords who had given up on the area and were no longer maintaining their properties. Many other houses were owned by brokers who were not maintaining them and who were intent on selling them to blacks or Puerto Ricans. Other poorly maintained houses were bank foreclosures; the banks tried to get rid of these, often selling them at deep discounts to speculators. Banks sometimes hold onto buildings in receivership for years in the hope of finding a new owner, but not in these circumstances. Speculators also neglected maintenance, hoping that Model Cities would take their property for urban renewal. A growing number of abandoned or tax-lien (in rem) properties were owned by the City of New York, which also just let them sit. Practically all the blocks showed a quality drop, some of them from "good" to "fair," most from "good" or "fair" to "poor."

Ignored by the city's housing agencies, the East New York Model Cities Policy Committee presented its own program to the city in August 1969. The program called for: (1) the refinancing of mortgages and other steps to avoid foreclosures, (2) use of nonprofit developers to repair and reoccupy vacant properties, (3) provision of financial and technical assistance to homeowners who needed to make home improvements, and (4) use of environmental improvement funds by block associations. All these proposals were ignored.

The lack of response was right in line with administrator of the city's Housing and Development Administration, the 1976 proposal by Roger Starr, for "planned shrinkage" as a way of dealing with devastated communities.[6] His idea was to halt rehabilitation and new construction in deteriorating neighborhoods, move the remaining population out, and cut back on police, fire, subway, and other services.

A 15 percent vacancy rate in the tenement area when the Vest Pocket plan was approved in 1967 was eliminated by the end of 1968. Relocation from the Vest Pocket sites had become increasingly difficult; housing conditions had become progressively worse. Nor did the future look bright. Only 340 units had been rehabilitated through 1970. While another 2,000 new and rehabilitated units were expected during the next two years (it actually took four), there wouldn't be any increase in the total housing stock because of the high foreclosure and abandonment rates.

By the winter of 1969–1970, hundreds of families were doubled up, lodged in welfare hotels, or squatting in apartments without heat, hot water, or other services. "Rent strikes and squatting are spreading," warned Lillie Martin, executive director of East New York Housing Services. During that winter, dozens of such families regularly attended Model Cities planning meetings to press their case for one of the rehabilitated units being readied for occupancy in the coming weeks and months. Few of the neediest got such apartments. Key money was demanded, and political favoritism dominated tenant selection.

In 1970, the East New York Model Cities Policy Committee further proposed that the emergency repair program be empowered to rehabilitate vacant buildings. Again, there was no response from the city or FHA. Several organizations, including Central Brooklyn Model Cities, the East New York Development Corporation, the East New York Restoration Corporation, the Bedford-Stuyvesant Restoration Corporation, and the Urban Coalition proposed programs for repair and re-occupancy of vacated dwellings owned by the FHA (which now owned at least 40 percent of all the vacant houses). Up to 1972, only fifty of the most deteriorated FHA buildings had been offered to Model Cities. More progress was registered during those years by community volunteers, who repaired and re-occupied two vacant buildings on their own.

The buildings in fair to good condition were largely owned by better-off blacks, Puerto Ricans, and the remaining whites. Despite their financial problems, the more stable homeowners took care of their buildings as well as they could. Even so, over the years, many homeowners were overwhelmed by the financial pressures and faced foreclosure.

CATASTROPHE—AND MEDIA INDIFFERENCE

In February 1970, the East New York Model Cities Housing and Physical Development Plan was completed. It called for more than 3,000 units of new and rehabilitated housing, two major recreational facilities, a shopping center, a high school, additional park space, and more day-care centers in the one- to four-family area. Though its completion was a triumph for local community resolve, the plan was doomed. The federal government stopped approving new urban renewal projects, eliminating the funds needed to reduce land costs for housing and other elements of the Model Cities plan. Then, federal housing subsidy funds were also withdrawn. Only six of some thirty-five sites were approved for acquisition, and only four of these were actually acquired. On none of them did construction take place.

In March 1971, my office undertook the fourth in its series of vacant building surveys. Since 1969, an additional 200 buildings had been vacated, mostly in the one- to four-family area. Since the start of these surveys in 1967, some 500 buildings had been vacated, and 200 of these had been torn down. These 500 buildings contained about 2,000 units of housing, 12 percent of the Model Cities housing stock of 16,700 units. These totals excluded all areas then in development, themselves major pockets of vacated and demolished housing before they were selected. The Vest Pocket housing sites and the East Brooklyn High School site contained an estimated 3,000 units of housing.[7] Together with the 2,000 vacant or demolished units outside the site areas, 30 percent of the East New York Model Cities housing stock—some 5,000 units out of the initial 16,700—had been vacated or demolished.

Vacant buildings were not restricted to the "worst" areas in East New York. In 1967, for example, there were about twenty vacant residential buildings in a thirty-block area of better three-story brick buildings bounded by Pitkin, Van Siclen, New Lots, and Pennsylvania Avenues. By 1971, there were 110 vacant buildings in that area. All the "better" areas were similarly hit. Homeowners and tenants were terrified, fearful of vandalism and fires.

The situation in the East New York sector east of the Model Cities area was at least as bad. Surveys of the area out to Fountain Avenue showed more than 100 vacant buildings in February 1967, and almost 200 in August 1968. In addition, 110 buildings had been demolished. While the area was not surveyed after that, police estimated, according to the *New York Times* magazine on Sunday, March 28, 1971, that there were 1,000 vacant buildings in all of East New York. Because 300 to 400 of these were in the Model Cities area (the police count may have included up to 100 vacant buildings on Vest Pocket sites), from 600 to 700 buildings were vacant in the rest of East New York.

As a result of this high rate of housing destruction, earlier estimates of what it would take to stabilize the community's housing stock had to be drastically revised. Prior to the March 1971 vacant building survey, I felt that another 2,000 to 3,000 new and rehabilitated units (in addition to the Model Cities plan proposals) would be required in the Model Cities area. These new and grim vacant building statistics, indicating a continuing and even accelerating rate of abandonment and destruction, suggested that almost all of East New York might require redevelopment or extensive rehabilitation before the desired stability could be achieved.

I was so upset by the findings of the survey that I prepared a special report, "Putting a Stop to the Destruction of East New York." It was completed in April 1971, and was distributed widely throughout the community. The first paragraph began as follows:

> The unprecedented and continuing rate of abandonment, vacancy, destruction and demolition of housing in the East New York community has dispossessed thousands of families, has created a housing crisis of unbelievable proportions, and raises serious questions about the approaches and procedures being followed in renewal efforts in the area. In the Model Cities area alone, over a five-year period, almost 5,000 units of housing have been lost to the community through building vacancy, demolition and the renewal program. Less than 400 units of new and rehabilitated housing have been completed within the same period. Almost 1,000 units scheduled for completion in 1971 and an additional 1,000 units in 1972 are almost balanced by an expected loss of 1,700 units during those two years. After 1972, things get worse. Despite renewal, by 1976 the net loss of all units in the Model Cities area will rise from 27 percent in 1971 to 30 percent in 1976.

The response to the publication of the report was incredible. My office was deluged with calls from homeowners and community leaders, demanding a meeting to discuss the findings. On May 4, 1971, Frank Rivera, Chairman of the East New York Model Cities Housing and Physical Development Committee, called a protest meeting for May 11. I had never seen such an outpouring of community heavyweights as I did on that night. Everyone was mindful of the city's indifference to East New York's plight; outrage was everywhere. At a follow-up meeting on May 18, the East New York Ad Hoc Committee of Housing Leaders was created, its twenty-six members broadly representative of neighborhood churches, businesses, and community organizations. The attendees decided that, since neither the city nor the federal government would help, the community would have to help itself. Right then and there, a few vacant houses were selected, which the community would repair and move needy families into.

It was also decided to get publicity for the effort and to expose the problem and the city's inaction to public view. We (I was very much a part of this) decided to hold a press conference on June 17, 1971. We figured the media would not come to East New York, so we would call the press conference in Manhattan. With the help of Raymond Rubinow, then president of the J. M. Kaplan Fund, we were given free use of a pleasant meeting room in the offices of the nonprofit Brotherhood-In-Action, at Seventh Avenue and 40th Street, just three blocks from the offices of the *New York Times*. Using the information and expertise of activist friends, we prepared a press release, which was sent to almost seventy newspapers, radio shows, and TV stations.

On the morning of June 17, we visited the site of the two houses being opened up and prepared for occupancy. Volunteers were already at work. Piles of trash were being removed; a couple of broken windows were being replaced; neighbors were promising to provide beds and other furniture. We then left for Brotherhood-In-Action, and, by noon, half a dozen East New York leaders and I were all set up, with maps and copies of our release, ready to tell our story to the world.

We waited till 2:00 P.M. Not a single media person showed up. Not a single person called. It was one of the most disappointing days of my life. I was utterly exhausted, feeling as though I had let all these good people down, and was at a loss to explain the total lack of response. The East New York leadership was also visibly disappointed but stoically accepted the lack of response as further evidence of the indifference of the white community to minority needs.

We were all relative neophytes in those days. Had this happened a few years later, we would have marched en masse over to the *New York Times* office on 43rd Street, walked into the editorial offices, and demanded coverage. And we would have gotten it!

But it was a damned good release, and I'm reproducing just a few choice paragraphs below:

> Housing leaders in East New York today announced their *Repair and Reoccupy Our Homes* program, a communitywide action to open abandoned and vacant buildings to use by the community. "We are tired of having our buildings foreclosed and demolished, our community ruined by the failure of the city and federal government to take action," said Frank Rivera, chairman of the East New York Model Cities Housing and Physical Development Committee. "We can't afford to lose any more housing, so we are taking action ourselves."
>
> Work is proceeding on several vacant buildings in East New York. Half a dozen volunteers are repairing a two-family building at 601 Warwick Street, while others are repairing 526 New Jersey Avenue. One building is owned by a Philadelphia man, while the other is owned by an out-of-town bank. The Warwick Street building repair is

being spearheaded by Reverend Jacob Underwood, pastor of the Grace Baptist Church, and Hector Rosas, executive director of Brooklyn Hispanic Civic Organization, while the New Jersey Avenue job is being pushed by East New York Housing Services, aided by Father Capillo, of St. Gabriels Roman Catholic Church, who is raising funds and providing blankets, beds, and other materials. Debris is being removed, walls and ceilings repaired, apartments painted, and water pipes hooked up to sinks, toilets, and bathtubs. The entire effort is unaided by any government sources, a spontaneous volunteer community reaction to the city's failure to act.

"Nothing is being done about the abandonment problem," says Reverend Underwood. "The FHA, the banks and insurance companies, and the City are all at fault. Exploitative practices are at the root of the problem. Real estate brokers buy houses cheap and sell them for twice the price to families who can't afford the upkeep. FHA approves the higher value and doesn't investigate the financial condition of the buyer. When the excessive payments bring about foreclosure, tenants are evicted, the banks get their money from FHA, and another vacant building is subject to vandalism, fire and eventual demolition."

The East New York Restoration Corporation, formed by community people on the Bedford-Stuyvesant model, has visited many of the banks and other institutions responsible for foreclosures, including Eastern Service, United Institutional Service, Chase Manhattan, Inter-Island, and Springfield Equity, in an attempt to halt the precipitous foreclosures. They haven't gotten anywhere with their idea of repairing and reoccupying fifty FHA-owned vacant buildings. Without programs to repair, refinance, and reoccupy buildings, a temporary halt to foreclosures will be meaningless.

Frustration, bitterness, and despair were on everyone's lips. The community was being destroyed more rapidly than it was being improved. The renewal program was dead; the FHA was helping to destroy East New York. The Model Cities program had produced little of help to the community. The media were uninterested. Citizen participation was all but dead (fewer than 100 votes were cast in the 1972 Model Cities election). Many leaders moved out of the community.

As for the FHA involvement? That scandal deserves and gets its own chapter. It's a story I delight in telling—next.

12

The FHA Scandals

JOSE GONZALES, a slim, bright, articulate minister of the New Lots Baptist Church and chairman of CBENY (Council for a Better East New York) first brought to my attention the idea that all was not right with the mortgage lending business: "Do you know that a Hispanic or a black broker cannot get an FHA-insured mortgage? But if you go to Inter-Island or Eastern Service, you can get it?" In early 1970, this was my introduction to the already out-of-control FHA scandal.

The scandal was precipitated by the passage, in 1968, of an amendment to the Federal Housing Act, which extended mortgage insurance to thousands of East New York homes in previously redlined areas and found many FHA officials ready collaborators in crime.

As noted by the Reverend Gonzales, the East New York mortgage market had become strangely selective. Minority brokers were not the only ones unable to get mortgage commitments. White homeowners could not sell their homes directly because they could not get mortgage commitments, either. If one contacted the right broker, however, mortgage funds and FHA insurance flowed freely. Homes were sold with basic deficiencies in wiring, plumbing, heating systems, roofs, walls and even beams, though the FHA required that houses sold under its insurance program be in good repair. Home improvement loans at high interest rates were often tacked on to mortgages. Most of the purchasers who were getting mortgages, moreover, turned out to be poor financial risks. With low incomes, facing high carrying charges, and living in houses badly in need of repair, the homes of poorer purchasers were foreclosed soon after the mortgage commitments were made. In the worst cases, lenders even advanced the $200 down payment required for a home purchase by a family that couldn't begin to meet income requirements.

Community leaders were certain that the banks, private mortgage lenders, and certain brokers were making huge profits from these questionable transactions, while the community suffered from the resulting foreclosures and the evictions that went along with them. (FHA accepted foreclosed buildings only if all tenants had already vacated the premises.) They took their suspicions to East New York's Congressman Frank Brasco and HUD officials in 1970 and 1971 in an effort to get an investigation started. They named many of the suspect firms operating in the area, including Eastern Service (which was later indicted), and helped uncover one of the most invidious, widespread, and expensive conspiracies in the nation's housing history.

Wide-ranging investigations did finally get under way. Grand juries met to consider alleged wholesale violations of federal and local laws in Boston, Detroit, New York, Philadelphia, Chicago, and elsewhere.[1] Indictments were returned in all these cities; seven HUD employees were also dismissed for wrongdoing. Total losses from the foreclosure schemes alone reached $2 billion. In the Section 235 and 236 scandals, the sales of 43 percent of the existing homes showed significant deficiencies, including falsification of applications and fraudulent certification of repairs. Money was lost in excessive fees, unwarranted land markups, rapid depreciation, and lucrative tax write-offs.

The shocking nature of the conspiracy and the lack of ethics among government employees and respected firms was fully revealed in the New York City investigations, which resulted in the indictment of ten firms and forty persons. These included FHA employees, eight real estate firms, seven lawyers, including Herbert S. Cronin, a $27,000-a-year chief underwriter for the FHA, and the firm of Dun and Bradstreet.[2]

In a case typical of those alleged in the indictments, a speculator would buy a ghetto house for $5,000 (borrowed from the Eastern Service Corporation at 6 percent) and bribe an FHA appraiser to appraise it for $21,000. A purchaser, usually black or Puerto Rican, would be told that, though he had an income of only $5,000 a year and FHA requires income to be at least half the purchase price, he could still buy a $21,000 house with the speculator's help. The broker would apply to Eastern for a mortgage, inventing additional income for the purchaser, calling him, for example, a self-employed painter in his spare time. Eastern would then steer its Dun and Bradstreet credit check through Arthur F. Prescott, a vice president of D and B, who would confirm the false information.[3] Harry Bernstein, of Eastern Service, would then be able to get FHA approval of a mortgage—a process that normally takes a week to a month—by phone in fifteen minutes.[4] Eastern would charge a closing fee of 10 to 15 percent though 1 percent was all the law allowed.[5] The mortgage was promptly discounted and sold to the Federal National Mortgage Association or the Government National Mortgage Association for 95 to 98 percent of its value. The purchaser would find it difficult to keep up payments; the mortgage would be foreclosed and any remaining tenants in the building evicted. The mortgage lender had already received his money; the federal government suffered the loss. The "homeowner" and any tenants were out on the street. Total losses in Brooklyn were estimated at up to $250 million.

Not everyone working for the FHA was crooked. The scam did not die in the face of an honest (that is, thousands of dollars lower) appraisal. It would then operate through an unscrupulous tradesman or contractor who would certify expensive repairs or alterations when they had not in fact been made.[6] After the building was vacated, a local real estate agent would be given the property to resell. Depending on his honesty, the cycle might begin again. In one case, according to U.S. Attorney Anthony Accetta, a house had been sold, foreclosed, and sold again six times in an eighteen-month period.[7] "I don't see how anyone who is black or Puerto Rican could have faith in the white system after being shaken down like this and then losing his house two months later," said Accetta.[8]

Political chicanery was responsible for much of the scandal. The final coup de grace in the New York City case was the guilty plea of Donald C. Carroll, director of the FHA Hempstead office, to an "information" (not quite an indictment) that he had promoted two men in his office to key positions in return for an agreement by Stanly Sirote, president of the Inter-Island Mortgagee Corporation, to pick up $1 million in unauthorized mortgage commitments (and a $30,000 loss in their resale value) while Carroll was vice president of the Lawrence-Cedarhurst Federal Savings and Loan Association of Cedarhurst, Long Island.[9] Carroll agreed to the promotions to give the men "greater responsibility and discretion in the performance of their official duties corruptly for and on behalf of Sirote."[10] Sirote was indicted for paying $30,000 in bribes and for financing trips to Puerto Rico for federal employees.[11] At the time of his indictment, Sirote was in the process of selling the Inter-Island Mortgage Corporation. He and his family "stand to make several million dollars on the deal," according to the buyer, Granite Management Services Corporation.

It was now clear why minority brokers and white owners could not get mortgages except through Inter-Island or other brokers in on the scam. They were cut off at the pass by FHA officials in the Hempstead office who were working on behalf of Sirote.

Donald C. Carroll's was "a political patronage job that was given to Carroll as a result of his contributions as a committeeman," Suffolk County Republican Leader Edwin M. Schwenck told the New York Post.[12] George Romney, secretary of HUD (U.S. Deptartment of Housing and Urban Development), was unable to dismiss suspect officials in Florida because of their ties to Senator Edward J. Gurney, Republican of Florida.[13] Lawrence S. Katz, director of the FHA in Milwaukee, ran one of the best programs in the country, including sales of homes to welfare mothers, and was untainted by scandal. Yet he was replaced because he did not meet the patronage requirements of the Wisconsin Republican Committee.[14] Even Romney wasn't totally clean; he refused to disclose the names of fee appraisers involved in fraudulent sales until ordered by the court to do so.[15]

In February 1972, Romney, previously the chief executive officer of American Motors, blasted "the fast-buck artists, speculators, and un-scrupulous developers moving into the subsidized housing markets" who seemed to have "got their training in the used-car business." Shady get-rich-quick schemes abound, declared Romney, involving re-altors, builders, developers, and even some housing authorities."[16] On resigning as HUD secretary, Romney emphasized that Washington did not have the answers and charged that the cities themselves didn't care. The nation "needs one example" of a city concerned with saving its res-idential areas, as well as its downtown and business areas, he declared in a speech at the Economic Club in Detroit, "but," he exclaimed bit-terly, "we don't have one."[17]

While the investigations were continuing and the causes of failure were being uncovered, the machinery put in motion by the granting of thousands of federal mortgage insurance policies continued to grind out the results. By 1973, the FHA owned more than 1,600 buildings in Brooklyn alone.[18] Practically all were vacant, and were rapidly infecting the surrounding areas.

In 1975, multimillion dollar scandals continued to plague the big cities, with little corrective action being undertaken.[19] According to the New York Times, a HUD departmental study group reported that agency "officials believe there is a need for overwhelming preponder-ance of conclusive evidence of wrongdoing before any action should be initiated." As a consequence, action was seldom taken to retract a mortgagee's approval of a mortgage or to suspend a mortgagee from participating in the program.[20]

Some few were caught. In November 1975, one Stephen Rosenbaum was indicted for bribing FHA and VA officials to approve inflated mortgages on rundown houses in poorer areas of Brooklyn and Queens.[21] In 1998, Nadine Malone, president of Madison Home Equities, one of the city's largest mortgage lenders, agreed to pay $50,000 to settle charges that she had abused a federal mortgage program.[22] Malone allowed false income statements to be submitted and failed to disclose her ownership of companies that sold homes to low-income buyers who then used Madison to finance the deals. Four other firms were accused by HUD of similar violations.

AFTER THE SCANDALS

As a result of the scandals, there was finally a break in FHA's hard-nosed stand against repairing and reoccupying vacant buildings. It sold 277 properties to the New York City Housing Authority and another fifty to the Urban Coalition (mostly outside the Model Cities area).[23] In 1972, it also offered 200 properties to the city's Housing and Development Administration, with more in the offing.

The agency remained adamant about repossessing vacant properties, however, and, in July 1972, a suit was filed in Brooklyn Federal Court by nine tenants on behalf of hundreds who had lived in or were living in one- to four-family houses that had been foreclosed by the FHA. Legal Services lawyers argued that the "vacancy requirement" was "arbitrary, capricious and contrary to law." The suit was not successful on the vacancy requirement, but it did succeed in stopping the bulk sale of FHA-owned properties at distress prices, a practice that had only fed the speculation fever.

Having failed to overturn the vacant building requirement, Legal Services lawyers then fought the vacancy requirement through the National Environmental Policy Act (NEPA).[24] Neighborhood groups in Brooklyn (including some in East New York) brought suit against the FHA in February 1973, seeking to force FHA to evaluate the impact of the vacant-delivery requirement on the affected Brooklyn neighborhoods.

The suit was decided in favor of the tenants in 1974. HUD was enjoined from requiring vacant delivery until it had developed guidelines for when buildings should be vacated. It did not do so, and tenants no longer had to be evicted in the event of foreclosures. The foreclosures, of course, continued.

In 1974, HUD finally agreed to rehabilitate fifty buildings and to turn them over to the East New York Development Corporation for marketing, sales, and counseling of new owners.[25] The East New York Savings Bank made $1 million in mortgage money available for the initial stages of this plan. Ultimately, community leaders hoped, 750 buildings owned by the FHA in East New York would be rehabilitated and sold to new owners.

VENGEANCE ON THE VICTIMS

While advances were slowly being made in repairing and reoccupying vacant properties and in the prevention of bulk sales at distress prices, the federal establishment seemed hell-bent on punishing East New York and other ghetto areas victimized by the FHA scandals. Instead of ending the exploitation that was destroying the community, the feds turned off the oxygen that was keeping hope alive.

On January 5,1972, and over the following two months, citing widespread waste and corruption, HUD suspended all subsidized housing programs and issued strict new guidelines for urban renewal, effectively ending the program. On February 27, 1972, the Senate Banking and Currency Committee approved legislation that would locate 20 percent more very-low-income housing units in the suburbs under the 236 program, leaving that much less funding for East New York and other ghetto areas. The FHA scandals played a role in creating the new guidelines.

By July 1972, a blacklist was being set up by FHA officials that banned loans in deteriorating, mostly black and Puerto Rican sections of Brooklyn.[26] Reform legislation foundered in the House of Representatives.[27] Fifty-nine local housing authorities were experiencing "serious financial difficulties," and seven were "verging on insolvency."

As of March 31, 1972, 26 percent of the mortgages insured under the Section 236 program (which subsidized multiple-dwelling projects) were in default, reflecting the growing financial failure in the subsidized field. Most of the projects were built in the suburbs by for-profit sponsors who had utilized the tax shelters provided by rapid depreciation sections of the law. Once the tax shelters were used up, in seven to ten years, many sponsors let the property revert back to the government.

Representative Wright Patman, of Texas, chairman of the House Banking and Currency Committee, criticized past housing legislation, saying that it gave too much to special interests and too little to consumers. He battled the National Association of Home Builders and other real estate groups that complained, among other things, that his reforms "would put these state agencies in direct competition with private builders."[28] The NAHB was also upset by the success of nonprofit sponsors that had proved they could sponsor, develop, and maintain Section 236 apartment projects. Nonprofits were soon required to furnish a 5 percent equity in new projects (previously no equity had been required), a requirement that summarily ended their participation.

In December 1975, the U.S. Commission on Civil Rights criticized the federal government for failing to build housing for poor and moderate-income families and asked for a new effort to build at least 600,000 units of such housing each year between 1976 and 1978.[29] No one in power paid the slightest attention.

What we had here was a total failure on the part of city, state, and federal governments. George Romney was right—not one city cared enough about its residential areas to try to save them. All levels of government were in thrall to the real estate industry, all too willing to ignore the industry's criminal acts, its community-destroying activities, its undisguised racism, its enthusiasm for segregation, its lust for profits. In the East New York feeding frenzy, it was open season on blacks and Puerto Ricans.

Some officials wanted to do away with ghetto communities altogether. Roger Starr, then administrator of the city's Housing and Development Administration (HDA), coined the term "planned shrinkage" as a way not only of clearing deteriorated areas but of removing their occupants, as well. He looked toward shrinking the number of low-income people, citing half a million lost jobs in the city since 1969, and said, "We seem to have great difficulty in attracting industry here. If we don't have sufficient jobs, people will leave the city."[30] That translated into less housing for blacks, Hispanics, and Asians.

Other city officials took issue with Starr. Deputy Mayor John Zuc-cotti, for example, defended the devastated communities' right to re-build and also doubted that large areas of the city could be closed off. Of course, none of the officials took a single step toward curbing the ex-cesses of brokers, banks, the FHA, or the city's own agencies.

In 1975, in the twilight of the devastation, the HDA finally put to-gether a token Small Home Improvement Program (SHIP), through which eighty-eight East New York vacant buildings would be repaired and resold with FHA insurance.[31] The project involved all the actors in the play, including the FHA, the East New York Savings Bank, and the East New York Development Corporation, and was started with a Fed-eral Community Development allocation of $1.6 million. As with many of HDA's programs, few buildings were actually repaired and reoccu-pied. In a community that had 125 mortgage failures a year, the SHIP program had enough legal service funds to help just twenty-four build-ings within its twelve-block service area.

EAST NEW YORK REVISITED

At the end of 1971, my work for East New York Model Cities came to an end, and I attended to work for other clients for the next few years. I still kept an eye on East New York, however, and took great delight in the exposure of the FHA scandals. By 1975, I was very curious as to how the community had fared since 1971.

I wondered whether the FHA scandals had brought abandonment to a halt and whether the area was still being destroyed. I also won-dered whether the rehabilitation and reoccupancy of housing was mak-ing a noticeable difference. Despite the news that hundreds of buildings were being transferred by the FHA to the city and other groups, I had the feeling that not much was being accomplished.

At my own expense, and with the volunteer help of Lillie Martin, long the director of East New York Housing Services and by then exec-utive director of Multi-Service Center #3, we undertook another vacant building survey in September 1975. The results were not pleasant. Be-tween 1971 and 1975, another 450 buildings in the Model Cities area had been vacated and 240 demolished. Five hundred buildings now stood vacant in East New York. Another 100 buildings had been vacated and demolished on newly acquired residential and industrial renewal sites.

The 550 newly vacated buildings contained an estimated 2,100 housing units, 13 percent of Model Cities' original total. Altogether, some 43 percent of the Model Cities housing stock had been destroyed since 1966. An additional sixty-seven buildings (containing about 200 units) foreclosed by the FHA were still occupied by tenants, thanks to the 1974 court ruling.

As a result of this large-scale foreclosure, abandonment, demolition and accompanying deterioration, large sections of the Model Cities area had been destroyed. New areas, some twenty to twenty-five blocks, almost a sixth of the total, had deteriorated to the point where they could not be rehabilitated. The worst destruction had taken place in the east, in the area between Van Siclen and Barbey (north, south, and west of the East Brooklyn High School site), where between fifteen and twenty blocks were all but destroyed. To the east, outside the Model Cities area, similar devastation was apparent.

Housing needs in East New York had escalated to very high levels indeed. Very little of the community's housing was in acceptable shape. The broad categories of need found in the Model Cities area in 1976 are shown in table 1. Basic to recovery of the area was elimination of the abuses in the real estate market. The withdrawal of bank mortgage funds from the area would have to be reversed. Brokers would have to be strictly supervised. The practices that had culminated in the FHA scandals of 1972 would have to be ended (houses with poor wiring, bad plumbing, leaking roofs, rotted beams, and deteriorated plaster walls were still being sold at greatly inflated prices). Establishment of a local FHA office, use of public appraisals, strict monitoring of sales, and double-checking of sales prospects, among other safeguards, would be needed to eliminate the unsavory, illegal, and destructive practices.

Table I

Housing Improvement Needs in East New York

Housing needs	No. of units
Normal maintenance, minor repair	2,500
Foreclosure and abandonment prevention	1,500
Repair and reoccupancy of vacant buildings (existing and anticipated)	2,700
Rehabilitation/major repairs	3,100
New construction	6,000
Total	15,800

Deferred payments, grants, loans, tax forgiveness, refinancing, and issuance of mortgage and improvement grants and loans would all be necessary to prevent foreclosures and abandonments.

A preliminary estimate indicated that upward of $400 million would be required to put East New York back on its feet. More than $300 million would go for new construction and about $50 million for rehabilitation and repair of some 6,000 units. Between $10 and $20 million would go to foreclosure prevention, $20 to $40 million for community facilities, a shopping center, and other non-residential uses. Major commitments would be required by both government and private lending institutions. Every year that no action was taken, the price tag would rise by another $20 to 25 million.

No action was taken. My report, "East New York Revisited," issued in March 1976, was received in silence by government agencies and in East New York. The most dynamic leadership was gone; those who were left knew it was useless to call for help. East New York entered a long sleep.

13

The Community School Board Disaster

NOTHING WOULD HAVE pleased East New York's education activists more than the chance to run their own schools. And, during
the upheavals surrounding the integration issue, they almost got the
chance. Frustrated and disgusted by the education bureaucracy, they
wanted and fought for meaningful community participation. By the
early 1960s, more than a dozen studies had recommended stronger
local boards that would have closer ties to their communities and to district superintendents, but no changes were made. The Board of Education's unwillingness to share its power, plus its failure to act decisively
to integrate the schools, stimulated a record amount of opposition to
central control.

During 1964, there were three school boycotts, two by blacks and
one by whites (Parents and Taxpayers), all of them against the Board's
plan for integration. At its height, several hundred thousand children
absented themselves from school, resulting in a loss to the Board of
more than $2.5 million in state aid.

The following year, a schools consultant, Marilyn Gittell, issued a
sharply pointed critique of the existing system.[1] She lamented the declining role of the mayor, the Board of Education, and the superintendent of schools in setting educational policy, and deplored the correspon-
ding rise in the power of the professional bureaucracy. She called the
decentralization of bureaucratic power and the expansion of nonpro-
fessional influence the first objective of any effort to change the system.

In 1965, despite the mounting criticism, a new Board of Education
plan created thirty local school districts, each containing an average of
twenty-eight schools and 35,000 pupils. Again, the local boards were
granted no powers and were insulated from district superintendents by
having to report directly to the central board.

Incensed by this bureaucratic rebuff, Milton Galamison, of the black
Ocean Hill–Brownsville area, organized a boycott of 600 schools to protest the lack of community participation. In the fall of 1966, parents boy-

cotted I.S. 201, in Harlem, to stress the need for teacher accountability. In March 1967, Isaiah Robinson, chairman of the Harlem Parents Committee, issued a blueprint for decentralization called Operation Excellence. The proposal called for local control of the educational process and the organization of schools into intermediate and feeder school complexes, or educational parks. During 1967, also, students boycotted more than a dozen schools in an effort to remove their principals.

Finally, government took notice. After two years of riots and civil disorder, housing and education in ghetto areas were given high priority. On April 30, 1967, following action by the state legislature, Mayor Lindsay appointed an Advisory Panel on the Decentralization of the New York City Schools and asked it to come up with a plan for decentralization. Chaired by McGeorge Bundy, president of the Ford Foundation, the staff was headed by Mario D. Fantini, also of the Ford Foundation (which had long been influential in school planning and educational issues). Fantini, to his credit, employed Marilyn Gittell as a consultant and also called on Isaiah Robinson and myself, among others, for assistance. A great sense of urgency inspired the effort. Change was in the wind.

THE DEMONSTRATION DISTRICTS

In May 1967, in response to its most outspoken critics, the Board of Education established three demonstration districts as experiments in local control. One of these, in Milton Galamison's Ocean Hill–Brownsville district, was implemented in six elementary, one junior high, and one intermediate school.[2] Governed by a board of ten parents, five teachers, five community reps, and one administrative rep, the demo district was empowered to "select and appoint personnel, initiate and approve programs, and request budget appropriations and to allocate same."

Rhody McCoy, who helped Milton Galamison organize the 600-school boycott in 1965, was named district superintendent. When he took office, only 1.4 percent of New York City school supervisors were black or Puerto Rican, though more than half the schoolchildren were. Within one year, the Ocean Hill–Brownsville demo district had two black assistant superintendents, male and female black principals, one Chinese principal, and many minority teachers and staff. Teachers from all over the country applied to work in the district.

The major difference in the approach to teaching in the demonstration district was the belief that the children were educable.[3] In a single year, the positive evaluation of teachers by parents rose from 38 percent to 77 percent. Pupil reading and math scores improved each year of the three-year period for two of the districts; pupils were not tested in Ocean Hill–Brownsville because the local board did not believe the tests were well constructed. Nevertheless, in her evaluation of the demonstration districts, Marilyn Gittell stated that "we must conclude that the districts . . . seemed well on their way to making a significant educational impact on their students."[4]

Many educational innovations were tried by the Ocean Hill–Brownsville demo district, with varying results. One popular program was the assignment of a bilingual teacher to a single class at every class level. This bilingual presence reduced hostility to the school and led to increased communication with parents, who could now talk to the teacher. One program that did not do so well was Project Learn, in which pupils followed programmed materials at their own pace. It did not seem effective to many teachers and parents and was dropped. The good news was that new ideas could easily be tried in the experimental district, whereas this had been almost impossible under the old school rules.

The most striking finding about the impact of local control on pupils was children's response to the statement "Every time I try to get ahead, something or somebody stops me." Most minority children answered yes to the statement, but in Harlem's I.S. 201, 79 percent of the fifth graders interviewed said no. Again, pupils were not interviewed in Ocean Hill–Brownsville, but a similar response would have been likely there. The teachers' belief in the children's ability to learn, as well as children's feeling of kinship with the racial and ethnic makeup of the staff, was felt to be responsible for the response.

On November 8, 1967, after working for just over six months—a record for major advisory commissions—the mayor's Advisory Panel on Decentralization issued its recommendations in what came to be known as the Bundy report, so named after its chairman.[5] Community school boards should receive a clear grant of new authority, said the report, which proceeded to outline their proposed new powers:

> A total allocation of annual operating funds, authority for all primary and secondary (high school) education within their boundaries, the power to appoint and remove District Superintendents. Existing ten-

ure rights of teachers would be preserved, but tenure of new personnel should be awarded by the District. New and wider authority over curriculum, budget, personnel and educational policy would be given to the district. The Board of Examiners would be eliminated.

East New York and other districts were that close to getting true local control. But it was not to be. Early in the spring of 1968, Rhody McCoy returned nineteen teachers and other professional personnel to the central Board, claiming they were actively working to sabotage and destroy the Ocean Hill–Brownsville Demonstration District.[6] If this had been an all-white community, it would not have caused a problem, teachers are returned to Central (they were not fired) every day. But the number of returns and the ostensible cause raised the hackles of the UFT (United Federation of Teachers). Al Shanker, UFT's president, demanded that the teachers be reinstated and that Rhody McCoy be fired. The teachers were reinstated, but not all were returned to teaching duties; Rhody McCoy was not fired; Albert Shanker was not satisfied.

Early in September 1968, Shanker took the UFT out on strike. Within hours, only 5 percent of the teachers and 3 percent of the pupils were still attending New York City schools. Those black (and the few white) teachers who crossed the picket lines in an effort to keep some 400 of the city's 900 schools open with skeleton staffs ran into a bitter barrage of invective: "Commies!" "Fascists!" "Nazi lovers!" "Nigger lovers!" shouted the strikers. Teachers who crossed the picket lines at P.S. 63 were called "scabs."[7] Negotiations during September and October failed to end the strike. On October 25, 1968, a UFT rally outside City Hall drew a surprising 40,000 supporters, who carried signs and cheered Shanker's statement that "We are not about to let our schools be taken over by Nazis and gangsters."

THE SCHOOL DECENTRALIZATION BILL

The strike ruined any prospects for a strong decentralization bill based on the Bundy proposals. Many legislators now viewed decentralization as tantamount to turning the city schools over to black militants.[8] Ultimately, a watered-down version was negotiated between the Board of Ed and the UFT, and resolute political lobbying by both in Albany resulted in a law that was a travesty of the original intent. On April 30,

1969, the *School Decentralization Bill* was passed by the state legislature and promptly signed into law by Governor Nelson Rockefeller.

How badly were the Bundy recommendations decimated? First, almost one-third of the pupils, those attending high schools, were not covered by the decentralization plan. A second major disappointment was the continuation of the Board of Examiners, which conducted tens of thousands of appointment and promotion tests every year. While the community school boards (CSBs) would have jurisdiction over all the elementary and junior high schools in their district and could appoint their own district superintendents, they had to accept policies, programs, instructional materials, union rules, and a host of other restrictions established by the Board of Education, the UFT, and other supervisory units. Most teachers were still assigned by the central administration, and local board authority was limited with respect to most civil service employees. The local boards were empowered to hire and fire other employees and teacher aides. The local boards could submit proposals, help select architects, and review preliminary plans for construction, remodeling, or enlargement of schools under their jurisdiction, but they enjoyed no real power there, either. The agreement with custodial staff prevented local boards from having any control over school maintenance and utilization.

Some good survived the rout. The NAACP Legal Defense Fund successfully sued the Board of Examiners, charging that it discriminated in its examination procedure for principals. As a result, community school boards were able to appoint principals from a list of eligibles who had not passed the Board of Examiners exam, resulting in the appointment of forty-five minority "interim acting principals" out of 108 appointed by the first CSBs. With major restrictions, CSBs in districts where schools scored in the lowest 45th percentile of reading achievement were also permitted to hire teachers locally.

THE COMMUNITY SCHOOL BOARD ELECTIONS

The Bundy plan called for direct election of CSBs by the parents of school children or a mixed "elective-appointive" process. The decentralization law gave the vote to all residents, however, which opened the way to the capture of local school boards by organized groups.[9] Far higher percentages of whites than blacks or Puerto Ricans came out to vote in the first elections. While only 8 percent of the voters turned out in largely black Morningside/Manhattanville on the Upper West Side, for example, 23 percent voted in a white Queens district.

The first community school board elections were held in the boroughs on March 19, 1970, but had to be rerun on May 28 in Manhattan because of boundary disputes in a few districts. In that first election, the Catholic Church elected 95 of the 270 CSB members, a hefty 35 percent, and in six of the eleven Church-dominated boards, there was evidence of bloc voting. The UFT elected another forty-six, ending up with influence on nineteen of the boards. While Board of Education employees were not eligible for election in districts to which they were assigned, twenty-four Board of Ed employees were elected to other community school boards, and received time off to attend to Board duties. Together, these groups accounted for 61 percent of the newly elected community school board membership. Community corporations (poverty programs) and other organized groups also elected many members. The Jewish Defense League successfully frustrated the attempts of black and Puerto Rican parents to control the Lower East Side CSB. (That seesaw struggle continues to this day.)

Though more than half the city's school children were black and Puerto Rican, 72 percent of the first CSB members were white. In twelve districts with 85 percent or more black and Puerto Rican pupils, only six boards had a majority of minority members.

EAST NEW YORK'S COMMUNITY SCHOOL BOARD

In East New York's District 19, with a pupil population that was 83 percent black and Puerto Rican, 13.3 percent of eligible voters elected seven whites, one black, and one Puerto Rican. Despite the active participation of black and Puerto Rican community people on school issues, the well-organized John F. Kennedy Democratic Party club pulled out the vote and dominated the outcome. The Kennedy Club ran the CSB for more than fifteen years, aided by willing black allies such as Council member Priscilla Wooten.[10]

The CSB membership was replete with Democratic Party member names. Ed Griffith had been a District 19 school board member before being elected to the State Assembly; Priscilla Wooten was a school board member before being elected to the New York City Council.[11]

Frances Abbracamiento was school board president for two terms while she was co-leader of the Club. In the 1975–1977 term, the school board president, Michael Long, was a member and, later, head of the state Conservative Party; Vito Battista, who was elected to the New York State Assembly as a Republican and ran for mayor on the Parents and Taxpayers ticket, was a member, as was his secretary; two other Democratic Party politicos were also members. With only one black and one Puerto Rican on the 1975–1977 CSB, East New York was the last local school board with so few minority representatives, despite its overwhelming majority of black and Hispanic voters and children.

Democratic Party control of the CSB basically gave it an enormous patronage base, not only among the school aides and paraprofessionals employed but also among the teaching and supervisory staff. The teaching staff and the CSB played ball with each other; education of the children was not a major part of the agenda.

The new CSB actively discouraged community participation, causing the two minority members to resign as of June 30, 1972. The community angrily protested its lack of involvement at public meetings, but without seeing a change. When ten vacancies for principals occurred, three PTA members were allowed to sit in on interviews and recommend choices for selection, but only two out of the ten principals finally appointed were the choice of the community. The CSB followed normal selection procedures for supervisory positions; though district reading scores were well below the 45th percentile, the hiring and firing of teachers still took place under the centralized guidelines. Closed executive meetings were held weekly. Open meetings were held monthly to announce what had been decided in private. The UCC (United Community Centers) successfully sued the board, forcing an end to its illegal closed meetings in 1978.[12] The board then made its decisions over the phone or at informal gatherings in private places. Business went on as usual.

Local school activists and parents now found themselves protesting, picketing, and demonstrating in front of the local school board, rather than before the Board of Education. The Board of Ed was now further insulated from the demands of its clients by another level of bureaucracy. That level, the local CSB, watched educational budgets being heavily cut by 1977 without raising a peep.

As in many other low-income communities, the parents associations were uniformly weak; at membership meetings, twenty parents was a huge turnout. In November 1975, fourteen of twenty-eight parent association presidents were employed in local schools, making them beholden to the principals and the CSB.[13]

UCC representatives started attending CSB meetings around 1974 and attended almost every public meeting for the next ten years. The UCC used these meetings to criticize the board on a wide variety of issues; getting no response, the UCC decided to try to elect school board members. It formed Concerned Parents for Better Education, held meetings, conducted voter registration drives, and sponsored candidates nights.

While voter participation in District 19 fell from 14.4 percent in 1975 to 11.3 percent in 1977, the figure was still relatively high among ghetto communities. In New York City as a whole, fewer than 6 percent of eligible voters cast ballots. UCC's Integrated Education slate polled 485 first-place votes out of a total of 5,802, enough to elect one of its nominees to the nine-member board.[14] The UCC ran a campaign in the next two elections, as well, electing the single member both times. Its "success" mattered not a whit.

THE BURGEONING DISASTER

Nor did time improve the education climate. Black leaders and administrators interviewed in 1978 felt that the central Board and the UFT had too much power. Local boards should have more power over the expenditure of funds, policy, contract negotiations, and the use of school buildings, they said. They felt that decentralization had benefited the black community mostly by adding minority educators, but were split on whether this had had a positive effect on the education of black schoolchildren.[15] They complained that many of the boards were politicized and had other than education agendas. A sizable majority felt that the boards were not representative of the community, and especially not of parents. Both leaders and administrators felt that Board of Ed employees and UFT members who served on local boards had inherent conflicts of interest and that this practice should be outlawed.

Much of the UFT's power became visible through decentralization. It had gradually developed a stranglehold on educational programs and policies. "Since 1965, virtually all state and federal funds for compensatory education granted to the city were spent on programs spelled out or controlled by the provisions of the UFT contract."[16]

In the 1960s, the UFT aggressively fought against the compulsory transfer of teachers to ghetto schools and opposed reorganization of junior highs so as to foster integration.[17] It sought (and may have recently won) the right to allow teachers to expel disruptive students from the classroom as part of its contract negotiations. (Some readers may think teachers should have that right, but consider the abuses that could result, especially in minority communities.)

The UFT contract mandated that teachers *not* be judged on the basis of performance in the classroom or whether they produced students who can read![18] Teachers and principals were accountable only to themselves under the contract and through similar arrangements to the Council of Supervisory Associations.[19]

In addition, if a school adopted a new program (e.g., teaching reading through phonics), a senior teacher (who was given preference in transfers) could enter the school even if she or he opposed the program. That teacher did not have to accept the program or work with it.

The UFT contract also mandated student tracking. On each grade level, stated the contract, classes should be divided into two categories, "difficult" and "less difficult" in terms of reading achievement.[20] Pupils were placed in one track or the other. Tracking has not proven effective; in fact, when students of different achievement levels were placed in the same class, all students gave evidence of greater improvement.[21]

The UFT strongly influenced educational policy through its membership on community school boards until it was banned from CSB membership in 1989. In 1987, school employees and elected officials still held more than a quarter of local board seats and were a majority on some boards.[22] Parent observation of teaching was not permitted where UFT had CSB membership (nineteen of the thirty-two boards), but CSBs with no UFT members did permit it.

So negative was the UFT's influence that teachers in some schools organized the Teachers Action Caucus, challenging the UFT's retrograde positions on school policy.

THE FAILURE OF CENTRAL AUTHORITIES

If central authorities had tried to make decentralization work, major educational improvements might have been possible, even given the weakness of the decentralization law. But five separate studies made in the late 1980s and early 1990s sharply criticized central authorities for failing to do their part.[23]

The major findings of these studies indicated that central authorities overregulated and competed with local school boards, rather than assisting and supporting them. Central had mandated strict budget categories and had even held back funds over which community school boards had independent statutory authority. It failed to allocate resources to districts in an equitable manner, never consulted with local boards, and failed to involve the boards in policy development or UFT negotiations.

The reports unanimously recommended that the Board of Examiners be abolished.[24] The Gill report (see note 24) noted the Board's inadequate screening of new employees and its many biases; others scored its maddening promotion procedures. The PEA (Public Education Association) report complained that the Board of Examiners sharply inhibited the recruitment of personnel by local school boards.

Central authorities made no attempt to monitor educational performance or to assist or intervene when needed. They badly mismanaged business and managerial support for the CSBs, creating difficulties in the day-to-day operation of the schools. Central was aware that some districts were out of control fiscally but did nothing about it.

The Board of Education's inspector general's office was seen by many observers as lax and lenient, and most of the reports recommended that it be made independent of the Board. An attempt to improve the situation occurred in 1990, when Ed Stancik was named Special Schools Investigator by the Dinkins administration. That office has thirty-five investigators and concentrates on sex abuse and other crimes that can be prosecuted. The unit has an 81 percent conviction rate.[25] Schools Chancellor Harold Levy, appointed in 2001, reconstituted the Board's own Office of Special Investigations, staffing it with more former police officers and giving law enforcement training to civilian investigators. The unit is still poorly staffed, with only thirteen investigators to handle a soaring caseload of more than 7,000 complaints a year. Both offices have come under repeated attacks because serious sex offenders have fallen through the cracks and because the offices are perceived as weak and lenient and as lacking accountability.[26]

While all the reports agreed that political patronage had seriously compromised the efforts of some superintendents to run their districts effectively, this was not found to be a widespread problem. School employees and local elected officials were among the worst offenders; they were guilty of improprieties and of ignoring conflict-of-interest provisions. The Gill report and others called for detailed standards for superintendents, principals, and fiscal officers to prevent the appointment of unfit applicants.

All the studies recommended changes that would reduce the ability of special interest groups to control election results. While proportional representation allowed minor party candidates to be elected with less than a majority vote, its time-consuming, hand-counting procedure opened it to corruption, and its use was legally ended in 1998. Nevertheless, it continues in use; the state legislation ending proportional representation was struck down by the Justice Department, which felt that it was injurious to minority representation. Another change is being used; eligible voters now vote for only four of the nine members in any election year, in hopes of reducing the ability of organized groups to control an entire board.

Though not part of the CSBs, high school administrators also came under attack. In effect, they were fully accountable to no one. In 1978, field superintendents were reestablished for the high schools, but the need for fully staffed administrative units similar to those in the thirty-two CSB districts was undeniable. In 2001, district supervisions was being imposed on high schools on a case-by-case basis.

On the basis of these findings, it is easy to see why community school boards were failing. They were being overregulated on the one hand and almost totally neglected on the other. When wrongdoing was not punished and poor performance was not addressed, participants began to feel that anything went. Exploitation of the system was more common than one would expect. One principal in East New York's District 19, known as "The Cookie Monster," enlisted her staff to sell junk food to pupils at a 300 percent markup.[27]

ACHIEVEMENT IN DISTRICT 19

Even the one bright spot in the picture has lost some of its luster. It was early thought that increases in minority staff would inspire minority children to learn, but it turned out that race and ethnicity of the teaching staff had little to do with learning. In District 19, the proportion of minority teachers rose from 38 percent in 1987–1988 to 49 percent in

1995–1996. All to the good! Yet the 20 percent increase did not produce an increase in District 19 reading scores.

While differing standards, use of different tests, and alleged widespread cheating during the 1970s and 1980s make it difficult to compare reading scores over time, a sampling of the most comparable results shows the hard reality: no basic, long-term improvement in reading skills has been achieved.

Table 2
Percentage of Students Reading at or above Grade Level

School year	District 19	Citywide	Gap between city and D-19
1981	38.3	49.6	11.3
1986	43.1	51.1	8.0
1992	36.3	46.4	10.1
1995	36.2	47.5	11.3

Source: New York City Board of Education

The bottom line is that the average community school board has had very little influence on educational quality. Over the years, minority membership on the East New York Community School Board has risen appreciably, but educational success has not accompanied the change. The CSB could say that children needed more reading programs and that it wanted to see an improvement in scores but that it had to rely on the professional staff to come up with new approaches. The CSB had few unallocated resources, and, since most of the curriculum was mandated by central authorities and by UFT contract, it could implement few if any new ideas.

Improvements and declines in reading achievement according to Corina Grant, a member of District 19's community school board for the past thirteen years, can be directly traced to budget increases or reductions, the presence of quality teaching, and the condition of buildings and equipment. Budget increases and/or supplemental funds can result in reduced class size, additional remedial programs, increased individual attention, and experimentation with new approaches, all of which help to improve scores. But poor districts just don't get their fair share. A 1987 Community Service Society report found that "poor districts are almost always shortchanged in the 35 percent of resources which buys remedial and enhancement programs."[28]

The trick in teaching is to have teachers who know how to teach and who are consequently respected by students, parents, and coworkers. The best teachers can get themselves assigned to schools with the best pupil populations, and they often opt for that road, leaving less gifted children shortchanged. During the past several years, Grant reported, many highly qualified and successful teachers have left District 19 or retired, leaving the schools more and more in the hands of less experienced instructors. Teachers fresh out of school, with no break-in assistance, are thrown into difficult classrooms and expected to swim. An inordinate number quit soon after they start.

Programs and equipment are also in short supply. District 19 is one of seven school districts in which no elementary schools have a specific focus on science and math, nor are the schools participating in the Urban Systemic Initiative, a program that encourages the study of science through improved curriculum, staff training, and equipment.[29] Many districts have six to twelve such schools.

Schools with these programs generally have a high (for New York City) 10:1 ratio of students to computers. District 19 does have one middle school that focuses on science and math, and another middle school that receives extra funds for health and human services training. These are the only District 19 schools with a 10:1 ratio of students to computers. Few of the district's other schools have computers, though they are gradually getting some.

Many of the district's schools are old and decrepit. Peeling paint, broken systems, and generally deplorable conditions are typical of the district's older schools. The really old ones have no gyms, no cafeterias, and little or no play space.

Conditions such as these are hardly conducive to learning. It is hard to produce educable children if your hands aren't free to lift spirits, if patronage affects appointments, if your coworkers are in despair because of poor working conditions, if you can't try new ideas or respond to emerging needs, if you can't repair, paint, and fight for those new computers. If CSBs had been given the power visualized by the Bundy report, if board members had been able to make a difference, corruption and chicanery might never have made the inroads they have.

It is also worth pointing out that, when a former chancellor, Rudy Crew, began to take action against CSBs that were guilty of educational failure and corruption, he suspended only five of the thirty-two CSBs elected in 1996 and replaced several of the superintendents who served those boards. While such actions helped to maintain the integrity of local boards, the chancellor's actions (actually the paucity of actions) suggest that blanket condemnation of the CSBs was totally unwarranted.

THE POLITICALLY UGLY

One would have thought that the legislature was on the right track when, in 1989, it banned school employees and elected officials from serving on CSBs. But, on December 31, 1996, the state legislature passed a bill that virtually destroyed local boards. Taking effect in April 1998, the bill took away all the executive and administrative powers of the boards. The district superintendents now control the budget. No longer do the boards hire and fire employees, manage and operate the schools, make repairs costing less than $250,000 per year, operate social centers, cafeteria, or restaurant services, appoint teacher aides, employ counsel, or, submit proposals for school facilities. Instead of the local boards, the district superintendent now selects new principals and supervisors, though parents do have a voice in the screening process. These powers and more are given to the district superintendent; all other personnel appointments are controlled by the chancellor. All in all, these changes represent a stunning loss of the few powers local boards did have.

How did this legislation come to pass? By the ugliest of politics. In the May 1996 CSB elections, the Por Los Niños slate had beaten the Jewish Defense League forces and came out on top in Manhattan's District 1. Sheldon Silver, Speaker of the State Assembly, smarted under this defeat in his home district.

After the 1996 election, also, a third of the superintendent jobs were open. A Queens district sent in its selection, which Chancellor Rudy Crew rejected, saying the woman candidate was not qualified. But she was qualified; support for the district's candidate was overwhelming, and Rudy Crew had to reverse himself. He found he could refuse to appoint a CSB's choice only for cause.

But Crew was determined to control the system. Somehow, he convinced Assemblyman Steve Sanders that he, Crew, should be the ultimate authority on school issues, working through superintendents that he would select. Sanders agreed with taking away some CSB powers but also wanted to further empower parents. Together, they approached Sheldon Silver with their ideas.

Silver went along with stripping the local boards of their powers. In this, he was avenging the Por Los Niños victory in the 1996 elections by making the boards powerless. On the other hand, he insisted that the appointment of district superintendents remain the province of the CSBs, because he felt the JDL forces in District 1 could control the selection of the district's next superintendent.[30] On those terms, he agreed to passage of the vindictive and ill-advised school governance law described earlier in the waning hours of 1996. The bill was passed in the dead of night; most legislators had no idea what they were adopting.

The bill required CSBs, utilizing a screening committee that included parents, to submit to the Chancellor of the city school system four candidates for district superintendent (taken from an approved list), from which the chancellor would select one. In practice, following another abortive attempt by Crew to name a superintendent, most boards submitted a single name, which Crew unhappily approved.

Sheldon Silver was also indebted to Crew for a favor. Earlier, William Ubiñas had been hired as district superintendent of District 1, had sold out to the (JDL) Jewish Defense League forces, and was then fired by CSB 1 after he had served a year as superintendent. With Silver's help, Ubiñas was then hired by the New York State Department of Education—and shortly thereafter, fired. Crew did Silver a favor by giving Ubiñas a one-year consulting job with the city Board of Education. Silver was therefore indebted to Crew.

In this way, flying in the face of all the evaluations, central authorities have been reinvested with almost total (unaccountable) power, while local school boards have been relegated almost to their pre-1970 position of impotence.[31]

After passage of the law, Rudy Crew continued to try to gain control of the district superintendents. When reading scores came in lower than hoped for in May and June 1999, Crew announced that he was going to fire five superintendents who were not doing a good job.[32] District 19's superintendent, Robert C. Riccobono, was assured that he was not one of the five, but, after he returned some principals to the central board, they appealed to Priscilla Wooten, who complained to Crew, as a result of which Riccobono was put on the to-be-fired list. He received a letter of termination in July 1999. No good reasons were given for the termination. In fact, Riccobono was doing a good job as superintendent and was getting along well with the local board. He had actually been turning the district around; there had been a slight increase in the reading scores of the East New York district.

The CSB and Riccobono appealed his firing to the Board of Education, which upheld the firing. Riccobono then appealed to the State Board of Education, which found he had been wrongly dismissed. Crew was later succeeded by Harold Levy, who appealed the state's decision to the State Supreme Court, which found against the Board of Education. While Harold Levy did a high-wire act (on the one hand appealing the decision, on the other moving toward a settlement) in Riccobono's case, he was very much in the Rudy Crew mold, seeking to dictate the selection of district superintendents and thus to control them.

In May 2001, Levy got into a running feud with the Lower East Side District 1 school board, which declined to add his protégé, the district's acting superintendent, Helen Santiago, to the list of potential hires.[33] Santiago, who got her current post at Levy's request, did not make the initial list of five finalists. Though one finalist was disqualified, the board's search committee refused to add Santiago's name to the list to be submitted to the full CSB for consideration. In a curious turn of events, Riccobono, who hadn't worked for more than two years, was being considered as a potential fifth name. Levy was furious; he threw Amy Velez, a new CSB member, off the board for trumped-up charges. As of April 2002, he had refused to name a permanent superintendent, satisfied to have Helen Santiago continue as acting superintendent. The battle was heating up.

IS THERE A FUTURE?

Despite the rigidly centralized control of New York City's educational system, the report of the state-appointed Marchi Commission noted that hundreds of school districts in the state carry out all the functions performed at the citywide level in New York City and recommended pilot and demonstration studies to further decentralize the system.[34]

Major cities around the world have long recognized the need for making government more responsive to needs at neighborhood and community levels. Local districts in London, Berlin, and Paris have their own submayors, operate local marriage bureaus at their borough halls, and provide appropriate services at the district level. The twenty-eight London boroughs, for example, raise half their revenues locally, are responsible for most roads, public health, electricity, street maintenance, garbage collection, parking facilities, baths and bathhouses, public libraries, museums, parks, and open space, maternity and child welfare services, tuberculosis clinics, dairies, personal welfare and children services, education in part, and housing. While such decentralization is not always superior to centralized operations, local control certainly deserves a chance to prove itself in the City of New York.

However marginally the objections to local power were weakened by school decentralization, the idea of giving local communities some additional powers looked promising to some. The idea was explored by the Scott Commission in its report on restructuring the government of New York City, published in 1972.[35] Where power can be exercised at the local or city level equally well, says the report, "we choose the level closest to the people." The authors, Edward N. Costikyan and Maxwell Lehman, named twenty-five to thirty services that local district governments could be made responsible for. The real guts of government (building and developing housing, as opposed to its management, for example) would remain centrally controlled. The local district could provide social services but not dispense welfare funds, hand out parking tickets but not have its own police force. The taxing power, budget power, and eminent domain power would remain firmly in city hands.

But the idea of conferring any local autonomy on minority or other districts was (and still is) anathema to New York politicians. The Scott Commission report died a-borning.

Aside from being permitted to operate social service, antipoverty, and youth programs and to participate in housing, planning, and urban renewal, local communities have little or no actual power. While the city could grant local communities substantial powers even now, statehood for the City of New York (or the metropolitan area) could put such changes on a fast track. Jimmy Breslin and Norman Mailer came up with the idea of making New York City the fifty-first state during Breslin's run for the mayoralty in the 1970s. If the city were a state, every district within it could have the autonomy enjoyed by the City of New York and still be under state guidance and control. Each district could become a city, with its own taxes, laws, courts, police, fire, sanitation, education, health, and other services (or most of them, anyway), as well as its own housing and development programs. Hoboken, New Jersey, does it all, and with a population of only 50,000. Black communities would have the same opportunity to run themselves as white communities. And we'd also have two additional senators working for us. Do I hear a call for a referendum?

14

Rebuilding in East New York

MY EYES WERE initially opened to East New York's progress during my first visit to the area after a twenty-year absence. Guided by Marshall Stukes, one of the original members of East New York's Housing and Urban Planning Committee, I revisited the housing built under the Vest Pocket Housing and Rehabilitation Program during the early 1970s (see map 3).

We started out on Pennsylvania and Pitkin Avenues, where we saw the health center we had planned. Across the street was the Reverend Underwood's project, which he still runs. Then we went down to Blake Avenue, where we visited the housing sponsored by the Long Island Baptist Church.

Next, we hit the Remeeder project (four buildings, 260 units) which had been developed by the Community Redemption Foundation (CRF), with a number of highly esteemed local men (no women) on its board of directors. After many years of working with a politically connected management team that had brought the project to the brink of foreclosure, a questionable deal was cut to save the project (see chapter 10). "There's big bucks to be made in management," Marshall explained, "big bucks."[1] Corruption is a way of life in East New York—as it is under similar circumstances everywhere.

Next on the tour was Unity Plaza, the two-block New York City Housing Authority project, with a large park in the center, which was empty. The project was named Unity Fiorentino in honor of that small Italian man, an active member of the East New York Housing and Urban Planning Committee who had worked for racial integration during the 1960s and 1970s.

No children or even adults were out on this beautiful day. The sunken amphitheater is never used; rarely are the playground and its equipment in full use. There was a very nice play area with play camels that children could climb on. When this open space was planned, not much thought was given to what should take place there. It cries out for

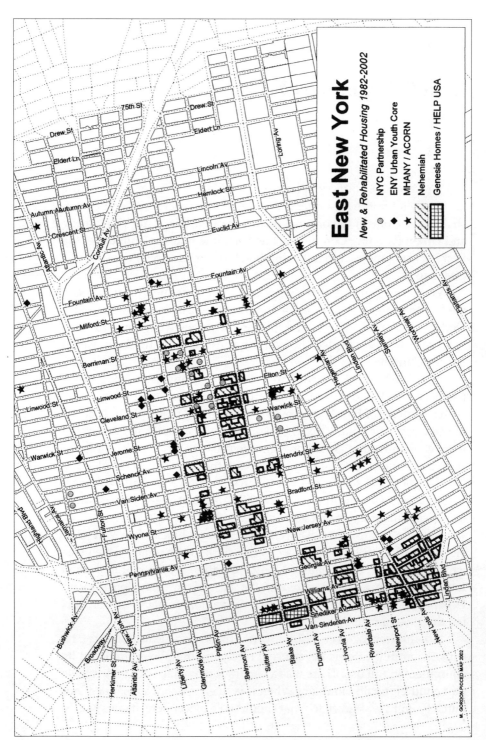

East New York

New & Rehabilitated Housing 1982-2002

- ◉ NYC Partnership
- ◆ ENY Urban Youth Core
- ★ MHANY / ACORN
- ▨ Nehemiah
- ▦ Genesis Homes / HELP USA

M. GORDON PICCED MAP 2002.

MAP 3

a task force of professionals and residents to create something useful out of it.

On Pennsylvania Avenue, underneath the street sign, is another street sign that reads Granville Payne Avenue. What a treat—the community thought enough of these men to name projects and streets after them. Priscilla Wooten sponsored the street name designation.[2]

On another building, passersby are informed by a big four-foot-by-four-foot black sign that the building is protected by a tenant patrol. While it was satisfying to see the old projects we had planned, the main eye-opener on this and subsequent trips was the enormous amount of new and rehabilitated housing. East New York had achieved a remarkable recovery from its depressed state in 1975. When we left it in the 1970s, less than one-third of the housing stock was viable. Today, more than 2,500 new and rehabilitated housing units are liberally sprinkled throughout the community.

A basic factor that had helped to ignite all this action was the existence of vacant land and buildings alongside the impoverished community. One-sixth of East New York's land area was vacant; 4,500 units in existing buildings were also vacant, and most of these buildings were owned by the city or the FHA. While homelessness and high rents proliferated, vacant land and buildings were begging to be occupied.

This chapter details some of the more dramatic housing initiatives and also looks at progress on the commercial, industrial, and social services fronts. While the progress is impressive, there is still a long way to go.

THE NEHEMIAH HOUSES

The spark and a major presence among the new construction has been the Nehemiah houses, named after the biblical prophet who rebuilt Jerusalem. The Nehemiah Plan was launched in the early 1980s with the help of the developer and civic reformer I. D. Robbins, who insisted that low-cost, single-family houses could be built for low- and middle-income families on city-donated parcels of land in blighted neighborhoods. Thirty-six East Brooklyn congregations, brought together by the organizer Mike Gecan, of Saul Alinsky's Industrial Areas Foundation (IAF), took the idea and ran with it.[3]

Mike Gecan reached East New York through the Reverend Heine-meier, a Lutheran pastor in Brownsville, who earlier in his career had taken several days of IAF training. Gecan was invited to a meeting of about fifteen clerics and church members on April 6, 1978. Gecan would not bother with the group, he said, until it raised $300,000, obtained thirty member churches, and got commitments from those members to pay dues of from $500 to $3,000 a year.

On January 15, 1979, seven congregations officially formed East Brooklyn Churches (amended to East Brooklyn Congregations in 1988, when a synagogue joined). Seven more joined by year's end, and a dozen took the ten-day IAF training. Johnny Ray Youngblood, pastor of the St. Paul Community Baptist Church, a dynamic and powerful presence in East New York, was finally persuaded to send two of his best people for the ten-day IAF training regimen, and they came back aglow with enthusiasm. As a result, Youngblood himself went to Chicago for ten days of training to learn the ways of Saul Alinsky.

There, Youngblood came to the attention of Mike Gecan, who saw that Youngblood was at ease with the Catholics and Lutherans around him, and was a rare combination of leadership and fellowship. The two became friends. Youngblood invited Mike to a St. Paul's service and introduced him to the congregation.

The idea of rebuilding Brownsville and East New York thrilled Mike Gecan. He recalled Youngblood's sermon about Nehemiah, who rebuilt the walls of Jerusalem. He then recalled EBC's director telling him about a retired builder, I. D. Robbins, who claimed that he could build a one-family house for $36,000 that a family with an income of $12,000 could afford.

Gecan arranged to meet Robbins and promised to raise a $12 million revolving loan fund. Gecan and Robbins were soon reaching for the brass ring. The revolving loan fund would advance the money for construction of 1,000 row houses, the loan to be repaid as each row house was sold. Early efforts to raise the $12 million failed, however. They were turned down by nine banks and several religious denominations. Finally, after giving Missouri Synod church officials an unforgettable tour of Brownsville's housing chaos, they received the Synod's commitment for a five-year, interest-free loan of $1 million.

With this start, they appealed directly to Bishop Francis I. Mu-gavero, of the Roman Catholic Diocese of Brooklyn. He liked the Nehemiah plan and gave the group invaluable access to the highest levels of government, introducing EBC leaders to Governor Mario Cuomo and ultimately to Mayor Edward I. Koch, a real boost, since otherwise they would never have gotten to see Koch. Koch and Robbins were enemies. At the meeting, Bishop Mugavero did the talking. "Well, Ed, we've got $12 million, and we're ready to build." Gecan and Youngblood looked at each other with shock—they had about $2.5 million at that point. Ed Koch was clearly impressed.

When the bishop put forward EBC's request for land condemnation, tax deferral, and interest-free loans for $10 million (enough for 1,000 homes), Mayor Koch cut in: "There's no money."

"Then steal it," said Mugavero, "and I'll give you absolution."

"You got it," the mayor promised.

The plan received extraordinary support from the area's churches. The Roman Catholic Church, the Episcopal Church, and the Lutheran Church ultimately pledged the bulk of the $12-million loan fund.[4] Finally, on a blustery and overcast afternoon, October 31, 1982, a crowd of 6,000 churchgoers from forty-two churches, dressed in their Sunday best, came to the ground breaking.

Early in the building phase, a group of very tough guys calling themselves the Neighborhood Coalition tried to dictate who would be hired on the job site. In response, EBC assembled from among its members fifty equally tough guys, former policemen, and rough characters, and invited the tough guys to a meeting. EBC told the tough guys they would hire anyone the tough guys suggested, but only if they had the proper qualifications. If they didn't like that approach and wanted to play rough, they would get more than they bargained for. The tough guys never returned.[5]

Twenty months later, on June 14, 1984, a couple named Herbert and Leolin Schleifer moved into 668 Mother Gaston Boulevard, the first Nehemiah home. Nearly half the new homeowners moved directly from housing projects; most came from within a three-mile radius. The price tag for the completed house was about $50,000; the income of Nehemiah house buyers averaged only $25,000.

The Nehemiah houses wouldn't win too many design awards. The two-story homes, with unfinished basements, were eighteen feet wide and thirty-two feet deep, with two or three bedrooms and a bath upstairs and a kitchen, a living room, and a half-bath on the ground floor, for a total of 1,100 square feet. A patch of grass and a concrete parking space out front completed the package. Ron Shiffman, director of the

Pratt Institute Center for Community and Environmental Development, was critical of the quality of the Nehemiah housing, calling it second rate.[6] Other professionals echoed that opinion. While they are not the most glamorous houses, says Mike Gecan, none have fallen down or have failed to give good service in seventeen years.[7]

Some 500 Nehemiah houses have been built east of Pennsylvania Avenue, and, after a battle with City Hall, the EBC has completed another 680 units west of Pennsylvania Avenue. The newer houses are 1,300 square feet and are now manufactured housing, built in a portion of the old Brooklyn Navy Yard.

The new houses cost from $94,000 to $110,000 each, and many of the new owners put another $50,000 into finishing the basement or making other desired improvements. The newest buyers have incomes of between $25,000 (the minimum) and $60,000 annually. There are thousands of applicants on the waiting list; buyers are chosen by lottery.

The great majority of the newest owners come from within a five-mile radius of the project site. While the earlier owners were likely to be city employees, transit workers, or the like, newer owners are more likely to be at the bank manager level, or at least a step above tellers. Many of the new owners are female heads of households.

Home ownership has proved to be an enormous attraction. People are willing to live with difficult conditions if only they can have their own homes. It makes it all the more tragic that so many would-be homeowners were bilked by the FHA scandals. The new buildings have also given new hope to the surrounding neighborhoods. Owners of nearby property now believe that the area has a future and are fixing up their own buildings.

While the first groups of houses were easily located on vacant or nearly vacant land, in December 1994, EBC proposed to tear down nine fifteen-unit apartment buildings containing 135 apartments and to replace them with far fewer single-family Nehemiah houses. It also proposed to displace a number of homeowners to make way for the mass-produced building technology. In an emotional hearing before the City Planning Commission, an EBC organizer, Ken Thorbourne, complained that the apartment buildings were unmanageable and would become a cancerous sore if left in the midst of the Nehemiah development. The Williams Avenue buildings did have a horrendous history. They had started as a rehabilitated coop in the mid-1970s as part of the Vest Pocket Housing and Rehabilitation Program. The coop fell apart after members quarreled; the city took over and appointed a series of terrible managing agents. After ten years without heat, the buildings had fallen into almost total disrepair and were at the mercy of drug dealers and addicts.

More recently, after a suit brought by Legal Aid against the New York City Department of Housing Preservation and Development on behalf of the tenants, the buildings had been brought under control and repaired; services had been restored and the few vacant buildings reoccupied. Discussions were under way on the creation of nonprofit housing management under East New York Urban Youth Corps and/or the city's Tenant Interim Lease program. EBC ultimately lost the battle, and had to build around the Williams Avenue buildings. Homeowners who spoke up at the City Planning Commission hearing were also spared.

The Nehemiah houses have made living in East New York attractive once again. Middle-income blacks have begun buying homes in the area, resulting in sharp increases in home values between 1996 and the present.[8] Houses are being better maintained; homeowners are painting, gardening, making repairs.

In November 2000, with EBC as sponsor, work began on a $192-million shopping complex, the Gateway Center, in the Spring Creek area near the Belt Parkway.[9] Stores such as Target, Home Depot, Marshalls, and Bed Bath and Beyond have signed on as anchor tenants in the 640,000-square-foot center. Once the mall opens in 2002, a new neighborhood, Gateway Estates, will be developed, including 600 new Nehemiah row houses (400 single-family and 200 two-family) for low-income working families. The mall will be a welcome addition to the still poorly served East New York area.

ACORN'S MHANY

The struggles to create a viable rehabilitation effort are also worth recording. Squatters, advised by organizers for ACORN (Association of Community Organizations for Reform Now), occupied twenty-five vacant buildings in East New York, causing a political uproar.[10] ACORN warned the police a day in advance of its intended action at 412 Vermont Street. Eight persons, including State Senator Thomas Bartosiewicz, were arrested for breaking into the building, and they all vowed to reoccupy the building the next day. Tom Kelly, spokesman for Mayor Ed Koch, called the move "illegal, unsafe and the city is already in the process" of trying to renovate the buildings. But ACORN had been trying unsuccessfully to get the city to permit it to renovate the buildings for several months.[11]

It was the desperate need for affordable housing while the city sat on 4,500 vacant units that inflamed local passions to the point where squatting made sense. Typical of the squatters, Jacinto Camacho moved into his house on 925 Glenmore Avenue as a squatter in 1985. "I found about 100 addicts running up and down the stairs. I worked from six in the morning to eight at night clearing out the garbage . . . four times they wanted to evict me, and ACORN defended me." He talked politely to the drug dealers, and the police made many visits; ultimately, the dealers left. "What I did was illegal," Mr. Comacho said, "But if you don't try, you don't get anything. I slept here two winters without heat or electricity. I never had any weapons—just my own hands and the help of God."[12]

Impressed by the sincerity of the residents but put off by the in-your-face squatting actions of ACORN, the Brooklyn borough president's executive assistant, Marilyn Gelber, asked PICCED, the Pratt Institute Center for Community and Environmental Development, to mediate the situation. Ron Shiffman, the Institute's director, persuaded ACORN to promise to abandon squatting, which calmed city officials. Over the next year and a half, with help from Brooklyn officials and from HPD administrator Felice Michetti, the New York City Board of Estimate unanimously approved a program to give those same illegal squatters, transformed into homesteaders and incorporated as the Mutual Housing Association of New York (MHANY), fifty-eight city-owned buildings, money for technical and architectural aid, and another $2.7 million as a revolving loan fund for rehabilitation.

Since 1985, the Pratt Planning and Architectural Collaborative (PPAC) has worked with MHANY on the rehabilitation of vacant city-owned buildings in the area. The buildings range from single-family houses to nine-unit buildings, which are cooperatively owned. Families build up equity in their unit by the work they have put into them. Resale rights are restricted. When a family decides to move, MHANY has the first option to buy the unit at the restricted resale price (plus any earned equity, which goes to the coop owner), keeping the unit affordable.

As of 1998, 112 buildings containing some 360 units had been rehabilitated by MHANY. Prospective tenants must contribute forty hours
of labor (painting or cleaning back yards) in order to be put on the waiting list for an apartment. A typical two-bedroom apartment rents for
$425 a month (less for smaller units, more for larger ones), just about the
level that most East New Yorkers can afford.

Perry Winston, senior architect of the Pratt Collaborative and project manager for MHANY from 1990 to 1995, called the program "one of
the best I have worked on from the point of view of long-term affordability, size of units, quality of materials, opportunity for resident participation, involvement of small local contractors, pace of production,
and cumulative impact on the physical environment."

Despite the substantial amounts of housing rehabilitation, primarily low- to moderate-income rental, the need for affordable apartments
is still overwhelming, not only for the largely poverty-stricken population of East New York but also for young families who are just getting
out of school and who have found jobs but who can't find affordable
housing.[13] By the end of the year 2000, private apartment rentals were
going for from $750 to $900 a month, while these young people could
afford only $400 to $450.

THE EAST NEW YORK URBAN YOUTH CORPS

On a subsequent tour of East New York, led by Perry Winston, we visited the Nehemiah houses, MHANY projects, and many other rebuilding efforts, including those of the East New York Urban Youth Corps.[14]
The dynamic Martin Dunn headed the ENYUYC until 1998, producing
440 units of rehabilitated housing out of forty burned-out buildings
during his tenure. The vacant shells were transformed into affordable
housing for families, AIDs sufferers (in a joint effort with Housing
Works), senior citizens, and the formerly homeless. ENYYUC opened
two Beacon schools, offering arts and literacy programs, cleared some
eight blocks of drug dealers, and opened a teen center in partnership
with the police department. Once-cautious government agencies and
foundations were pouring in money. ENYUYC's budget increased from
$500,000 to $6 million, and it had a staff of eighty. But, when Martin
Dunn refused to award any more contracts to contractors who were associated with district leader DaCosta Headley but who did shoddy

work (see chapter 15), he was summarily fired.[15] Other staff members
quit in support, and the ENYUYC quickly fell from grace. Foundations
withdrew their support; official agencies put projects on hold or simply
dropped them. The group has nevertheless rehabbed the Williams
Street buildings and added them to its management portfolio.

THE GENESIS HOMES PROJECT

Genesis Homes, bounded by Hinsdale, Dumont, Snediker, and Blake
Avenues, is a project of HELP USA Inc. It is a beautifully designed permanent residence for 146 families who were originally homeless. Created by Andrew Cuomo, Secretary of Housing and Urban Development
in the Clinton administration, HELP USA is a dazzling example of how
to create new lives through the intelligent use of housing and social
services. Most people would give their eye teeth to live in this splendid,
square-block housing development, with its internal walkways and
park. Formerly homeless families are given the chance to live there and
to develop their skills, enabling them to compete in mainstream society.
    HELP USA targets all the problems that accompany homelessness,
including poverty, unemployment, crime, drug use, and disease. The
program's approach generally follows the path of work not welfare,
providing incentives for independence, favoring prevention over intervention, promoting low density and diversity, and encouraging not-for-
profit operation of the housing produced. The project has a tenant court
and helps to train leadership.
    HELP USA programs are aimed at getting people ready for work
via academic remediation, work in the Genesis Homes' store, tutoring
for school work, and computer training. Another initiative is AMISTAT,
which is developing school curricula with input from the community
aimed at giving the people what they think they need. It has a boys and
girls club for recreation, with attendance required at antiviolence meetings, and also provides help in getting GED and tutoring. Finally, it offers training in nutrition, in running day-care centers like the Cypress
Hills program (discussed later in this chapter), and in security work.
    Across the street is HELP 1, the organization's first project, with
189 units of transitional housing, completed in 1989. HELP 1 prepares
people to move into Genesis Homes. A third HELP USA building was
nearing completion toward the end of 2000. Located on Snediker be-

tween Blake and Dumont Avenues, it contains fifty-two apartments, half rented to the homeless and half rented to low-income working families. Rents range between $400 and $600 monthly. The building also houses a medical center. Rounding out the HELP USA's Neighborhood Plaza concept is a planned community center on an adjacent lot, which will include space for retail shops, day-care and afterschool programs, and adult activities. The community center is to be followed by another residential building containing sixty-nine units.

COMMERCIAL PROGRESS

Retail stores have increased in number over the years, but they are still outnumbered by vacancies. A windshield survey in August 1999, done by driving up and down the streets of East New York, revealed more empty stores than occupied ones and a slew of vacant lots that had once contained stores, as well. Occupied stores were generally marginal and included groceries (mostly bodegas), barber shops, pharmacies, pizza parlors, small supermarkets, laundromats, storefront churches, fish stores, dry cleaners and diner-type eateries.

In the central portion, the only real shopping street is Sutter Avenue, and it contains little more than convenience outlets. While the vacancy rate is lower on this street, there is still an average of two empty stores per block.

The majority of the stores in East New York are bodegas, catering almost exclusively to their immediate neighborhoods. Most are suspected of selling drugs, or running numbers operations, or other illegal activities, and they are so clannish that it is difficult to find out just what is happening. Many bodegas have signs and posters covering their windows, so it is hard to see what is going on inside. Blacks do not shop there except for immediate needs.

Nor do residents patronize the few supermarkets in the area because the lines are long and the operators are not responsive to community needs or desires. Those with cars (only about a third of the residents) go to Queens to big supermarkets where the service is a lot better. Of course, people who don't have cars have to patronize the local stores.

High on the list of community complaints in the 1980s were grievances with local markets—short-weighting, overpricing, sale of spoiled goods.[16] EBC (East Brooklyn Congregations) organizers identified ten of the worst offenders, and late in the spring of 1981, on a Saturday afternoon, "EBC shopper inspectors" descended on the stores, filled their carts with sour milk, moldy fruit, week-old meat, and rusty cans and took their carts very publicly (to the delight of shoppers) to the checkout counter. Management was terribly embarrassed. The inspection team left each place with a list of violations and a contract to correct them. Three stores resisted signing the contract, but, at a meeting attended by 400 residents, they were that told either they had to correct all violations within three weeks or they would be closed by any means possible. In typical hard ball, Industrial Areas Foundation–fashion, they were then told to leave. They signed.[17]

The middle-income community would like to have anchor stores, major supermarkets that would be responsive to the people and would serve them better than in the past. The EBC recently attempted to acquire a large parcel at Sheffield and Belmont for a Pathmark store, but the city sold the site before it could be acquired.

On the entertainment front, the fourteen-screen Linden Boulevard Multiplex Cinemas opened in mid-May 1998, the only movie theater in this long-neglected community.

AFFORDABLE INDUSTRIAL SPACE

For more than twenty years, East New York has been working to reawaken interest in its vacant industrial space. In 1980, the forty-four-block East Brooklyn Industrial Park was established by the New York City Public Development Corporation in the northwest quadrant. Bounded by Atlantic Avenue, Sheffield Avenue, Sutter Avenue, and Powell Street, the Park has also become one of two industrial Business Improvement Districts (BIDs) in the city and is administered by the LDCENY (Local Development Corporation of East New York).

During the 1980s, the LDCENY packaged cheap city-owned parcels and moderate-interest loans for local business. Under the direction of Rick Recny and Jeff Stern, the LDC helped develop 300,000 square feet of space for manufacturers, foundries, and freight operations and grew into a $900,000-a-year corporation. The effort ground to a halt when Recny and Stern resigned, following years of self-serving political pressure from DeCosta Headley.

Thanks to the strong economy, the availability of cheap industrial space, and the crackdown on crime, East New York has become attractive to industry once again.[18] In the past few years, a number of new companies have moved in, many to the East Brooklyn Industrial Park, others to the Fairfield or Twin Pines districts, south of New Lots Avenue. They range from Hena Inc., a coffee roaster, to DXB Video Tapes Inc., a high-tech videotape, DVD, and CD producer, to Renaissance Woodcarving, a custom furniture manufacturer, and to Distinctive Displays Inc., a producer of showroom, trade show, and retail displays. In addition, weedy lots, once strewn with trash and inhabited by vagrants, have been snapped up as future sites for distribution and manufacturing facilities.

Affordable (and suitable) space is growing scarce, even in East New York. "Five years ago, you probably had at least twenty properties available at any given time," says Avi Feinberg, a partner in City One Real Estate, in Greenpoint. "Now, you can only show a third or less of that."

In response, prices have risen. A one-story building, which rented for $3 to $4 per square foot five years ago, now commands $5 to $6 per square foot. On the sales side, one-story industrial buildings that sold for between $20 and $35 per square foot five years ago now go for $55 per square foot.

Dominick Vitucci, whose Dom's Truck Sales has been based in East New York since 1963, is among those who have cashed in on the neighborhood's rise. Three years ago, he purchased a long-dormant, burned-out industrial building. He paid $400,000 for the 32,000-square-foot space and then poured $500,000 into renovations. Before the work was even finished, he had signed up his first of two tenants. The second tenant committed to the space the morning Mr. Vitucci ran a classified ad for it.

The LDC manages the East Brooklyn Industrial Park, marketing properties in it, acting as ombudsman between firms and city agencies, and acting to improve area security and maintenance.[19] It helps businesses take advantage of incentive packages, acts as a grievance center for complaints about issues such as illegal dumping or unfair ticketing, and has promoted the end of redlining, which prevented many businesses from getting insurance.

The LDC is working with the Neighborhood Shield program (see Chapter 16) through which offenders on probation perform community service in the Industrial Park.[20] The probationers clean up graffiti, remove debris and street trash, and do painting and other light maintenance. The experience could lead to jobs for some of them and is also expected to reduce littering and vandalism as the young people experience being part of the community and doing something for it.

Another improvement in the Industrial Park has been a visible reduction in drug selling and prostitution. The police, under Deputy Inspector Secreto, have been doing more community policing and are doing a better job of following up on complaints. As a result, you don't see as many drug deals or women walking the street as you did just a year or two ago.

While the LDC is sponsoring commercial revitalization along New Lots Avenue, there is little evidence of success on this front. The LDC is nevertheless working to develop the New Lots Plaza, a retail center, on the farmers' market site at New Lots Avenue and Barbey Street. It also helps with the East New York Farms and Farmers Market programs (discussed later) and gives small loans to minority and women-owned businesses.

In these and other ways, the LDC is coming to life and is enthusiastic about its prospects. It is seeking to expand the boundaries of the industrial zone so that more firms can become eligible for benefits (e.g., tax relief, cuts in utility costs). It is working to attract or develop incubator industries, which could mean more jobs for the community, and is also seeking businesses that are compatible with the residential community around them.

There is much more to be done, of course. Despite the recent success, 40 percent of East New York's industrial space is still vacant, much of it derelict. Now is the time to rationalize a land use plan for the community. The toxic and other objectionable industries along Van Sinderin Avenue and elsewhere will have to be dealt with; and whether the entire 144 square block industrial zone should remain industrial and how it should interface with the residential community also needs to be addressed.

PRATT PLANNING

Following the community conflict with EBC over the Williams Street multiple dwellings, it became apparent that longer-range planning responsive to residents' needs was required. Myrvin Garnett, a member of Community Board 5, persuaded Rosalie Genevro, director of the Architectural League, to hold an urban design ideas competition. During 1994, in preparation for the competition, the Architectural League and the community board organized neighborhood forums in different parts of East New York, asking residents to speak to the area's strengths and weaknesses. Out of these discussions came a long list of the top areas of concern in East New York that formed part of the brief for the design competition. These included community involvement, tolerance, violence and drugs, safety, jobs, economic development, education, youth centers, cultural events, housing, health, and transportation.

Concurrently, the Pratt Institute Center for Community and Environmental Development (PICCED) was awarded a grant from HUD to facilitate the local planning process in East New York and in four other Brooklyn communities through HUD's Community Outreach Planning Centers (COPC) program. PICCED's application for COPC was supported by several major East New York groups. They began meeting monthly in the spring of 1995 to develop a long-term planning process and its substantive aspects.[21] The group was open to other community-based organizations (CBOs) and to residents.

As a good way to jump-start PICCED's work under COPC, its architectural subset, the Pratt Planning and Architectural Collaborative (PPAC), entered the competition. Its senior architect, Perry Winston, who had worked for five years on the MHANY rehab project in East New York and who had grappled with the residential fabric of the area firsthand, organized the PPAC design team.

In response to the neighborhood concerns listed in the brief, PPAC developed seven housing prototypes that could fit into scattered sites as small as twenty feet wide and were able to accommodate options for single-, two-, and three-family occupancy. One of the options allowed ground-floor retail, a scheme that responded to the expressed interest of local merchants to own their own store. Too often, they struggled to make a business succeed only to have the rents raised, forcing them to relocate or to go out of business. Apartments above the ground floor were also said to increase illumination on the street, reducing the threat of dark and empty sidewalks. Unfortunately, programs to fund new low-rent, mixed-use construction on small sites do not yet exist.

In addition, PPAC proposed two youth centers at scattered sites, rather than one large one, so that they would be located within walking distance of more youths. It also proposed a new athletic field near one of the youth centers, a new high school, and a new indoor/outdoor swimming pool on New Lots Avenue.

New opportunities for commercial development along Sutter Avenue and Livonia Avenue commercial strips were also identified. The PPAC proposed a new two-story commercial building with ground-floor retail to serve Nehemiah residents and people coming to and from the Livonia Avenue stop on the "L" subway line. While several new supportive housing projects had been approved for construction on Pitkin, all lacked ground-floor retail. In a study undertaken in the spring of 1996 by Pratt graduate planning students, a twenty-five-block long strip of Pitkin Avenue between Sheffield Avenue and Euclid Avenue was examined in detail. It was found to contain ninety commercial establishments, twenty-five vacant storefronts, and fifty-five vacant parcels, averaging about two building lots each.[22] The nodes at Van Siclen, Shepherd, and Euclid Avenues, all near underground subway stops and with available vacant land, were strong candidates for mixed-use development.

Pratt's PPAC designed viable groups of buildings for the three nodes, at an estimated construction cost of $105 to $130 per square foot. Not surprisingly, banks could not be found ready to lend money in East New York for such developments, nor could many would-be entrepreneurs pass the financial requirements for obtaining the needed loans. Most lending sources also dislike mixed-use buildings, though they make the most sense in East New York and many other neighborhoods.

These and many other proposals developed by the twenty-five entrants in the Architectural League competition received a great deal of attention when exhibited in the community and in many meetings and discussions thereafter. The community planning board and its 197a committee (so called after a paragraph in the city charter that permits a locality to formulate its own plan for future development) adopted many of the PPAC's proposals, including many of the suggestions for Pitkin Avenue, and realized that they could work together with the COPC and supplement one another's efforts. The board would benefit from COPC's ability to increase citizen input, and the priorities developed at these forums would gain political weight if included in the board's 197a plan.

Funding for most of these projects has not been forthcoming. One might have expected the LDC to take an interest in subsidizing commercial development, but its feeling is that if an entrepreneur doesn't have the money for a substantial down payment or investment in a business, he shouldn't be in it, nor were they about to throw money at it. Yet, commercial revitalization is an issue of such importance that an ongoing conference of CBOs, banks, Pratt, the EBC, the LDC, and the city should be convened to see what needs to be done and what can be done to jump-start commercial development.

HUMAN AND SOCIAL SERVICES

As the area has regained some of the population it had lost over the previous decades and as the area's crime rate has been dramatically reduced, community organizations have begun to pursue more comprehensive community development strategies. These include child-care centers, afterschool programs for local youth, community-based health services (including an AIDS residence and treatment center), industrial business retention programs, employment and job-readiness training, and an area-wide community security initiative. Sustaining the momentum of these revitalization initiatives in the context of government devolution of responsibility and a rapidly changing political and budgetary environment poses special challenges to the community.

On that same October 15, 1999, tour, participants were introduced to some of the dramatic results of these efforts and to some of the local activists who were involved in the social and economic rebuilding of the East New York community. The tour stopped at the health clinic, now the East New York Diagnostic and Treatment Center, at Pitkin and Pennsylvania Avenues, which offers a variety of medical, dental, and other services including extensive out-reach programs (chapter 7 gives some details).

We also visited the United Community Centers child-care center on New Lots and Schenck Avenues. At the center, we saw five preschool classes for children ranging in age from two to four years, and three afterschool classes for children aged five to twelve years, with twenty children in each. The children are from households on welfare, off welfare (workfare), with working mothers and some special-needs children. An increasing number of household heads are clericals working for private industry. The operation is very impressive. It is housed in an exceptional building designed by Bob Mangurion and Lester Walker, who transformed the interior of a former garage into a series of exciting spaces, including a rooftop play area. The director of the center is Mel Grizer, a longtime UCC activist.

Altogether, some nineteen facilities, under contract to the Agency for Child Development, part of the city's Administration of Children's Services, are serving more than 2,000 children in preschool and after-school programs. This is truly great progress, though the Citizens Committee for Children estimates that East New York (Community Board 5) contains another 3,000 children from infancy through five years of age whose family incomes are less than 200 percent of the federal poverty level and who are not receiving needed child care.

Mel Grizer, executive director, says that the UCC would like to expand its operation by adding a building on part of the adjacent vacant lot. The lot is owned by the city, which is willing to sell it but won't sell it till Councilwoman Wooten approves the sale. This she has refused to do; Wooten has typically blocked projects proposed by critics, just as she has gone out of her way to help or reward her supporters.

The UCC center is across the street from the New Lots Reformed Church, a landmarked building, and nearby are the New Lots branch of the Brooklyn Public Library and the New Lots Community Church and Day Care Center. These and other neighborhood organizations finally got four-way stop signs put up at Schenck and New Lots in March 1997, after twenty years of pressure and demonstrations, including blocking the street.

THE CYPRESS HILLS LOCAL DEVELOPMENT CORPORATION

What can be done locally is shown by the efforts of the Cypress Hills Local Development Corporation (CHLDC), north of Atlantic Avenue, led by its executive director, Michelle Neugabauer. In the 1970s and 1980s, the area went from 70 to 80 percent white to 30 percent black and 50 percent Hispanic, a change accompanied by an economic decline not quite as drastic as that in East New York. Over the past decade, the population has become increasingly Latino; today, some 70 percent of residents are Dominican, Puerto Rican, Colombian, or Honduran, while about 20 percent are black and 10 percent are white.

The organization started in 1983 with a $34,000 budget, sufficient for two staff people. Through hustling and other hard work, by showing results, and by aggressive fund-raising, the organization established a budget of $2.7 million for FY 2,000. It has fifty-five full-time staff people and about 100 part-timers, most of whom work in the various centers as activity leaders or teachers of various skills. The LDC has afterschool programs at all the schools, running from 3 P.M. to 9 P.M., with parents' nights, sports programs, and other activities. It has eight offices and activity centers.

Funding of $1.4 million from twelve different government sources indicates a growing recognition that local community efforts can be productive and well worth the money invested. Another $1.1 million comes from corporate and foundation support, and $200,000 is listed as Earned Income and Special Events. More than $840,000 is contributed by The New York City Department of Youth Services and Community Development.

By comparison with the rest of East New York's commercial progress, Cypress Hills has fared rather well, though vacancies are still a problem. CHLDC has a strong ongoing marketing campaign to rent stores, especially near the subway entrances in the dozen blocks between Crescent and Cleveland Streets along Fulton Street. More than 122 shops have benefited from CHLDC's capital assistance program, which has awarded grants exceeding $1 million since the program began in 1985. Over the years, about half the vacancies have been filled.

A little further west, the LDC hopes to establish a minimall at Van Siclen and Fulton, a subway stop on the "J" line. The LDC is about to purchase the 20,000-square-foot site from the city. It has secured an anchor tenant, and financing is in hand. The project is budgeted at $1.9 million and is partly a response to a 21 percent increase in population over the past two decades, creating a large, unmet demand for retail services. Thus far, the LDC has attracted two supermarkets, including Key Foods, to the area. It is hoped that the minimall will bolster the retail area west of Van Siclen, where a third or more of the storefronts are still vacant. Crime and drug selling are major problems for the commercial strips.

East of the Cleveland Avenue area, there are many more occupied stores and a greater variety of retail and other uses: a Bargain Center, Chinese restaurants, Hispanic restaurants, a music store, bargain stores, real estate and insurance brokers, furniture stores, party suppliers, sales/service/TV/stereo shops, churches, cleaners, a cafeteria, a liquor store, electronics stores, and a travel agency, along with some vacancies. A still higher-quality retail area is found on Liberty Avenue, between Atlantic Avenue and Conduit Boulevard running out to the Queens line.

Among the LDC's more noteworthy programs is the Family Day Care Network. The group seeks to increase safe, quality day-care options for the predominantly low-income mothers. It has trained ninety-five women in day care, forty-three of the women have received their Family Day Care Providers licenses. Ten of these women run fully operational centers, and three have expanded to Group Family Day Care licenses.

The Cypress Hills 21st Century Community Learning Center offers more than fifteen programs in adult and youth education and in recreation and leadership development. More than 600 community residents have registered for these programs. The Good Find Thrift Shop/La Buena Compra, Inc., now two years old, provides retail training experience for unskilled workers. Another 200 people have received career training and assistance in reaching their goals.

The 2000 summer youth employment program placed 376 young people in various government work sites; CHLDC itself provided work for fifty, eleven at the Good Thrift Shop alone. Its summer community center was in operation, with day camp, classes, recreation, athletics, and other programs, all conducted at I.S. 302.

In 1983 CHLDC linked up with LISC (Low Initiatives Support Corporation) to build housing, rehabilitating close to 200 units to date. People from outside the area are buying these two-unit properties for $160,000 to $180,000, even $200,000. As a result, most of the readily available properties have been reoccupied. Many of the still-vacant buildings are owned by absentee owners who are just hanging onto them, hoping to get a lot of money for them some day.

CHLDC is now rehabilitating six city-owned buildings that will provide fifty-seven affordable housing units. And, in 1999, the group acquired nine partially occupied two- to four-family houses from the City of New York and has closed on $1.8 million in financing to rehabilitate these buildings through the LISC-HPD "Neighborhood Homes" program. After rehabilitation, the homes will be resold to low- and moderate-income homebuyers. Current tenants will be protected with three-year leases, a less than satisfactory compromise.

The LDC works with property owners to repair and maintain their property, helps secure grants and loans to homeowners for repairs, organizes tenant associations, educates prospective homebuyers, assists in preventing mortgage foreclosures, and provides information on fire prevention. Thousands of landlords and tenants have been helped by the program.

Local banks have a relatively poor loan record in Cypress Hills. The total value of loans made by the seven local banks between 1993 and 1998 ranged from $6.5 million to $9.6 million annually. In 1998, these banks made a paltry $7.6 million in loans, almost half of which were for home purchases. Banks or their mortgage companies accounted for only a third of the $102.2 million in loans made in 1998; two-thirds were made by predatory, subprime lenders at higher-than-average interest rates. By comparison, in Bay Ridge, Brooklyn, 78 percent of the mortgages were made by banks or their mortgage companies; only 22 percent were made by subprime lenders. In addition to closely monitoring bank lending practices, the LDC maintains its pressure on the local banks to increase their lending in the Cypress Hills area.

The LDC affirms that much remains to be done in relation to deferred home maintenance, reoccupancy of vacant buildings, and correction of violations in multiple dwellings. In the rental housing arena, a two-bedroom apartment is currently renting for $700 to $850 a month, whereas what people need are apartments that rent for $400 to $450 a month. As a result, there is considerable doubling up, as well as apartment sharing, illegal conversion, and rapid residential turnover.

To what can we attribute the LDC's success thus far? First and foremost, the LDC board, consisting of residents and local businessmen, was adamant in refusing to allow local politicians to get a foot in the door. Second, LDC benefited from an executive director and staff who tirelessly pursued program and funding opportunities. Third, the LDC paid dogged attention to the community's needs, as in its monitoring of bank lending policies over the years. At some point, Neugabauer believes, the banks will cave in and give the area its due.

COMMUNITY GARDENS

Perhaps the most astounding achievement of all is the proliferation of community gardens. East New York has been "blessed" with hundreds of vacant parcels throughout the community, and community people are landscaping and growing flowers and vegetables on about ninety of them. They are mostly tended by older blacks that have worked the land in the past. Teens and even preteens are working as interns with many of them.

With so many gardens in operation, a scheme to grow produce commercially and to sell it at local farmers' markets has been initiated. Called East New York Farms, the effort is being coordinated by a coalition of three East New York community groups (UCC, LDCENY, and Genesis/HELP USA). In 1990, East New York Farms was one of five groups in the United States to be awarded a two-year Hitachi Foundation grant for sustainable community development projects, which served as seed funding for the project.

The gardens are on month-to-month leases from the city through the Green Thumb program, and seeds, needed materials and expertise from the Cornell Coop Extension service are being paid for through the Hitachi grant. A full-time garden coordinator and a part-time market manager were created at UCC and LDCENY respectively. The garden coordinator recruited community gardeners to sell produce at the market and organized the youth interns referred by Genesis/HELP USA into work teams that assisted the participating gardeners on a rotating schedule from April through mid-November. The market manager assigned stall space at the market and collected minimal fees from the gardeners to cover the cost of equipment (e.g., pop-up tents, tables, scales) made available to them. Courses are being offered to the gardeners in how to grow produce and in basic business skills; assistance with resources is also being offered. Success will nevertheless require commitment and determination; the results cannot yet be foreseen.

The enterprise had its first full season in 1999. After some delicate political maneuvering to gain access to the city-owned site, the farmers' market was established on a vacant lot at Barbey Street and New Lots Avenue. During the 2000 season, six of the fifteen participating gardens brought their produce to the East New York Farms Farmers' Market and sold it there; an Orange County farmer was also recruited so that a wider range of produce could be offered. Some local crafts vendors exhibited and sold their products, as well. In addition, $20 worth of Women, Infants, and Children (WIC) Farmers' Market Nutrition Program (FMNP) coupons were approved for use at the market, and this has helped sales a great deal.[23]

Results of the 2000 season were encouraging but not conclusive. While the market generally did good business, with gross sales of

$19,000, the quality of the produce was poor and the number of vendors sometimes low. Some of the gardens that produce food are among those the city is trying to sell to developers.[24] It is not easy to get this project into full swing; there are stumbling blocks all along the way. The fact that it is being tried at all is remarkable; it uplifts the spirit.

In the 2001 season, the same number of community gardeners were back at the market; they were selling a greater quantity of produce. That year also saw the first issuance of FMNP coupons targeted at senior citizens. In July, this resulted in vanloads of senior citizens arriving before the market opened. Produce stands sold out before the day was half over. Two additional upstate farmers were recruited to help handle the increased traffic. Market attendance rose from an average of 300 to 750 shoppers each Saturday in August. Even after the FMNP coupons were used up in September, local customers continued to patronize the market. Gross sales for the 2001 season totaled $62,200. Plans are being made to construct a permanent shed to provide shade and to establish a permanent presence on the site.

There we have it. There is much to be thankful for in East New York over the past twenty years. Still, there are major problems, which have yet to be addressed. In the chapters that follow, we revisit the cancerous core of poverty and recount the corrosive impact of aggressive policing.

15

The Hard Road to Recovery

WHILE GREAT PROGRESS has been made in many areas of East New York life, the elimination of poverty and social instability is not among them. A threshold was passed in the 1960s when a mass of impoverished, ill-educated, and low-capability households were thrown together in this alien and violent landscape, made all the more scary by the virtual lawlessness and by the studied neglect of the uniformed services, the education system and social services. The human damage that resulted has never been alleviated or even basically addressed. The area remains a nuclear meltdown, a hotbed of alienation, violence, illiteracy, fear, and grinding poverty. While concentrated in the tenement and multiple dwelling areas in East New York, it is widespread throughout the community.

Government has never seen fit to address the problems created by the senseless welfare dumping of the 1960s. At best, the community is dealt with as all other low-income communities are dealt with; at worst, it meets with studied neglect. It receives band-aids where major surgery is indicated.

Many organizations are fighting to improve the situation, none more effectively than St. Paul's Community Baptist Church under the leadership of the Reverend Johnny Ray Youngblood. The East Brooklyn Congregations (EBC), with its fifty-plus member churches and thousands of members, has had the greatest impact on community life by bringing many improvements to the community. The United Community Centers, organizations like the East New York Urban Youth Corps (despite its shortcomings), and many of the area's churches acting individually do their part. In its neighborhood, the Cypress Hills Local Development Corporation is doing a wonderful job. Add the Pratt Center to the mix; it has helped focus the community's thinking about its future and helps to design the needed changes.

All this effort has reached only a few of those in deep poverty and/or deeply involved in gangs, drug or alcohol abuse, or other criminal or antisocial behavior. Aggregate all these efforts, and perhaps a few thousand people on that desperate level are being given some kind of help or guidance. Unfortunately, there are 50,000 who need multiples of that kind of attention.

The self-serving nature of East New York politics, which often stands foursquare in the way of progress, also blocks recovery. It is a politics of petty tyrannies and ruthlessness that leads to a disregard for human life and for the community that elected officials are supposed to serve. Replacement of these despots by new political leadership in recent elections may bring with it a welcome commitment to serve the community.

HOW THE OTHER HALF LIVES

As we revisit the poorest of the poor living in East New York, we see them in even more desperate straits than they were in the 1960s and 1970s. By 1990, the Seventy-fifth Precinct, which covers East New York, regularly placed among the top two or three citywide for violent crime. East New York won the moniker "Murder Capital of New York" in the early 1990s, when it recorded 340 homicides in a single year, a record.

Between 1980 and 1990, the area's population remained relatively stable; the average age continued to hover around eighteen years. In 1990, single-mother households predominated, accounting for 42 percent of the total. By the year 2000, a great deal had changed. The population of Community District 5 had risen by 7.3 percent, to 173,198. The average age had risen to twenty-four years. Single-mother households had dropped to 31 percent of the total in and around the Weed and Seed area (still a high figure), and to 21 percent in the rest of East New York.[1]

In 1990, in addition to single-mother households, married couples accounted for 32 percent of the population, while other family types (adults and children) totaled 6 percent; other households (those with no children) accounted for the remaining 19 percent. Educational attainment was low. Only 27.5 percent were high school graduates, 12.9 percent more had some college, and 6.3 percent had gone beyond college. By contrast, 53.3 percent had not completed high school.

Almost 45 percent of adults were not in the labor force; an additional 10 percent were unemployed; only 45 percent were employed.

Although median income rose over the decade, from $13,568 in 1979 to $18,229 in 1989, it was still comparatively low.

Of the eighteen community districts in Brooklyn, East New York contained the second highest number of welfare recipients. In 1996, it also registered 1,648 foster-care placements and 1,880 cases of abused and neglected children. With its AIDS incidence more than doubling each year, East New York counted more AIDS cases than seventeen states.[2] The infant mortality rate was comparable to that of Panama.

Among New York's community districts, East New York had the eleventh highest percentage of birth to teens (16.7 percent).[3] An incredible 40 percent of its households have incomes under $10,000; 30 to 40 percent of its children receive public assistance, and 91.4 percent of its public school children receive free lunches. Only half of eligible mothers and children receive WIC (Women's Infants and Children) coupons, handed out at health clinics to be used to buy milk and food. Head Start capacity in 1998 amounted to only 286 seats.

Other indicators of community health and medical condition also seriously impact family life. East New York ranks high in the number of abandoned buildings, lead paint violations, and hazardous materials storage (a problem that is getting worse). Between 9 and 12 children per 1,000 are hospitalized for asthma (a rate twenty-one times higher than that for the hardest-hit areas of more affluent communities).[4] East New York also had 3,083 seriously emotionally disturbed children and youth in 1997, the highest number in any New York City community district.

Any one of these health and medical problems can seriously upset a family's life. When they are added to the raging drug and alcohol use, involvement of family members in trouble with the law, joblessness, and low levels of education, many families' desperation and hand-to-mouth struggle to survive are readily explainable.

The lack of affordable housing is arguably the most serious detriment to stabilization of the lowest-income population. In the South Bronx and in East New York, more than 35 percent of renter households in 1996 faced severe affordability problems. Indeed, one of the most often repeated complaints of both East New York and Cypress Hills activists is the lack of affordable apartments. The going rate is $700 to $850 a month, but most families can pay rents of only $400 to $450. In 1996, 35 percent of East New York residents were paying more than one-third of their already low incomes for rent. Young couples just starting out can't enter the current rental market.

Much of the problem for the city's poorest families is the totally inadequate housing allowance for welfare clients. From 1975, when the shelter allowance was more than adequate, the value of the allowance ($286 in 1999) has fallen far behind the current median rent average of $700. The allowance continues—unchanged—at the 1975 level. Now, of course, welfare families face total abandonment by the system.

Even working people are finding it more difficult to pay the current rents. Rents have gone up by an average of 33 percent, while real incomes have been flat.[5]

A survey of 300 adult students in St. Rita's Roman Catholic Church's basic education class revealed just how desperate the housing famine is. "More than half of them are renting rooms," Father Peyton said. "They're people with average incomes of $7,000 to $15,000."[6] Many members of his church are too poor to rent an apartment, much less buy a Nehemiah home.

It should come as no surprise that the vast majority of homeless families come from the poorest minority communities in New York City. Bedford-Stuyvesant and East New York together contain 21 percent of New York City's homeless population. More than 88 percent of all shelter residents are black or Latino. Over a recent five-year period, one in every twelve blacks experienced homelessness.

A 1997 survey of homeless families found that 92 percent of the adults were unemployed and that the median household income was $10,400 (in 1997 dollars).[7] In another study of newly homeless families, 94 percent were found to be receiving public assistance (sometimes in combination with child support), on the waiting list for public assistance, or receiving SSI (Supplemental Security Income).[8] The same study found that 45.5 percent had left a doubled-up living arrangement; another 16.6 percent had been evicted, mostly for nonpayment of rent. Domestic violence accounted for another 8.3 percent of the homeless; 4.8 percent had sought shelter because of the unlivable condition of their own housing.

More than 60 percent of doubled-up families reported they had slept in the living room, the dining room, or the hallway or on a sofa or the floor. It is clear that the enormous number of doubled-up households (200,000 during the 1990s) resulted from the shortage of affordable housing and the inability of poor households to enter the housing market.

The relationship between poverty and crime is undeniable. Father

Peyton spoke of another growth "industry" in East New York—the stealing and stripping of cars. He pointed to scores of abandoned car shells that have been stripped down for parts and left on the streets and complained about the many auto body shops and salvage yards in the area.[9]

A full 65 percent of the nation's prisoners never completed high school. Thirty-three percent were unemployed and another 32 percent were making less than $5,000 a year at the time of their arrest.[10] These statistics clearly support the thesis that poverty is the single greatest influence on criminal behavior.

It is not just those convicted who are drawn into the prison system. Children may end up in foster care. Many families spend an inordinate amount of time visiting prisoners or seeking legal assistance. Many families face eviction from projects for failure to pay the rent because of lost income.

Housing condition is another factor that contributes to instability in the community. Fires in abandoned and occupied buildings are a constant threat; 791 structural fires were reported in East New York in 1997. A sizable 42 percent of East New York's housing is rated in fair to poor condition. Only 20.3 percent of East New York residents owned their own homes in 1996. And, while 80 percent of the streets were rated clean in 1997, potholes abounded.

As the population of East New York ages, the elderly will become another distressed class. They will have tiny Social Security benefits (many as little as $400 a month or even less) and will have to pay a horrendous portion of their income for rent—up to 60 percent is not unusual for the elderly poor. The elderly are rapidly increasing in number, yet no provisions are being made to house and service them in a decent fashion. Many are disabled, but do not receive adequate health services. At worst, the elderly will simply add to the burdens of the community, living in an extended family structure cramped for space.

Tragedies are commonplace. Kate Worthy's husband died, and she was left to deal with a growing brood of ten that had become an outlaw clan.[11] "They became uncontrollable," she said. "I have to get out of that apartment. I'm not gonna die like this." The future was written for the Worthys when Kate's daughter Brenda married a heroin user named Ray Asbury. The change from hope to daily disaster came fast. Soon Brenda was an addict. Ray and Brenda had five children: three boys and two girls, Renee and Omean, both of whom had children before they were fifteen. All those kids grew up in a festering world of syringes, dope buys, strangers, and stupefied parents. The second wave was AIDS, which killed Ray Asbury at the age of forty-two in 1988. Brenda was stricken with the disease a year later. Renee and Omean and their children were on their own. The third wave, crack, blew the doors down. Into this chaos rolled cars loaded with weapons purchased from gun stores in Virginia, guns in brown boxes delivered by mail order.

In New York City, in 1997, 18 percent of all youths carried a weapon, 4 percent carried a gun, and 9 percent carried a weapon on school property. The percentages for East New York are probably twice as high as those averages. Trying to control the contagion of weapons, Thomas Jefferson High School installed metal detectors at its doors.

East New York is one of only four community districts that had more than 350 juvenile arrests in 1996; the rate was 43 per 1000 juveniles. A total of 1,547 New York City youths were placed in New York State Office of Children and Family Services facilities, where the average stay is one year. The number of New York City juvenile delinquents on probation has remained fairly constant; in 1997, there were 4,359 citywide, about 145 of whom were on probation in East New York.

Table 3
East New York Juvenile and Youth Arrests (1996)

Juveniles—Under 16 years of age	
Felony arrests	361
Misdemeanor arrests	43
Youths—16–20 years of age	
Felony arrests	994
Misdemeanor arrests	836

Source: New York Police Department

The average length of stay in New York City juvenile facilities was sixty-five days in 1998. Some 325 juveniles are in city secure facilities. Each of the nine community districts with the highest youth felony arrest totals, including East New York, accounted for 3.4 percent of the total citywide arrests. These districts (mostly minority ghettos and other poor districts) have a predisposition to violence and crime. The remaining fifty community districts each contributed an average of 1.4 percent of the felony arrest total, a far more manageable burden.

By almost any measure, the poorest areas and minority areas are chronically unstable and are breeding grounds for criminal activity and antisocial behavior. Officers in the Seventy-fifth Precinct and people all around the neighborhood say they are encouraged by the drop in violent crime. There has been a 70 percent drop in homicides since 1993; in 1999, there were thirty-two homicides, down from forty-one in 1998, at least in part because of the booming economy. Nevertheless, the breeding ground has not changed. Criminal behavior rises from the ashes; the poorest in the community remain alienated from the rest of the world.

EBC (EAST BROOKLYN CONGREGATIONS) ORGANIZING VICTORIES AND DEFEATS

Without doubt, the appointment of the Reverend Johnny Ray Youngblood as pastor of St. Paul's Community Baptist Church and the establishment of the EBC (East Brooklyn Congregations) in the Saul Alinsky mode of the IAF (Industrial Areas Foundation) were tremendously important in the community organizing movement in New York over the past thirty years. Not that there haven't been other bold and courageous community efforts and organizations, but the "best in show" honors belong to Youngblood and the EBC.

The Reverend Youngblood came to St. Paul's in June 1974 and moved swiftly to turn that debt-ridden church around.[12] The church had barely eighty members, was housed in an unused social club, needed major repairs; for example, it had dozens of electric sockets that lacked bulbs. With the help of Sarah Plowden, a church assistant, the Reverend Youngblood decided to make one improvement the congregation could see every week. The first week, there was a fine drawing of the church in the church bulletin. Next, an oak door was given a new veneer. Next, Bible verses replaced southern belles on the church bulletin cover. He found that the church had overpaid its utility bills by $2,300, recovered the money, and used it to rewire the church (and to light the unlit bulbs), to install new tiles, to add fresh paint, and to make other improvements. Having shown the possibilities, after three months, the Reverend Youngblood called for all church members to tithe themselves for 10 percent of their salary. Despite grumbling by some, the church began to pay its debts and much more. People saw their tithing used to pay college tuition for several youths and to invigorate or create new church clubs, and they realized they no longer had to hold chicken dinners to raise money.

In 1979, St. Paul's was able to buy much larger and more impressive quarters, a vacant synagogue on Hendrix Street. On December 24, 1989, more than 1,000 people attended Christmas Eve services. By then, there were 5,000 people on the church rolls, with 1,800 tithe-payers. Yet expansion and new projects stretched even this solid source of income. The church operating budget was $4 million, supporting a staff of fifty-five. There were adult education classes, the Yoke Fellows program (discussed below), a credit union, a playground on the vacant lot next door, vans to bring the elderly to church, and much more than can be recounted here. Yet, aspirations sometimes outdistanced capabilities; a $145,000 payment on a new youth center was past due; another $1.5 million was due in May toward an enlarged sanctuary.

This giant of a man, who almost singlehandedly reinvigorated religious institutions throughout East New York, not only inspired the better-off residents but also appealed as well to those who had very little. His association with the EBC and the IAF proved to be equally dynamic, resulting in many victories, as well as occasional defeats. Mike Gecan, lead organizer for the IAF, was so impressed with the tithing system at St. Paul's that he engaged Sarah Plowden and Icie Johnson to teach it to EBC members from other churches. Many churches began to support themselves and were no longer at the mercy of their sponsoring agencies.

As a result of EBC pressures over the years, city agencies have installed 3,000 missing street signs, completed the long overdue renovation of a park and swimming pool, and demolished 300 vacant and irreparable buildings. The EBC built the Nehemiah homes and won guarantees of college scholarships and entry-level jobs for graduates of Brooklyn's most troubled high schools. From obscurity and political impotence, the EBC vaulted onto television's *20/20* and into the *Congressional Record*.[13]

The EBC developed an action team of 135 members, who held several hundred house meetings to identify and help solve local problems. At one such meeting, women complained about a changed bus stop that was no longer convenient and made people more easily subject to attacks. The Reverend Youngblood told them to get up a petition, get 2,000 signatures, and take it to the Transit Authority. "Forget Ed

Griffith; forget Priscilla Wooten. We'll work with you, but you got to do the organizing."[14]

The EBC Action Team met often in 1990, began its meetings by reporting on EBC's ongoing campaigns, and followed with action programs aimed at getting results. At a higher organizing level is the EBC "strategy team." It has twelve members, all of whom have received "ten-day training" in the Saul Alinsky community organizing gospel. They have been putting that gospel into action for the past ten years. Among them is Father John Powis, a veteran of the Brownsville decentralization struggles, and the Reverend Youngblood, along with Catholics, Protestants, and Jews, men and women, blacks, whites, and Hispanics.

At one of its mass meetings, the EBC invited leaders from the police department, the educational bureaucracy, the medical community, and the local political apparatus. The EBC demanded that they say yes or no to EBC's initiatives. By 7:30, vans from EBC's fifty-four member churches and synagogues started to arrive. The St. Paul's contingent alone numbered nearly 400 persons, all in yellow sweatshirts emblazoned "He Is Lord." The Reverend David Benke exhorted the crowd, ending his speech with "We say tonight, powers that be, listen up. The clock is done ticking. Time has run out. At eight-fifteen tonight, you're either with us or against us. And I say to you, EBC, we're either in action with those who can and do, or we're in active battle with those who can't or won't. Are you ready?" The crowd screamed its approval; people whooped and stood and shook their fists.

At the meeting, the good news came first. Tom Hall, assistant executive director of Saint Mary's Hospital, announced that the hospital would open a primary care facility on Atlantic Avenue (it has yet to open). Next, the chancellor of the City University announced a commitment to house the EBC's enrichment academy on the campus of Medgar Evers College in Crown Heights. The announcement and a second announcement in Spanish set off two rounds of cheers. Another speaker wrung from school officials on the stage a schedule for repairing broken roofs, fire doors, playground equipment, and toilets in Bushwick public schools (much of this still awaits action).

It was then explained that Lee Brown, the police commissioner, had skipped the meeting. But EBC was not about to let the issue die. Lee Brown was appointed police commissioner of New York City at least in part because of his commitment to community policing. In fact, the

Reverend Youngblood had met with Lee Brown in Houston and had been impressed. Due to Brown's failure to institute community policing, the EBC finally released the Reverend Youngblood's letter criticizing Brown to the press. "A major black minister attacking a black police commissioner—that's good copy," said Youngblood.

The EBC has not been satisfied to pursue purely local concerns. Along with ACORN and several unions, it pioneered the living-wage policy (started by the IAF in Baltimore), which requires many firms doing business with the City of New York to pay its employees a living wage, starting at $8.20 an hour and going all the way up to $15 for a cook or chef.

Recently, the EBC has gone national. On March 4, 2000, Johnny Ray Youngblood wrote an article for the *New York Times* publicly exposing the unwillingness of the presidential candidates to meet for half an hour with 100 bishops, rabbis, and ministers to discuss the basic community's need for work that pays a living wage and for affordable housing. Neither Bush nor Gore agreed to meet with the EBC.

In a dramatic effort to get the candidates to pay some attention to the issue, an affordable manufactured house—complete with doors and windows, kitchen, living room, and dining nook and mounted on a trailer—was parked outside the New York State Democratic Committee's office on Madison Avenue on June 24, 2000.[15] To underscore their seriousness, 700 members of IAF groups in Washington, Boston, Baltimore, Philadelphia, and New York attended the demonstration. Except for a small piece in the *Daily News*, the major media ignored the demo.

In recognition of his leadership, Johnny Ray Youngblood was made a co-leader of the Industrial Areas Foundation, along with Mike Gecan, filling a post vacated by the former IAF leader Ed Chambers.

Students of community organizing will recognize the powerful and well-organized thrust of both the Reverend Youngblood and the EBC toward improving conditions in the East New York community. While the poorest have been affected to some degree, when we review the results, not much of a bread and butter nature has been achieved—drugs, alcohol abuse, lack of housing for the poorest, unrelenting arrest policies of the police, the lack of social and economic help the poorest families need all continue to plague the area. The churches can help those who are in a condition to accept help and who are able to take advantage of help when it is offered, but this does not reach the hard core of poverty in East New York.

Mike Gecan, EBC's lead organizer, insists that EBC parishioners come from all economic levels, including the very poorest. What EBC members have that non parishioners do not have is a religious institution that cares about them and gives them a role and a stake in making things better. He believes that the way to reach the poorest people is to give them institutions and groups they can join, something that can engage them.

Still, the possibility of a clash between the upwardly mobile religious groups and the dead-end poverty cultures in East New York exists. Conflicts have already occurred, as in the Williams Avenue houses affair, when the Nehemiah builders sought to demolish low-rent apartments in favor of single-family homes. And, while the demonstration for affordable housing on Madison Avenue was a step in the right direction, the manufactured house on display was a means of providing home ownership for moderate-income families—a good cause, but far from meeting the needs of the poorest East New Yorkers. One must also look toward the future and wonder what role the Nehemiah homeowners will play in the community once they are well organized.

LESSONS IN EDUCATION

The then Schools Chancellor Fernandez finally did meet with EBC leaders in a Nehemiah home and officially approved the Enrichment Academy plan; the EBC Enrichment Academy is now housed on the campus of Medgar Evers College in Crown Heights.

Yet, locally run schools are anything but a panacea; the experience in East New York illustrates the colossal task that faces would-be educators.

Currently, the EBC operates three community high schools, one in East New York, one in Bushwick, and one in the South Bronx. The East New York school has 400 students. It has been very difficult to make progress with the students, who have already been through eight years of dreadful educational experience.[16] Many youths find it difficult to adapt to the rigid discipline at the academy; dropouts and drum-outs are common. The school has recently acquired a good principal, so a more solid performance is expected in the future. As with most schools, the high transience and dropout rates hinder educational progress.

Cypress Hills parents who felt neglected by the city's public schools have successfully opened their own Cypress Hills Community School. The school began with a grant from the New Visions for Public Schools Foundation and is housed in I.S. 302 and in an elementary public school. Adding a grade level every year, by September 2000 it taught grades K–5, and enrolled about ninety pupils.

Parents had the incentive and the authority to work with teachers in shaping every aspect of the school's operations, which were built around a demanding program that taught the children in English half the day and in Spanish the other half.

In addition to parent involvement, the school selected the teachers it wanted (from approved lists). Class size ranged between eighteen and twenty students. A governing council made up of teachers and parents reviews progress and establishes policy for the school, which has a relationship with the New York University Institute for Educational and Social Policy.

On completion of its third year in 1999–2000, the school had measurably improved results. The math test scores for third- and fourth-grade pupils were the highest in the district, although they were not high scores; the reading scores of the forth grade were also higher; although those for the third grade remained just a little above average. The parents were encouraged and are pressing the city for their own school facility.

A continuing problem at the school (as in most other ghetto schools) is the unusually high transience rate. A turnover of 50 percent during the school year is not unusual, and it interferes with classroom instruction.

The Cypress Hills Community School clearly demonstrates the enormous distance between current educational achievement, even in its most progressive form (small classes, local control), and what might be considered salutary results. The advances are genuine, but only a long-term commitment and the infusion of far greater resources will turn the educational system to good account.

Somewhere, somehow, the children must be reached—and reached deeply—to the point where they will want and be able to learn. In a place as physically dangerous and as morally corroded as East New York, one haven has been Saint Paul's, where college admissions were announced from the pulpit, where dances could be held without fear of gunplay, but where, unfortunately, a backyard playground had to be protected by razor wire. Dozens of youngsters were recruited into

St. Paul's Yoke Fellows program, where they committed themselves to study and succeed in high school and college.[17] Yoke Fellows were enrolled in the Park West High School in Hunter College; hundreds of relatives and well-wishers attended their graduation.

Ali was one such youngster. He had seen friends drop out and start selling crack, several of them landing in jail, one being murdered for a debt to his supplier. "You wanna make some money?" they would say to Ali. "You just carry this for me. I'll set you up with a couple of dollars," which meant, in the drug trade's glossary, a couple of hundred. Ali eventually joined the Yoke Fellows program.

In his final term at Park West, Ali was taking twelve courses just to graduate by the June deadline. He started at eight in the morning, continued past six at night, then rode the train ninety minutes to St. Paul's for pledging activities. More than once he fell asleep in his clothes and shoes, but he was adamant about adhering to the schedule, even refusing to consent to a knee operation until after his appearance in a school ceremony. Ali attended the ceremony, an all-night hazing session and celebration that was followed by the daybreak induction of the survivors as Yoke Fellows. Ali was one of the inductees.

THE POLITICAL MORASS

If any corner of the city cried out for courageous and honest political leadership, East New York did. And, if the abrupt white flight might have yielded any perverse advantage, it was to make room for black reformers on the order of State Assemblyman Albert Vann or Congressman Major R. Owens, who served other sections of Brooklyn. Instead, the same white political machine that had always dominated East New York continued to rule it through proven black allies—City Councilwoman Priscilla A. Wooten, State Assemblyman Edward Griffith, and Congressman Edolphus Towns.[18] The organization continued to oversee the vast patronage apparatus of Community Board 5 and the District 19 Community School Board.[19]

With Brooklyn Borough President Howard Golden acting as his mentor, Edolphus Towns had served simultaneously as deputy borough president and Democratic district leader for East New York before being sent to Washington. Wooten was a protégé of Samuel Wright (no relation to Bill Wright), a black councilman who, through much of the

1970s, controlled a $30-million network of schools, day-care centers, and antipoverty programs in Brownsville. Wright was eventually convicted of accepting a $5,000 bribe from a company that sold textbooks to School District 23, which had the lowest reading scores of any district in the city.[20] Wright had learned at the knee of the Brooklyn Democratic boss Meade Esposito, even assuming the leadership of Esposito's political club. Wooten also linked up with the Esposito Democratic machine early in her career as a school aide. As for Griffith, he had emerged from the John F. Kennedy Democratic Club, whose longtime leader, Mike Wollin, was ultimately rewarded for his machine loyalties with a judgeship. While Wooten and Towns sporadically drew scrutiny—she for residing illegally in a subsidized middle-income apartment, he for receiving a $1,300 kickback from a contractor in a sting operation—Griffith glided along, genial and innocuous, running virtually unopposed term after term.[21] (Towns avoided indictment only by returning most of the money.)[22]

While reading scores were sinking in East New York elementary and junior high schools, Wooten gained and held her City Council seat through her deep connections with the public education system and the money she could channel to her allies through her position as a council incumbent.[23] The local boards, until recently, had discretionary authority to fill up to 400 nonteaching positions each. To a great degree, Wooten controlled the hiring of these aides and paraprofessionals, turning them into a built-in electoral machine.[24] She got the votes not only of the teaching assistants but also of their aunts, uncles, and siblings. By controlling enough of those people, Wooten developed a substantial voter base. As a result of her far-reaching influence in the schools, she was able to get financial support for her campaign from teachers and administrators ($2,500), the teachers union ($3,000), and District Council 37's Local 372 ($4,500).

On the housing front, Priscilla Wooten has occasionally been an obstacle.[25] The New York City Department of Housing Preservation and Development was willing to honor a 1995 plan to give ACORN's housing arm, the Mutual Housing Association of New York (MHANY), $1.2 million to turn six abandoned buildings into affordable co-ops for nineteen low- to moderate-income households. Wooten refused to write an essential letter on behalf of the project.[26] Among the possible reasons for her refusal was ACORN's January 26, 1999, protest rally at Wooten's headquarters on Linden Boulevard. In the Williams Street fight, Wooten sided with the EBC, favoring the demolition of the 135 apartments.

Wooten and District Leader DeCosta Headley rule separate but sometimes overlapping fiefdoms. Headley is a hybrid product of the black power movement and the white clubhouse. He maintains a strong friendship with Assemblyman Ed Griffith. He helped run many Democratic campaigns and was then elected Democratic district leader for East New York and first vice chairman of Brooklyn's Democratic organization, posts that made his political support crucial.

Not long after his election, Headley began muscling in on ongoing development programs. In the early 1990s, Jeff Stern, then head of the Local Development Corporation of East New York, began contemplating the conversion of the vacant Biltmore movie palace into a business center that would help revitalize the New Lots Avenue commercial strip. As word of the pending project got out, DeCosta Headley began peppering Stern with phone calls.[27] He wanted the inside track on the potentially lucrative state and city reconstruction contracts, but none of the people he brought around to do the job had the needed qualifications. While Headley never actually pushed Jeff Stern out of office, Stern finally resigned after four years of constant pressure from Headley and others connected with him.[28]

Michael Brooks took over from Jeff Stern and began charging consultant fees for the Biltmore project, which he conceived of as a health clinic.[29] The Oxford HMO was interested, but Brooks was unable to help the group with the needed documentation and pathway toward acquiring the property. Five years later, the Biltmore still sat, in part because of Headley and in part because the building was an asbestos-laden mess. It has since been torn down and replaced by a boxy Juniors (Western Beef) supermarket, which opened in the summer of 2000.

During Brooks's tenure, according to documents obtained by *City Limits* magazine, the Local Development Corporation of East New York's budget deficit increased fivefold in just three years.[30] The businessmen and politicians on its board of directors did not monitor the agency head's performance, and no one was accountable for the $1.5 million the agency had received.

Headley was also key in the ENYUYC (East New York Urban Youth Corps) debacle. Headley was a major figure in Diversified Flintlock Construction and had gotten ENYUYC to give DFC a rehabilitation contract. Its work was unmistakably shoddy.[31] HPD was wary of giving

Headley any more work, but Wooten (whose reelection campaign was being run by Headley) put in a good word, and the agency's objections were dropped. A second contract was awarded but ended in disaster.[32] When Martin Dunn refused to employ Headley's firms (as soon as one firm was turned down, Headley created another) for other rehabilitation contracts, Winchester Key, chairman of the ENYUYC board, and a DeCosta Headley man, fired Dunn. Winchester Key took over the leadership role there and has since gotten ENYUYC appointed as the managing agent of the Williams Street buildings.

Each year, the New York City Council leadership gives each "cooperative" member about $150,000 in discretionary "member items" to spend on community groups of their own choosing. Much of Wooten's largesse has gone to groups that cooperated with her. Of nearly $25,000 she gave to senior groups, the largest amounts went to groups close to polling places that have voted reliably and heavily for Wooten. In 1995, she gave a $5,000 member item to the East New York Development Corporation, which receives a $395,000-a-year city Department of Youth Services grant to run an afterschool Beacon program.[33] Bernard Waiters, chairman and a long-time Wooten ally, donated $800 to her campaign in 1993, and his agency illegally gave the Wooten war chest another $300.[34]

As chair of the council's education committee, Wooten tried to stop a program allowing community groups to use school buildings for meetings because she wanted to have the right to choose which groups got to use the schools.[35] Revenge plays an active role in East New York politics—as it certainly does elsewhere.

Another clue to the staying power of East New York politicos became clear in February 1990, when Michael Leonard, a St. Paul's member who works as a probation officer, announced that he would run against Griffith. Within days, Griffith sent a certified letter to the Reverend Youngblood inviting the church to seek a state grant, with an application form attached.[36] Thirty minutes after the missive arrived, one of the assemblyman's top aides telephoned Leroy Howard, a Youngblood aide, with the suggestion that $7,000 was a nice round figure. This was the very same Griffith who had refused to write a recommendation in 1989, when St. Paul's wanted to build senior citizens' housing. The Reverend Youngblood refused to apply for the state grant, but Michael Leonard did abandon his campaign and soon afterward found himself invited to join a political club affiliated with the machine.

It was small wonder, then, that when the Reverend Youngblood spoke of politics, he often turned to Ephesians:

> For we wrestle not against flesh and blood, but against principalities, against powers, against the rulers of the darkness of this world, against spiritual wickedness in high places.

The East New York experience illustrates the problem besetting many low-income communities. The disaffection and hopelessness in East New York serve the political cabal well; only 29 percent of voting-age adults cast ballots in presidential elections, and far fewer vote in local races in off-years. Political leaders evade public accountability through the machinations of patronage and favoritism. Single parents, trying to raise children and looking for better-paying jobs, find it difficult, if not impossible, to monitor the activities of their elected leaders. The sad thing is that there are so many people willing to compromise the good will and the meager resources of East New York for their personal gain.

Very occasionally, everyone pulls together for the common good. When a Long Island based company, Atlas Bioenergy Corporation, announced a plan to build a wood-burning incinerator in East New York, Charles Barron (a former Black Panther, a long-time organizer, and a political ally of Jesse Jackson, Herbert Daughtry, and Al Sharpton), along with Rachel Godsil of the NAACP Legal Defense Fund, organized the East New York Community Committee Against the Incinerator. They were able to rally the community around the issue, a difficult thing to do because there were so many camps and so many people in politicians' pockets or people who would have been given jobs or programs had the incinerator project gone ahead. The Barron committee had battles with Towns and with Wooten, and battles with ACORN and with the borough president's office, all of which wanted to be in control.[37] But, since the committee was independent, everyone finally rallied around it. There was a demonstration by more than 300 people on July 15, 1995, on a 100-degree day. The Reverend Johnny Ray Youngblood came out, along with people from other churches and community groups. They uncovered a city law that prohibits most privately sponsored refuse-burning plants. That, plus the united community, defeated the proposal. East New York doesn't get the respect it deserves, according to Barron, at least partly because its public officials are out for themselves and are not accountable to the community.[38] They often stand in the way of progress because it's not coming through them.

The culture of the streets, the readiness to fight, the division of the world into friends and foes are as evident in East New York's politics as in the community's struggle to survive. Patronage and favoritism, support for the clique in power, and the pursuit of personal profit are all part of the reality.

Charles Barron successfully ran for Priscilla Wooten's city council seat in 2001. Term limits prevented Priscilla from running on her own, so she ran her son in the Democratic primary. Barron handily beat Wooten's son for the Democratic nomination and went on to win the election. In the 2000 election, Diane Gordon beat out Ed Griffiths for his Assembly seat. It's just possible that we're witnessing the birth of a new era in East New York politics.

TOWARD RECOVERING THE GHETTO

Community improvements aren't going to come about simply because community-oriented politicians are elected. They require the active collaboration of all the major forces for good in the community—including all the CBOs that were previously beholden to the outgoing political cabal. Certainly, many of the stalled projects will move toward implementation. Success on larger issues will require the active involvement and leadership of the East Brooklyn Congregations (EBC). While the EBC has preferred to go it alone up to this point, the success of political reform may make it possible to create a broad coalition of all the major East New York groups, actively working to bridge the gaps between the church going poor and the non church going poor. The political shift is, in fact, an opportunity for the churches (and other religious groups) to join with antipoverty and youth organizations to concentrate on finding out what the poor need and going after it in an organized and intelligent way. Greatly expanded efforts, built on programs such as those of Catholic Charities Brooklyn East, which focuses on health, immigrants' issues, job assistance, workers rights in sweatshops, and the forging of a youth coalition, are steps in the right direction.

If the entire community can be enlisted in the fight to bring needed changes to the ghetto, the community could present a powerful, united front to local and state governments, as well as to other ghetto communities. East New York could become the spearhead of a militant city-wide campaign to win much-needed ghetto improvements.

There are dozens of needs, of course, but a top priority should be an improvement in the economic condition of those on welfare and of the tens of thousands earning under $10,000 a year. Any economic relief provided to these lowest-income groups would be like rolling a huge stone away from the front of a cave, letting the sunshine in.

The evidence presented earlier in this chapter suggests two ways of making real progress. One is to take action to force New York State to raise the shelter allowance for welfare clients from under $300 to the current median rent average ($700 in 1996). The second is to secure major government commitments to build or fund affordable housing. An extra $100 a week for shelter allowances would allow welfare families to reduce their out-of-pocket costs for rental housing and to rent better housing. Every new affordable unit would allow another family to enter the housing market and/or to save $100 a week on housing costs. Success on these fronts would offer major benefits to the poorer community, helping to stabilize this out-of-control sector.

The next year or two will give us a clue as to how it will all play out.

16

Policing the Ghetto

THE POLICE PRESENCE in East New York is a volatile mixture of good and bad. It is much like chemotherapy and radiation; they destroy cancerous tumors but also greatly weaken or kill the patient. The pain can be unbearable.

In the 1960s and 1970s, as described in chapter 6, the police paid little or no attention to community complaints, arrested one-seventh of the youth of East New York in a single year, and were brutal, highhanded, and arrogant. In more recent times, not much has changed. Through most of the 1990s, the police were almost as unresponsive as ever, ignoring community complaints and allowing lawlessness enough scope to terrorize the community.

Starting in 1994, Commissioner William Bratton reshaped the NYPD into a more racially integrated and effective crime-fighting force. Crime in East New York, especially violent crime, has been substantially reduced. Still, the racial hostility, the continued antipathy to community complaints, the failure to defang many known criminal operations, and, perhaps most important of all, the continued emphasis on arrest and incarceration marks the NYPD as a fundamentally destructive force in East New York.

POLICE CREDIBILITY

The East New York community has characteristically been more abused than served by the police. Take the corruption scandal that shook the NYPD in May 1992. Captain Michael Dowd, of Brooklyn's Seventy-fifth Police Precinct, was arrested by Suffolk County police for drug trafficking between Brooklyn bodegas and Long Island bars.[1] At the time, Dowd was carrying eight ounces of cocaine. Additional cocaine was found in his locker, and $20,000 in cash was found in his home. He often received $5,000 to $10,000 from drug dealers in exchange for warnings about imminent police raids and the presence of federal agents. He also helped Dominican cocaine gangs with their drug deals by supplying them with guns, badges, and police radios, and by assisting in at least one murder.

The NYPD tried to look the other way. According to the Mollen Commission's investigation, the Dowd case demonstrated how NYPD Internal Affairs commanders worked hard to prevent the exposure of widespread corruption in the Seventy-fifth Precinct. For years, community people had told the police of known drug locations and were ignored. When the police did raid a location, the dealers knew about the raid beforehand and were never caught.

Most of the officers of the Seventy-fifth Precinct come across as alienated from the community and hostile to it. Greg Donaldson, in his book, *The Ville* (for Brownsville), writes very sensitively about youth growing up in Brownsville and East New York and about the housing police.[2] He reported what he saw, both good and bad, about youth and about the housing police. He also could not help reporting on the attitudes and actions of white Seventy-fifth Precinct police officers as they interacted with the housing police.

An example: A killing occurs in a housing project. Hundreds of people gather at the scene or are looking on from upstairs windows. Officer Fahey's reaction:

> "They should dynamite this fucking place." Then, looking up at the faces above, he shakes his head in a spasm of disgust. "Fuckin' baboons."[3]

At another such scene:

> "Fuckin' projects. Let 'em kill themselves," an officer nearby chimes in. "Like a self-cleaning oven."

These are the same NYPD officers who routinely beat helpless prisoners. In another case, a car was commandeered by a man who was then involved in a car accident. He was followed and cornered.

> He ran into a building. Four white NYPD cops followed the suspect up the stairs to the roof of the project building. As the housing cops fol-

low, the NYPD boys are already on the way down. They point toward the roof. When the housing cops reach the roof, the suspect is semi-conscious. Blood trickles from his right ear. "Damn," says J.R. disapprovingly. "Get a bus." A bus is an ambulance. The hospital report says that the prisoner has a broken femur, a bruised heart, and a fractured jaw. The arrest report surmises that the injuries were sustained in the car accident. The housing police have just witnessed a freebie. When a crime involves a car accident, some police officers respond enthusiastically, at least in part because they know they can administer a beating and blame the injuries on the collision. Officially, those officers had not been on the scene.

The few positive changes (such as returning phone calls and occasionally responding to community complaints) resulted from committed leadership in the seventy-fifth. Lieutenant Barrera was one such leader. When he said the precinct would do something about a problem, the police would act on that problem. He gained a lot of credibility, and, as a result, community leaders began coming to the precinct meetings. Unfortunately (and typically), as soon as his leadership qualities were recognized, he was promoted and transferred to headquarters at 1 Police Plaza. Another such leader was Joseph P. Dunne, formerly precinct commander of the seventy-fifth, then commander for all ten precincts of Brooklyn North. He was also transferred downtown and was appointed deputy police commissioner in 2000. It is said that the current precinct commander, Deputy Inspector Secreto, has also shown some interest in community policing and in following up on complaints.[4]

Most leaders and community activists would like to cooperate with the police, but they fear reprisals. They perceive widespread corruption. People still mistrust the police and tell them nothing; they also fear the drug dealers. Drug dealers are rarely caught because they match the police in radio and other equipment, are ruthless, and organize their trade in many apartments in project buildings. They have good lookout systems and have often avoided raids as if with prior knowledge—which can come only from the police. People who would like to finger drug operations are afraid of being betrayed by the police to the drug dealers and thieves. The few successes of the Weed and Seed program (discussed later) are atypical.

At an orientation program to acclimate 100 new policemen who would be working in Brownsville, held in the Brownsville community, ninety-six of the group were white, and all were terrified.[5] To preserve their own safety, many of these officers avoided situations that would put them in danger and used a lot of force if thrust into conflict situations.

COMMUNITY POLICING

Community policing effects a positive change both in the behavior of police officers and in their attitudes toward community residents. In 1991, New York City Police Commissioner Lee Brown, formerly the police chief and now a two-term mayor of Houston, Texas, introduced community policing through CPOP (Community Police Officer Program), and by 1994, almost 5,000 police officers were assigned to the program.[6] Brown advocated the appointment of mini-police chiefs within the department who would be responsible for their particular communities. He wanted to reemphasize the importance of the cop on the beat (as opposed to those in patrol cars and special units), "reestablishing a sense of law and order in neighborhoods that had teetered on the brink of anarchy for decades."[7]

East New York did get some community policing through CPOP for a while. The beat officers got to know the people in the community, and crime rates dropped thanks to their presence. Visible and available beat cops were well received by community activists. At city council hearings on the community policing program, community board leaders from all five boroughs strongly supported their community police officers. Ocean Hill-Brownsville leaders gave a ringing endorsement to the program: "There is a visibility of uniformed officers on foot patrol on a daily basis. These police officers are known by name to the residents and commercial establishments on their beat." The same community leaders decried the insufficient numbers assigned to the program, the rapid turnover of personnel, and the occasional incivilities. In East New York, as might be expected, the arrest rate also went down. This probably displeased police brass, however, and they withdrew the unit. Community leaders also welcomed the precinct management teams, which met regularly to deal with neighborhood problems. Community policing had won the hearts of ghetto communities, but not the hearts of police brass.

THE BRATTON/SAFIR ERA

When he became police commissioner in 1994, William Bratton "reengineered" the NYPD. He organized more than 300 people from every NYPD rank and bureau into twelve "reengineering" teams. His teams surveyed nearly 8,000 cops and eventually made more than 400 recommendations for change, of which 160 were eventually adopted.[8] Key among the changes, precinct commanders were given significantly more control over what happened in their precincts and made more accountable, as well.

Another reform was the introduction of Compstat meetings at headquarters at which precinct and borough commanders met with the top police brass to review progress in their areas. To help the brass understand what the situation was in each precinct, the Compstat office began to map complaints, robberies, shootings, grand larcenies, and murders in each precinct, utilizing computerized GIS (Geocoded Information Systems) mapping systems. Out of the mapping approach, a much broader scope of action emerged. For example, it was found that guns and drugs existed in overlapping geographic patterns. That realization resulted in the replacement of specialized drug units with so-called SNAG (Street Narcotics and Gun) units, which conducted aggressive, round-the-clock, buy-and-bust activities against gun and drug dealers in targeted locations. The rapidly expanding SCU (Street Crimes Unit), which was involved in the tragic Diallo shooting, was highly successful in harvesting guns from the street.[9] The success of SNAG units and SCU forces resulted in ever smaller commitments to community policing.

THE SHARP DROP IN CRIME

Between 1992 and 1998, citywide FBI Index arrests dropped by 19 percent, while murder arrests dropped by 34 percent. While citywide felony complaints fell by only 8 percent during the period, ghetto areas showed sharper drops. In East New York, FBI Index Crime complaints dropped by 40 percent. At the same time, felony arrest rates rose by 11 percent, a result of zero tolerance and concentrated police sweeps in high-crime locations.

These advances were not without cost. Between 1994 and 1997, citywide complaints of police brutality jumped by 62 percent, to which Commissioner Bratton responded, "That's too damn bad."[10] To Bratton, increased brutality was just another cost of policing the city.

The sharp drop in crime rates began before the Bratton regime and has continued since his departure. Critics point to "creative" reporting by police in which robberies are downgraded to lost property and murders to assaults. Unsolved homicides become suicides or accidental deaths. In his book, *Rudy*, Wayne Barrett showed that nonvisible (indoor) murders fell faster than visible ones in three of the five years from 1994 to 1998 (as well as overall), casting doubt on the theory that increased patrol strength and rises in misdemeanor arrests are associated with homicide declines.[11] Barrett also credited major improvements in life-saving techniques for the reduced number of homicides.

Still another interpretation is that a very small change can produce major results.[12] A gang shooting is like an arms race; it can escalate very quickly. Between 1982 and 1992, for example, gang-related homicides in Los Angeles County went from 158 to 618. Drive-by shootings went from 22 to 57 between 1979 and 1987, and to 71 in 1988; by 1992, they had reached 211. Very possibly, the sharp drop in murders in East New York (and in the city and the nation) resulted from a small reduction in shootings, which netted further reductions over time. Along the same lines, the new war between the Bloods and the Crips in Brooklyn (see next section) may well signal another rise in gang-related homicide.

Community views on the recent drop in crime vary, but no one credits zero-tolerance policing. Some believe that the recent drops are more related to the growth of the economy and to community policing than to tougher enforcement and jailing. Many feel that the 2,000 new and rehabilitated housing units constructed over the past decade, housing that filled in hundreds of vacant lots and buildings, have lit up the darkened community, significantly reducing the ease with which predators can strike. People now feel relatively safe in walking most of the streets of East New York.

THE WAR AGAINST THE GANGS

A major preoccupation of police throughout the country has been the war against the gangs. To carry on this war, there has been a proliferation of militarized antidrug and antigang law enforcement efforts, which further criminalize minority youth.

In Fresno, California, a typical sheriff's Operation Goldstar sweep involves sixty to eighty sheriff's deputies, augmented by investigators from the district attorney's office, probation officers, and liaison agents from the Drug Enforcement Administration, the Bureau of Alcohol, Tobacco, and Firearms, and the FBI.[13] Assembled at staging points and wearing typical SWAT-team regalia of combat boots, helmets, jumpsuits, and body armor, armed with H & K MP5s,[14] dogs, and battering rams, the Goldstar force sweeps problem corners in Fresno. The outfit's mission is to search for drugs, guns, and "warrant fugitives" who have failed to show up in court. A typical sweep bags between 75 and 100 prisoners a night.

While the NYPD has not yet donned the SWAT-team regalia of Fresno, the use of massive police force to overwhelm major drug and other gang-related criminality was initiated during the Bratton era. In the spring of 1996, for example, a spate of robberies in Brownsville public housing projects inspired a massive show of police force. A multipronged attack was mounted by patrol, housing, and narcotics officers joining in perimeter foot and car patrols, with the NYPD aviation unit surveying the tops of buildings for stockpiles of bottles and bricks. A temporary command post was established in the complex. Police showed photos of burglars to victims, transit police and patrol officers policed troubled subway stops, and the whole effort meshed well with the narcotics division. Police units made 700 felony arrests and more than 900 misdemeanor arrests over a seven-month period. The operation was responsible for a 25 percent decline in the precinct's crime rate over the period.

The police classify a "gang" as a group of persons with a structure that includes designated leaders and members who engage in or are suspected of engaging in unlawful conduct.[15] Officers are required to report any intelligence about a gang, a suspected gang, or a suspected gang member, including information about gang meetings, recruitment attempts by gangs, plans by gang members to organize or take part in protests, marches, and other public events, and self-styled events organized by a gang, as well as information useful in developing profiles and intelligence about gang activities. Legally, belonging to a gang is now the same as belonging to the Mafia. Organized crime and conspiracy legislation is now being used to prosecute and punish gang members and their families. Gang membership and even association with gang members has become a felony.

The recently formed NYPD Gang Division identifies and collects gang intelligence, investigates criminal gang activity, and arrests gang members who commit crimes. This unit works hand-in-hand with the Department of Correction's Gang Intelligence Unit. All are regionally linked to nearby state and local law enforcement agencies through a sophisticated federal network that involves a dozen federal agencies, including the FBI and the INS (Immigration and Naturalization Service).

The Security Risk Groups (SRGs = gang members) system was developed internally by NYCDOC (the New York City Department of Corrections) to track the activities of known gang members. The database is a joint product developed with the NYPD and includes name, gang affiliation, gang rank, date made, mannerisms, aliases, weapons, enemies, associates, warrants, prior arrest, front and side headshots, and physical characteristics, including photos of tattoos, scars, or other markings, for all known gang members. Major sources of information are informants who come through the jail system.

The SRG system contains the names and gang details of 13,000 individuals.[16] On a daily basis, an average of 2,100 identified gang members are in DOC custody. From its databases, the DOC has pieced together the full or partial organizational structure of more than fifty-five gangs and actively tracks about 100 of their leaders. Careful placement of SRGs in the jails and swift arrest, trial, and sentencing for in-jail violence have reduced prison stabbings by almost a third.

Many gangs were organized or have a strong presence in local jails and in state and federal prisons. The Bloods' New York City chapter was organized on Riker's Island.[17] Jails and prisons are notorious for rape, sex slavery, racism, and assault, which serve the interests of powerful elements of various jail and prison societies, as well as the administration. Through intimidation and the instinct for self-preservation, nongang inmates are persuaded to join gangs while incarcerated. Jails and prisons are gang recruitment centers, with some estimates placing gang membership in certain institutions as high as six out of every ten inmates.[18] Gang influence in jail has spread its tentacles to street life in the local community.

The police estimate that there are 6,000 Bloods and 5,000 Crips members throughout the five boroughs. "Sets" (as they are called) of these gangs are waging a violent war in the Sixtieth and Sixty-seventh

Precincts in Brooklyn.[19] Sets of both gangs are found in East New York. The East New York Bloods, mostly black, are the largest group and have several sets and about 200 members. They have entrenched themselves in Linden Houses, where they run one of the biggest prostitution rings in the city. At some point, a wholesale attack on the complex by police is expected.

The Crips, mostly West Indian or Jamaican, are in two locations in East New York: Cypress Hills and Linden Boulevard East. They may have sixty or seventy members overall. Violence is still the name of the game. As this is being written, in April 2001, word comes that three Crips members and/or associates shot and killed Ivan Martinez, age seventeen, for the price of a chicken-wing snack. Martinez was a hard-working Mexican immigrant who worked seventy-two-hour weeks at Tony's Famous pizzeria.[20]

The toughest, most ruthless gang in East New York is (or perhaps was) the Crime Family. It has 50 to 60 members and recently ran the Bloods out of the Unity Houses area, having shot some of them in the process. It even recruited some Bloods members to join the Crime Family. The gang has a vertical structure, according to police. It has two leaders, Brandy Russel and Tyrone King; under them is a group of four, under the group of four another group of four, then three descending groups of five. Tyrone King was recently arrested. Most of the others of the hierarchy are in jail; several are dead. The gang also received a massive setback in 2000, described later.

There are several smaller groups, some structured like the KMK gang, others not. Recent immigrants from Nieta, Salvador, feeling isolated and victimized, have formed their own gang.[21] The total combined membership of these smaller gangs might reach 100 to 150, so there are altogether 400 to 500 gang members in up to ten gangs. It is widely believed that most gang members end up in jail or dead. Some gang members do escape, however, and go on to other pursuits. There are also promising gang diversion programs, such as the Street Soldiers, organized by Joe Marshall in San Francisco.

Although crime is sharply down in the Seventy-fifth Precinct, police brass is still ordering a high level of arrests. This encourages police officers to make more quality-of-life arrests—a person drinking beer on the street, or yelling, or playing a boom box, or even hanging out with a bunch of young people, or caught in the stairwell of a project building. Transit police hide, then jump out and arrest fare beaters.[22] Total misdemeanor arrests in East New York rose from 3,205 in 1992 to 5,850 in 1998.[23] Misdemeanor arrests peaked at 9,560 in 2000, and were still above 7,100 in 2002, despite a drop in FBI Index Crimes below the 1992 level. Those arrested are handcuffed, booked, and fingerprinted and spend hours or days in jail. Most are sentenced to time served, receive a small fine, and are released.

These quality-of-life arrests can have serious repercussions. The arrest information is added to the gang databases and is used in later, more substantive cases if a person steps out of line.[24] The arrests clearly violate citizens' civil rights, since they are most often selectively enforced against people of color and the visibly poor.

Almost a third of those arrested for misdemeanors are under twenty years of age. Because of the Federal Education Act, which went into effect in the summer of 2000, federal college loans or financial aid are not available to anyone with a prior drug conviction. This could mean disaster for those very few college-bound youngsters from poor families.

In addition to a rise in misdemeanor arrests, the rate of felony indictments resulting from felony arrests declined a steep 37 percent between 1993 and 1999, more than five times the rate of decrease in felony arrests, indicating a pattern of deterioration in felony arrest quality, arising from either soft arrests or overcharging.[25]

The linking of local police terminals and arrest files with the databases of the INS further enhances the repressive nature of current law enforcement. Such systems can track, control, and intimidate whole populations. The collusion between police and the INS results in the de facto criminalization and political marginalization of documented and undocumented immigrants alike.[26] Immigrants fear the law more intensely, are docile in the workplace, and steer clear of politics.

Richard Perez, speaking for the National Congress for Puerto Rican Rights, brought the war on gangs and the politics of ghetto policing into serious question.[27] Perez maintained that the police seek to destroy the leadership of any large Puerto Rican (or other minority) gang that turns its attention to doing good for the community because it can become a major political force. King Tone, leader of the Latin Kings in Manhattan, effected a truce between the Latin Kings and other gangs. The police were opposed to these truces. They did not want to see the gangs become a political movement for change. According to Perez, the police preferred to see the gangs fighting and killing each other rather than attacking the fundamental discrimination against their communities.[28]

Up to a point, it is difficult to argue with NYPD strategies for fighting crime. But, when the department intensifies its arrest activity despite declining crime rates, many community leaders ask, why? Why not turn some of that police energy into an expanded cop-on-the-beat presence, which is known to deter crime? Why not take steps that will reduce the temptation to join gangs or commit crimes in the first place?

WEED AND SEED

Weed and Seed, a federal program started in 1998, was supposed to do just that—get the community to snitch on the bad "weeds" and get them put away while helping the good "seeds" through remediation, recreation, job search, and other aids. Significantly, the dividing line between "weeds" and "seeds" is small when viewed by the community. Many "weeds" are seen as "seeds" who didn't get the same breaks; many families are loathe to turn in "weedy" family members or neighbors. The Weed and Seed precursor was an East New York Urban Youth Corps program called PACT (Police and Community Together), which operated in a high-crime twenty-block area surrounding the Unity Plaza public housing project, home of the Crime Family.

PACT initiated the Community Security Initiative (CSI), in which two cops working the streets (community policing) gradually developed rapport with the local community. The community policing did reduce crime, resulting, predictably, in fewer arrests. "Fewer arrests" didn't please police brass, however, so the police were again withdrawn. A reduction in crime is pleasing to the local community, but high arrest activity pleases police headquarters. Guess who local police precincts are striving to please.

The new Weed and Seed program covers a fifty-six-block area bounded by Pennsylvania, Van Sinderin, Atlantic, and Livonia Avenues and has recently been expanded to include Linden Houses a few blocks away. The insufficient money originally made available for community-operated programs to help teen-age "seeds" has dried up; the main effort now is to convince community residents to report the criminal activity of "weeds" to the police. At the start of Weed and Seed, most people did not want to talk to the police. They were either involved in crime themselves or were related to criminals or their children were involved. Many of those who favored talking to the police were terrified of reprisals, but the needles and syringes lying on the ground near their apartment buildings convinced some residents to lean toward cooperation.

Finally, some progress was made. Under the Federal Trespass Affidavit Program, landlords of private apartment houses entered into an agreement with police that allowed officers to conduct vertical patrols from ground floors to the roofs and included giving them keys to all access doors. When the police found someone who did not live in the building and/or had no legitimate business in it, the police arrested the person and charged (usually) him with vagrancy. Crime in those buildings dropped; the residents saw results, became less suspicious of the police, and began to cooperate. The way police began to acknowledge citizen information or complaints was also a welcome change. Formerly, if you called in a complaint, police would come to your door, and then everyone would know you had talked to them. Now residents can call a special number; the police involved in the program take the information and don't show up in person. It makes complaining about criminal activity a lot easier (and safer).

In one of its more notable initiatives, Weed and Seed organized two marches and rallies in cooperation with the East New York Urban Youth Corps in an effort to curb the violence tearing the community apart. The first was the March for Life, held on March 25, 2000. It started at noon at Newport and Williams Avenues and ended at Sheffield and Livonia. Around 100 men turned out for the march in response to letters, posters in the community, and flyers. Passages from the scriptures were prominently displayed on the flyers. For the second march, the Stop the Violence Rally, 500 to 600 men turned out, as well as all the politicians. They marched from Newport and Williams two blocks north to Livonia and Williams, where a major rally was held. According to Dennis Taylor, current head of Weed and Seed, churches played a major role in the march. The Christian Life Center (CLC), a 14,000-member organization headed by A. R. Bernard, who recently opened a center in East New York, was one of the most active church participants.

These marches had a visible effect. While they may not have deterred youth from crime, they did bolster the determination of residents to rid the area of criminal elements. Shortly afterward, residents began sending more information about criminal activity to the police.

Through a group called the Coalition of Leaders against Crime, organized by Weed and Seed staff, the community came through with enough hard information that two Crime Family apartments were raided by narcotics detectives executing search warrants.[29] They came up with three loaded guns, four suspects, and a quantity of narcotics. Those arrested were between fifteen and twenty-nine years old.

In a second case, the Crime Family ejected a man from his apartment at 611 Blake Avenue, in Unity Plaza, and turned his home into a lucrative, around-the-clock crack store that terrorized neighbors.[30] The gang trashed the apartment, broke the toilet, and tore out wooden kitchen cabinets and dumped them in the hallway, along with bags of garbage. There were fights in the hallway and a steady stream of customers knocking on the door at all hours. Tenants informed the police about the situation; the Housing Authority also learned of the apartment takeover. Police raided the apartment, nabbed six teenagers, and returned the apartment to the original tenant, who swore he would never return to the neighborhood. The youths were charged with trespassing, burglary, and possession of sixty-eight vials of crack. The gang leaders, drug dealers nicknamed Bam Bam and Tyree, were still at large.

In November 2000, a massive police strike was finally directed at the Crime Family. Supplemented by forces from the ATF, the FBI, the DA's office, and special operations police, the four entrances to the Unity Plaza complex were sealed off while police went through the project buildings door to door. Because more murders and shootings took place in the Unity Plaza area than anywhere else in the area, the police action was very aggressive. They arrested many gang members, some of whom were quickly sentenced to twenty- to twenty-five-year terms. The leader, Brandy Russel (Bam Bam), escaped capture and is now a fugitive. Entrances to the project area were still sealed off as of December 2000. Though the main target of this operation was the drug-trafficking Crime Family, many nongang members were also caught in the dragnet. Heightened police aggressiveness, arrest activity, and brutality are de rigueur in these operations.

IMPACTS OF POLICE ARREST ACTIVITY

The profile-happy arrest, conviction, and sentencing of minority young people is excessively punitive and has created a de facto apartheid, a double standard of justice applied to ghetto communities and people of color. National and citywide statistics overwhelmingly illustrate a system that is self-defeating and out of control.

By 1990, 89 percent of first-time drug offenders with no prior record were being sentenced to prison for an average of sixty-eight months by the federal courts.[31] Only 79 percent of first-time violent offenders were sentenced to prison by those same courts, and those who had committed violent crimes were serving an average of less than fifty-seven months for those crimes. By 1997, U.S. Justice Department figures show that the average time served by persons convicted of murder, rape, robbery, and aggravated assault had dropped to only forty-nine months. Because of the lack of prison space, the actual sentences being served by those convicted of violent crimes have been decreasing since 1980.

By the end of 1994, blacks were being jailed at 7.7 times the rate of whites in all state prisons.[32] Although 64 percent of crack users are white, 91 percent of those sentenced under federal crack laws are black, and 6 percent are other minority; only 3 percent are white. Sentencing for crack possession is 100 times more severe than for cocaine. A person caught with five grams of crack receives a sentence of five years; 5.1 grams draws a ten-year sentence. For powdered cocaine, the same bill requires the possession of 500 grams to trigger an equal sentence. Crack cocaine is more prevalent in low-income communities because it is considerably cheaper than the powdered version of the drug.

As a result of sentencing guidelines and law-enforcement practices that prey on those living in poverty, by 1992 nearly one in three blacks between the ages of twenty and twenty-nine was under the supervision of the criminal justice system on any given day.[33] In some cities such as Washington, D.C., and Baltimore, 50 percent of black men between the ages of eighteen and thirty-five were being supervised by the U.S. Justice Department.[34]

Most of our nation's 810,000 opiate addicts are turned away each year by drug treatment programs because they lack funding. There is currently room to treat only about 115,000 addicts at any given time. Government can't find the $4,000 needed to treat an addict, yet willingly spends a quarter of a million dollars to incarcerate just one non-violent addict for a ten-year mandatory sentence.

Drugs are responsible for 25 to 35 percent of property crimes but only 4 to 5 percent of violent crimes. Alcohol, on the other hand, accounts for 3 to 4 percent of property crimes but a staggering 25 to 30 percent of all violent crimes. Yet we tax alcohol and create decades-long sentences for drug abusers.

A nearly inconceivable 4 million mostly poor U.S. citizens have already lost their right to vote because of a felony conviction. This includes 1.5 million African Americans, 14 percent of all black males. This stripping of voting rights seriously impacts the very urban areas where a healthy electorate is most needed in order to effect change. If the trend continues, it is estimated that 40 percent of the next generation of black men will have lost the right to vote.[35] In other countries, voting rights are restored after a prisoner has served his time. In most states, felons can get their voting rights restored after serving their time, but they must apply for them. In New York State, persons convicted of a felony lose their voting rights for as long as they are under the jurisdiction of the criminal justice system.

As a result of this punitive onslaught, and despite the greatest expenditures for new prisons in American history, the lack of space in the prisons has become a major problem.[36] The police arrest someone, perhaps at a drug location or for a felony, or frisk someone and find him with a weapon, and these perpetrators turn out to be on probation and have screwed up again. The courts—the judges—are reluctant to send them back to prison because there is no room. There is no room because the prisons are full of non-violent drug offenders serving unconscionably long sentences. For this reason, recidivist felons are often back on the street in days.

There is a move afoot in many states to ease the sentencing laws, reducing or eliminating mandatory terms and replacing prison with drug treatment, monitoring, and probation. New York is among them, but it lags far behind others in supporting the most needed reforms.[37]

PROBATION

In February 2000, the New York City Department of Probation launched Neighborhood Shield in the Seventy-fifth Precinct. It is a joint effort of the Department of Probation, the NYPD, the courts, the office of the Kings County District Attorney, and the Corporation Counsel, which seeks to sharply reduce recidivism among probationers.[38] The aim of the program is to steer the individual probationer away from criminal activity during the first 120 days, considered the most vulnerable period.

At the center of this initiative are Community-Based Response Teams (CBRTs) consisting of police officers and probation officers who conduct unannounced home visits, curfew checks, car spot checks, and vertical patrols in project buildings. After six months of operation, the teams had made 116 arrests, 90 percent of which were for misdemeanors and not all of which were for probation violations. As a result of the joint initiative, probation violations are now calendared five to ten times faster than before; the judge can swiftly impose additional restrictions on the probationer or even send him back to jail. Through this speed-up, the probationer is made aware that probation violation is a serious offense, leading, it is hoped, to a modification of behavior.

In addition to speedier disposition of probation violations, probationers are required to do fifty hours of community service doing such jobs as cleaning out vacant lots, removing graffiti from city schools, and street cleaning. When assigned to churches, probationers may paint or make repairs. In the East Brooklyn Industrial Park, they assist with debris removal and light maintenance. An attempt is made to match skills with needs. Young probationers are often surprised and pleased that people thank them for doing the work and often offer them sodas or other tokens of appreciation. Sometimes a person is hired by an agency for which he has done community service work.

Those at high risk for committing more crimes are identified at assessment and, in addition to performing community service, are required to come to the Neighborhood Shield office for two ninety-minute group sessions a week for ten weeks. The "Blue Group" is a highly structured, intensive, group counseling and therapy session that tries to change the way youngsters think about the world and to get them to realize the consequences of their actions. Many youths think they have to beat up a person or stab him if he steps on their sneakers and doesn't apologize. They don't consider what a stabbing will do if they are caught and returned to jail. As a result of these sessions, most high-risk youths get the message and do refrain from violence.[39]

Neighborhood Shield has also formed an East New York Community Advisory Committee that identifies probationers who are causing problems as well as resources that will help offenders make a positive adjustment. Through Nova Ancora, a local nonprofit organization, a youth who needs training to hold a job can get it. Other nonprofit support groups help with preparation and try to convince youngsters that success in poorly paying jobs can lead to better-paying jobs in the future. Drug addicts are required to go into drug treatment if it is available (they must be Medicaid eligible) or are sent back to jail. Psychiatric counseling and therapy are not available, although they are often needed.

Despite its limitations, Neighborhood Shield seems to be working. The most recent compliance rate, that is, the percentage of probationers who meet all requirements, including community service, is 93.7 percent.[40] This compares with 72 percent compliance throughout New York City and only 49 percent for those at high risk.

While probationers are dissuaded from committing further crimes, and while there are some heartening elements to the program, Neighborhood Shield must also be seen as yet another method for tracking and herding minority youths. The youths do not receive sufficient help to succeed in the outside world; the punitive element of the program is therefore its most prominent feature. More could be achieved if crisis management, job preparation, and community service were required courses in high school, along with the needed therapy and other behavioral resources—before the youngsters were arrested in the first place.

Preventive measures do work. The Brooklyn Attorney's office initiated a homicide prevention, intervention, and enforcement program in the Seventy-seventh and Eighty-first Precincts.[41] Of 200 individuals who applied, seventy-five were referred to services that included drug rehabilitation, job training and placement, and educational services. Since the start of the program, there has been a 42 percent reduction in assaults and a 75 percent reduction in shooting incidents compared to the preceding seven-month period. After at-risk women were armed with pendants and cell phones with which to quickly summon police, domestic violence homicides fell by a third. Yes, prevention can work.

THE COMMUNITY COMPLAINT PROBLEM

In 1985, the small businesses around the corner from St. Paul's Community Baptist Church were in trouble.[42] A fight staged in Key Foods would distract a cashier while a third youth emptied the till. Thieves would break into the clothing store overnight, taking costume jewelry and T-shirts. Purses were snatched, chains ripped from necks, car batteries stolen. The police were never around when you needed them.

St. Paul's Community Baptist Church tried to help out. To strengthen the commercial area, St. Paul's, under the leadership of the Reverend Johnny Ray Youngblood, bought seven store properties on Stanley Avenue just west of Hendrix Street for $363,000 in 1985 and five more stores for $296,000 a year later. On the first day, Rochester Blanks, a church official, rousted a crack addict from one store's basement boutique, and the Reverend Youngblood invited the police to raid it. Within the week, it was padlocked. The social club was evicted for nonpayment of rent. A medical clinic replaced the numbers operation in another store. A church member, Sylvia Eggleston, took over a badly mismanaged beauty salon. New sidewalks were laid, new awnings installed at church expense, and several residential buildings were purchased to house church officials who would keep an eye on things. Conditions were much improved.

Cut to early 1990. The commercial area was in trouble again. Robberies, thievery, and assaults occurred daily. The merchants hired their own overnight security guard, but they needed police protection, support, and action, which they were not getting. "If I call the police," complained the pizza parlor owner, "the boys say, 'Who called the police?' The police say 'The pizza man.' No brains. They could kill me and bury me before the cops come back." Calls to 911 often went without response for an hour or more.

Junior Roman, the dry cleaner, added fuel to the merchants' anger. While sleeping as usual in the rear of his store, he heard footsteps on the roof. He called 911 and was told an officer could not be dispatched on such a flimsy tip. By the time the private guard arrived, the cash register of the Chinese restaurant next door had been emptied.

The merchants aired their gripes at a meeting with Inspector Patrick J. Carroll and two sergeants from the Seventy-fifth Precinct. Ten or twenty boys committed most of the crimes. "A day doesn't go by," Fred Wein, the pharmacist, said, "when someone isn't robbed on the avenue between one and seven. If you would just put a car out there, you'd see them forming outside 640 Stanley after school. They go off in groups of three or four. They look for the easy prey." He lay open his palms on the table. "You see it every day. It's so simple. Give us two plainclothesmen; we can break it up in a day."[43]

Inspector Carroll says that he understands there has been a problem of "harassment" by "kids." He can certainly dispatch an officer on scooter every other day. What's more, Stanley Avenue is already covered under the Community Patrol Officer Program, known as CPOP. It is the beat of Officer Zito.

None of the merchants had ever seen Officer Zito. In its early days, getting CPOP to work was proving uncertain and difficult. There was poor cooperation and even hostility toward the program from other NYPD units. Some police officers derisively called it C-MOMS.[44] It was obviously not popular with Officer Zito.

Inspector Carroll admitted that something was wrong, but he offered little to the assembled merchants: Officer Zito would be more of a presence; if the merchants saw a gang of teenagers forming, they should call 911. The cops would like to pick up truants, but the Board of Education hadn't yet agreed to cooperate; maybe the van would be on the streets next week. "All I can tell you," Inspector Carroll said, ending the meeting, "is we have a worse problem on Euclid Avenue."

Possibly they did. As in East New York, police did not respond well to the continuing crime and drug-selling problems faced by the Fulton Avenue merchants in the Cypress Hills area (though the police were responsive to arson calls). Drug selling around Euclid and Fulton was ubiquitous. Similarly, the police rarely addressed the issues raised by residents; they always claimed there were more pressing needs for police attention. They still did things like ticketing cars parked on a street when a resident complained about something else.

The NYPD's failure to respond to community complaints is a major community beef. Activists and community leaders all tell similar stories. At a street fair, there is a van with eight cops sitting in it. Right outside, some young toughs are fighting, creating a scene. The police don't move. Are they waiting for a riot? If someone is playing loud music, the complainants are likely to be told that the police have more important things to attend to. If someone parks in your driveway, the police will not respond. At a meeting with police, someone complains about drag racing, and the police suggest that the resident bring up the subject at the monthly community/precinct meetings. The police sometimes promise to take action against prostitution or drug activity, then don't follow through, pleading more pressing business elsewhere.

One of the more egregious failures of the police has been the often violent struggles for a piece of the action on construction projects in East New York. Legitimate groups and shakedown racketeers have vied for control of construction since the early 1980s. One leader headed a very tough group of men who dictated who would work and who would subcontract on most rehabilitation and new construction jobs in Brownsville and East New York. Another group dictated construction hiring practices, imposing unnecessary financial burdens on these projects. The contractor of an ACORN project on Sheffield Avenue was forced to hire four (mostly unreliable) men at $10 to $15 an hour and pay $200 a week to the no-show leader of the group.[45] To show they meant business, some of these toughs have approached builders with shotguns, and have used them at least once. They threw the architect of one project down a flight of stairs and killed a superintendent of construction on another. A newly completed building was shot up by the group in another incident.[46]

The police never looked into these crimes, despite pleas and demonstrations—until murder compelled their attention. The police respond when there is a shooting or a threat of a shooting, someone carrying a gun or shooting one off in the air. That, at least, they recognize as "police business."

Because the number of construction projects has recently declined, the intimidation and violence have lessened. Yet the sparks are ready to fly. One of these groups of toughs is now demanding the contract to provide security at the Gateway Center, in Spring Creek, where the $192-million mall and another 600 Nehemiah houses are scheduled to be built; other groups likely will be demanding jobs—and more. Will the police ever take notice?

EAST NEW YORK IN JEOPARDY

The situation is one of continuing crisis. Though serious crime has been reduced, arrests for pot smoking and other misdemeanors have skyrocketed over the past several years, while many community concerns go unanswered. Much white crime goes unpunished, while blacks feel the full force of the law. Too many East New Yorkers are in prison serving excessively long sentences.[47] Thousands more are on probation or parole. The police continue to pursue a zero-tolerance strategy, increasingly criminalizing East New York's youth.

A high percentage of the community's male population has already been damaged or destroyed. As shown in table 4 on the following page, 28 percent of East New York's young men between the ages of sixteen and thirty-five were arrested in 1998; in that year, 22 percent were incarcerated or supervised by law enforcement authorities. Add up that kind of arrest rate over three or four years, and you have a devastated male population.

In the Weed and Seed area, up to 50 percent of the male population between sixteen and thirty-five were arrested in 1998.[48] In 1999, though felony arrests dropped by 12 percent, misdemeanor arrests fell by only 6 percent.[49] Since 1980, the female inmate population has also grown; 13 percent of the parolees in the Seventy-fifth Precinct were women.

If violent criminals were apprehended and put in jail for more reasonable terms, perhaps the community could stand being overseen by an aggressive and belligerent police force. But there is no such prospect on the horizon. Instead, the gangs are thriving, they are adding members in and out of prisons, and they are starting at a very early age. The six gang members arrested at the crack house at 69 Blake Avenue were ages fourteen to seventeen. Criminal behavior is ubiquitous at all ages, however, not just among the young.

Where do these criminals come from? From the 40 percent of the population that is on welfare, from the 35.5 percent single-parent households, from the 70 percent who haven't finished high school, from the more than 50 percent who are not in the labor force.[50] These are the people who can't pay the rent, who can't find jobs, who can't make ends meet. Becoming a gang member provides safety in numbers; a criminal career may even help pay the rent.

Every ethnic or racial group in the ghetto has developed one or more gangs. Many start as protective organizations, but most of them soon turn to predatory activity: robbery or burglary, dealing drugs or prostitution. The hallmark of East New York gangs is violence. To join one of the bigger, more violent gangs, you may have to shoot or stab someone. If you're a girl, you may have to sleep with twenty or thirty male members. As a result, it is estimated that 30 percent of the fourteen to seventeen year olds in East New York are HIV-positive. True or apocryphal, the reports are chilling.

My gut feeling is that the oppressive and nonresponsive law enforcement strategies pursued in the nation's ghettos have nurtured the growth of gangs over the past twenty-five years, as have the ghettoization of minorities, their short-changed educational options, the sad state of housing, health, and social services, the only too obvious

Table 4

Seventy-fifth Precinct Male Residents under the Jurisdiction of the Criminal Justice System (1998)

Type of Detention or Hold	16–34	Age 35+	All
ENY male population, 1990[a]	23,740	19,585	43,325
Number arrested, 1998[b]	6,711	3,614	10,325
Percentage of age group	28	18	24
Weed and Seed male population	1,021	1,606	2,627
Number arrested[c]	516	374	890
Percent arrested	51	23	34
Disposition of arrests, 1998[d]			
Jail[e]	299	161	460
State prison	427	230	657
Probation/jail-probation	424	229	653
Conditional Discharge[f]	1,705	919	2,624
Subtotals	2,855	1,539	4,394
Probation, from previous arrests[g]	751	405	1,156
On parole[h]	608	328	936
Prior State prison inmates[i]	950	512	1,462
Federal prison inmates[j]	31	16	47
Total under jurisdiction	5,195	2,800	7,995
Percent of males in Age Group	22	14	18

a Excluding males 0–15 years.

b NYPD arrest total for the Seventy-fifth Precinct, 1998. Women's imprisonment is estimated at 5 percent of total, on the basis of U.S. Department of Justice, Bureau of Justice statistics, and is excluded from all following totals.

c Based on 45.6 percent living below poverty level compared with 29.4 percent in the rest of the precinct.

d Disposition of adult felony arrests, New York State Division of Criminal Justice Services. Seventy-fifth Precinct accounted for the 4.6 percent of citywide arrests in 1998, using NYPD Compstat reports.

e Average stay in years based on forty-three-day average stay for jail sentences and time served.

f Average stay in years based on average duration of conditional discharge, estimated to be nine months.

g Probation totals from New York City Department of Probation.

h Total on parole from New York State Division of Parole for Seventy-fifth Precinct.

i Based on New York State Department of Correctional Services report on inmate population, less those imprisoned in 1998, January 1, 2000.

j Using an average stay of eighty-six months, based on U.S. Bureau of Prisons figures for 192 federal inmates from the Southern District of New York, minus 4 percent for Westchester County; the East New York portion is estimated at 3.56 percent.

discrimination in employment. From this perspective, the growing gang menace can be interpreted as a rapidly expanding rebellion.

The community's reading of the situation is that the proper way to handle the continuing crisis is to increase the services to the people in the areas of concentrated violence and crime. More needs to be done to reduce the impetus for youths to join gangs, to give East New York's youth something better to strive for, to belong to, to feel safe in. Young people also need help to kick drug and alcohol addictions. In East New York and other ghettos, people need less hard-on-crime strategy and more help in breaking the poverty cycle.

What would really make a difference is a civilian force equal in size to the police force, which would devote its energy to giving East New York youth (and the entire population) real hope in other directions, giving them the one-on-one assistance they need to cope with their problems, and rewarding them with stipends for the efforts they put in. The civilian force could open up real opportunities for ghetto residents to make it in this world and could offer gangs rewarding incentives to go straight.

Unfortunately, nothing like this is happening. The police pursue zero tolerance and the criminalization of ghetto youth in the continuing drive to justify still more expenditures on law enforcement and to strengthen the NYPD's hard-on-crime image. If it were sincerely interested in reducing crime, the NYPD would assign more officers to community beats, where their presence has deterred crime, and they would be happy with a declining arrest rate.

A baby step in the right direction is the truant holding area at the East New York Urban Youth Corps offices. In a large meeting room on a typical school day, perhaps sixty middle-school and some high-school pupils are seated.[51] They are truants, picked up by the police and brought to the UYC holding area. To the credit of the responsible authorities, the children are neither arrested nor fingerprinted. At times, that room has held up to 100 teenagers. Parents are notified to pick up their children. If they are not picked up by 5 P.M., the children are taken to the station house and released there. Perhaps half are playing truant for health reasons (sores, pregnancies, dental problems). Up to 6 percent have serious problems and are referred to a social worker on the premises. It has been found that recidivism is very low; over 90 percent of first-time truants have found school a better place than either the streets or the UYC holding room.[52]

Is that a glimmer of hope for the future? Maybe, but no more than that. So far, the few forward-looking steps made in decriminalization are still within the framework of the criminal justice system. East New York needs a reorientation of its "policing" system, a "reengineering" that will work for the community, not against it.

Epilogue

ESSENTIALLY, MY STORY is told. There are no ready answers, no brief full of prescriptions for the future, no panacea on the horizon. There is only unremitting struggle to correct the injustices and outrages of the past forty years.

To this point, we have witnessed the story of East New York's struggle to persevere and to improve its social and physical environment. While some outstanding progress has been made during the past twenty years, East New York has just scratched the surface of its thorniest problems. Its activist history has been long and tangled but remains a sound basis for renewed and successful efforts. The gains have been hard won, but some very good programs have suffered setbacks at the hands of political leaders with private agendas. Measures can be instituted to let more good ideas and programs flower and bear fruit. The awakened community has elected more responsive and progressive representatives, which may bring about a renaissance in forward progress.

All this is just the beginning. The major impediments to rejuvenation are encountered on a much broader front. The rigidity of the educational bureaucracy, the police obsession with criminalizing youth, the abuse of homeowners and renters, the neglect of the poverty stricken—all point to major hurdles yet to be overcome.

Take, as an example, the exploitation, discrimination, and greed that surround the would-be buyer of a house. If not financially secure, a buyer can be buffeted about, denied a bank loan, burdened with a home improvement package and a high interest rate, and generally put in harm's way—a ready candidate for default and foreclosure. We can help that would-be homeowner to avoid the worst excesses of the industry through operation of a home buyers' service, but we can't get the bank to give him a mortgage at a reasonable rate of interest.

To effectively deal with this situation, we may have to reach far beyond the near horizon. Can the home ownership financing techniques

(with their built-in safeguards) used for the Nehemiah homes be adapted for use throughout the community? What about starting a local bank
in East New York? Or a community-run brokerage?

This kind of look at the basic structure of a problem is desperately
needed. I believe that creative and ambitious solutions have to be pursued for many longstanding problems. The community will have to
muster the willingness and the courage to go out on a limb (a sturdy
limb is needed) to make ambitious but realistic demands. For example,
after a long history of ignoring local input, local school boards were
given some minor powers in 1972, most of which were taken away at
the end of 1996. The educational bureaucracy is back in complete control. As long as it (and the United Federation of Teachers) is in full control, there won't ever be any real improvement in learning.

The community's stance must be, and for the long term, a commitment to full or nearly full local control. East New York must some day
join the many thousands of locally controlled school districts, most of
whom have far smaller populations. With reasonable funding and an
accountable local school board, educating our children could be made
more relevant, more effective, and even fun.

Despite the efforts of school chancellors to take it away, local school
boards have retained one substantial power: they can still select their
own district superintendent. What's good enough for the repressive
schools bureaucracy should be good enough for the police, as well. A
perfectly reasonable demand is to allow local communities like East
New York to select their own police precinct commanders from an
NYPD-approved list of eligibles. Among the questions the community
might want to ask the applicants:

> What is your readiness to:
> Give high priority to community complaints?
> Initiate and/or expand community policing?
> End racial profiling and ease up on quality-of-life arrests?
> Support efforts to increase precinct strength?
> Be guided by a community advisory board?

None of these examples, nor the many more that could be itemized, can
even be approached, much less attained, without the visible support
and backing of a truly unified East New York. This might be achieved
by following in the footsteps of the Dudley Street Neighborhood Initia-

tive (DSNI) in Boston. This initiative is described in Christie Baxter's essay "Non-Profits: New Settings for City Planners," in *The Profession of City Planning*," edited by Lloyd Rodwin and Bishwapriya Sanyal and published in 2000 by the Center for Urban Policy Research at Rutgers University. The main thing the Boston community did was to establish an institution that could guide its revitalization process over time. Key to this was the creation of a neighborhood-led governing board. Its decision-making structure was developed through extensive negotiations within the community. Of the thirty-one seats on the board, twelve were reserved for residents, eleven for representatives of nonprofit organizations (including two religious organizations), four for business, one for city government, and one for state government; two seats were undesignated.

DSNI then created its own plan, basing it upon the strengths and needs of the community. The plan envisioned an "urban village" to be developed through a series of discrete projects undertaken over time. A key decision was to educate residents. Community participation was defined as the vehicle for community residents to become informed decision makers with the staying power and resources to move from decision making to implementation. Strategies for implementation were integral components of the planning process.

In a path-breaking achievement, DSNI received from the city the power of eminent domain in the neighborhood. The Ford Foundation gave DSNI a loan of $2 million to help carry out its new power. This allowed DSNI to create a nonprofit organization, Dudley Neighbors, Inc., to acquire and hold neighborhood land in perpetuity and to lease it to developers.

It is the idea of developing a representative governing body for East New York that is so intriguing. It could embody the whole of the social, economic, and physical development objectives of the community. If such a body existed, it could implement the bold suggestions and demands set forth earlier and have a major impact.

This is not to supersede or supplant the great strides made by EBC's Nehemiah homes or by ACORN's MHANY or the work of the other nonprofits that have been providing the community with a major service by producing low-cost and low-rent housing. Those efforts should continue and be expanded.

On another front, something positive should be done with the two-acre open space at Unity Plaza. This park area, which was not planned in detail in 1967, has never been fully utilized. The sunken band shell and amphitheater have never been used but could be the basis for an active youth recreational and educational program. If a Dudley Neighborhood–type planning body thought it worthwhile, it could organize a working coalition and bring community resources to bear on the problem. Similarly, a communitywide effort to speed commercial development could be launched, as could programs designed to relieve poverty, to meet the needs of youth, to raise the minimum wage, and to fight city hall for a fair share of resources.

What has been done up to now is all to the good. To wipe out the forty years of discrimination, deprivation, and destruction is going to take more, perhaps more than can be mustered over the short term. All I can do is to salute the community for its multiple efforts over the past several decades and to wish it much-deserved success in the future.

Notes

NOTES TO THE INTRODUCTION

1. At this point in East New York's history, the Hispanic population was overwhelmingly Puerto Rican.

2. *New York Times*, March 30, 1972.

3. The Enterprise Foundation, Columbia, Md., 1999 Annual Report.

4. *Rental Housing Assistance—The Worsening Crisis*, HUD, 2000.

5. "Brooklyn Sniper Kills Negro Boy in Race Disorder," *New York Times*, July 22, 1966.

NOTES TO CHAPTER 1

1. The study area was the central portion of East New York, bounded by Van Sinderin, Atlantic, and Fountain Avenues and by Linden Boulevard. The Board of Education's School District 19 and the NYPD's Seventy-fifth Precinct included Cypress Hills to the north, the area east of Fountain Avenue to the Queens line, and Canarsie, to the south. The population in 1990 was 164,000.

2. The statistics given in this chapter are drawn from Walter Thabit, "Planning for a Target Area, East New York," October 1967.

3. Richard A. Cloward, "Community Action for Housing Desegregation: Strategies and Problems," National Committee Against Discrimination, May 1966. In New York City, in 1959, Cloward notes, 325,771 persons were receiving welfare, but 716,000 appeared eligible to receive it. In a study of Manhattan's West Side, 52 percent lacked anything approaching adequate furniture. People were not informed of their rights and were denied welfare unlawfully, but nobody was watching out for them.

4. Survey of East New York tenants by my consulting firm, 1967.

5. Thabit, "Planning for a Target Area, East New York."

6. This Dutch heritage and its remnants (street names, a cemetery, churches) were highly valued by many of the middle-class blacks who first moved into East New York.

7. Samuel G. Freedman, *Upon This Rock*, HarperCollins, 1993.

8. Goldbeaters are people who pound gold into thin leaves for gilding.

9. New-law tenements were those built after passage of the Housing Act of 1901. It required more open space, larger rooms, and windows in every room, and required the upgrading of older tenements.

10. Freedman, *Upon This Rock*.

11. The following social analysis is based partly on discussions with the sociologist Malcolm Evans, January 1967.

12. Two of those who reviewed my manuscript were hoping for vignettes of what a street was like before and after the change from white to black. My own experience suggests that there were no glaring differences. In mostly white areas, most of the people on the street were white. In minority areas, most of the people on the street were black or Puerto Rican. When there were stores, people shopped in them; when the stores closed up, they didn't. Yes, there were more children on the stoops and in the streets; the streets were less clean, and there were fewer cars. Much of the violence and criminality and many of the fires took place at night, or at least out of sight.

13. Freedman, *Upon This Rock*.

14. For more detail on black churches and their role in the politics, culture, and life of the community, see Clarence Taylor, *The Black Churches of Brooklyn*, Columbia University Press, 1996.

15. New York Metropolitan Committee on Planning, "The Demand for Planning Services by Local Communities—An Analysis of Planning Needs in 26 Communities in New York City and Newark, New Jersey," New York, 1969. East New York was one of twenty-six communities reported on in 1966.

NOTES TO CHAPTER 2

1. A detailed historical account of life in the Delta and life after migration to Chicago is given in Nicholas Lemann's *The Promised Land: The Great Black Migration and How It Changed America*, Vintage Books, 1992.

2. NAACP Legal Defense and Educational Fund pamphlet, undated.

3. Juan Gonzalez, *Harvest of Empire*, Viking Penguin, 2000, provides a vivid account of the U.S. exploitation and impoverishment of Puerto Rico.

4. Ibid.

5. Ibid.

6. Irwin Silber, writing in *The Guardian*, December 31, 1975.

7. Ibid.

8. The following description is adapted from Alan Burnham, "The Dwelling in Greater Manhattan, 1850–1950: Part II, 1850–1890," published privately, 1953.

9. Ibid.

10. The continuation of rent controls, fixing rents at prewar levels, incensed landlords throughout the city. Though space was at a premium, they

were prevented from charging what the market would bear. Their answer was to cut services and neglect maintenance. Getting tenants to move was of limited value in most parts of the area, since rent increases that could be charged to new tenants were small (15 percent), and the new tenants were likely to stay on for years. Transient Puerto Rican occupancy and the creation of SROs was one of the few strategies that could rapidly increase rents.

11. The following is drawn from Committee on Housing, "Riverside, a Study of Housing on the West Side of Manhattan," New York Chapter, American Institute of Architects, New York, 1954.

12. Tenements built before 1929.

13. "Riverside, a Study of Housing."

14. A disastrous move, as it turned out. The ban is still in place, forcing hundreds of thousands of single persons to pay high rents for full apartments, to share apartments at high rents, or to live in illegal and often dangerous rooming units or sleeping alcoves.

15. AIA Committee on Housing, "Patterns of Urban Congestion," 1952.

16. *The Guardian*, June 30, 1971.

NOTES TO CHAPTER 3

1. Bayard Rustin, *A Way Out of the Exploding Ghetto*, A. Philip Randolph Foundation, 1967.

2. A telling account of the formation of the housing lobby, the development of its racist policies, and its control of the Federal Housing programs is provided in Charles Abrams, *Forbidden Neighbors—A Study of Prejudice in Housing*, Harper and Brothers, 1955.

3. Ibid.

4. Testimony of Ronald Shiffman, Associate Professor of Urban Planning, Pratt Institute, Director of the Pratt Center for Community and Environmental Development, and Chair of the New York City Housing and Community Development Coalition, before the New York City Commission on Human Rights, Commissioner Eleanor Holmes Norton, Chair, November 8, 1976.

5. New York Metropolitan Chapter, Planners for Equal Opportunity, "Inter-Racial Status of Publicly Aided Housing in New York City," May 1965.

6. Lewis G. Watts and others, "The Middle-Income Negro Faces Urban Renewal," Graduate School for Advanced Studies in Social Welfare, Brandeis University, 1964.

7. Norris Vitchek, "Confessions of a Blockbuster," *Saturday Evening Post*, 1962.

8. Testimony of Ronald Shiffman before the New York City Commission on Human Rights, November 8, 1976.

9. Ibid.

10. See Otis D. Duncan and Beverly Duncan, *The Negro Population of Chicago—A Study of Residential Succession,* University of Chicago Press, 1957.

11. Karl E. Taeuber and Alma F. Taeuber, *Negroes in Cities—Residential Segregation and Neighborhood Change,* Atheneum, 1972.

12. Elizabeth Wood, "A New Look at the Balanced Neighborhood," Citizens Housing and Planning Council, New York, December 1960.

13. An older apartment house area, with buildings containing from fifteen to forty moderate-rental apartment units and some two- to four-family buildings.

14. Interviews with four brokers, August 1968.

15. My firm undertook planning studies of East Flatbush in 1967–1968.

16. Walter Thabit, "East Flatbush at the Threshold," 1969.

17. The welfare assistance rate in East Flatbush Health Areas ranged between 2.5 and 17.7 per 1,000 families in 1965. By contrast, the nearest Brownsville Health Area showed a rate of 143.3 per 1,000 families. The declining housing quality in East Fiatbush could not easily be blamed on "welfare families."

18. Cease-and-desist procedures under recent laws allowed homeowners to petition the secretary of state to ask that brokers be forbidden to solicit. If solicitation continued, brokers could be punished or lose their licenses.

19. In fact, Brownsville did not get daily garbage pickup any more than East New York did. It is a fascinating commentary on city services that many black and white communities are convinced that services must be better in adjoining communities. In fact, most are poorly served, with ghetto areas receiving the worst service of all.

20. In mid-June, 1967, in East New York, the scene of riots between minority and Italian youths. One youth was stabbed in Linton Park following an incident in which black youths taunted white youths. Sixteen youths, all white, were arrested following the melee.

21. A common racist rallying cry. Residents of Rosedale, Queens, the scene of a pipe bombing, cross burnings, and other incidents in 1974, called it "the last frontier" of private homes for whites in southeast Queens.

NOTES TO CHAPTER 4

1. Unpublished paper, January 12, 1967.

2. The surveys reported here were conducted late in 1966 and early in 1967.

3. Report of James Norman, surveyor.

4. The director, Lillie Martin, was one of the program's strongest supporters.

5. Any further disruption of the already decimated commercial streets was rejected. It was also unlikely that subsidized new housing construction could

include new stores. Today, many vacant apartments above storefronts have leaky windows and are unheated, accelerating storefront deterioration, a further obstacle to reinvigorated retail activity.

6. Tenant surveys.

7. Recounted by the community leader in private conversation.

8. *New York Times*, Wednesday, July 20, 1966.

9. New York Metropolitan Committee on Planning, "The Demand for Planning Services by Local Communities—An Analysis of Planning Needs in 26 Communities in New York City and Newark, New Jersey," 1969.

10. For an intimate look at the Brownsville community, and its change from white to black and Hispanic, see Wendell Pritchett, *Brownsville, Brooklyn: Blacks, Jews, and the Changing Face of the Ghetto*, University of Chicago Press, 2002.

11. Ibid.

12. More than one program has been discontinued because it was too successful. One of the most memorable was an in-house HRB program that produced rehabilitation at half the per-unit costs of other programs. In response to real estate and construction industry complaints, it was summarily closed down.

NOTES TO CHAPTER 5

1. Martin E. Eisenberg, "Being Left in East New York; Tensions between Race and Class in Community Organizing, 1954–1980," Ph.D. diss., City University of New York, February 1999.

2. Ibid.

3. Ibid.

4. News Release, Office of the Mayor, City Hall, New York, February 23, 1966.

5. Freedman, *Upon This Rock*.

6. The following is drawn from district sanitation reports made available by J. T. Lennon.

7. Today's sanitation men had no idea what "tn-weekly" stood for in the 1960s.

8. District sanitation reports made available by J. T. Lennon.

9. Interview with Sidney Davidoff, Crash Clean-up Coordinator, January 12, 1967.

10. Eisenberg, "Being Left in East New York."

11. *New York Times*, January 29, 1968.

12. New York *Post*, December 8, 1971.

13. *Report of the National Advisory Commission on Civil Disorders*, Bantam Books, March 1968.

14. Ibid.

15. Deborah Wallace, "Roots of Increased Health Care Inequality in New York," *Social Science and Medicine* 31 (1990): 1219–27; Rodrick Wallace, "Urban Desertification, Public Health and Public Order: 'Planned Shrinkage,' Violent Death, Substance Abuse, and AIDS in the Bronx," *Social Science and Medicine* 32 (1991):801–813; Rodrick Wallace, "'Planned Shrinkage,' Contagious Urban Decay, and Violent Death in the Bronx: The Implications of Synergism," Epidemiology of Mental Disorders Research Department, New York State Psychiatric Institute, 1990.

16. In drawing on the sources I have named, I want to make clear that my experience in East New York did not include an *increase* in the number of fires. There were already too many fires, and they did contribute heavily to the havoc referred to later. While the reduction in the number of fire companies reduced the department's ability to respond quickly and effectively, the department had also been taking its time in responding to fires in East New York long before the cuts.

17. Priscilla Wooten felt that East New York didn't get its educational park because "we had no friends in city government." Interview, May 6, 1998.

18. Interview with Major Owens, then director of Brooklyn CORE.

19. Irving J. Rubin, "Analyzing Detroit's Riot: The Causes and Responses," *The Reporter*, February 22, 1968; interview, May 6, 1998.

NOTES TO CHAPTER 6

1. New York *Daily News*, November 23, 1996.

2. The materials that follow are drawn from "Youth in New York City: Out-of-School and Out-of-Work," Report of the Mayor's Committee on Youth and Work, New York City Youth Board, December 1963.

3. "Manpower Report," November 1965.

4. Drawn from the statement by Representative Shirley Chisholm before the Committee on Education and Labor, April 29, 1969.

5. *Diary of Philip Hone, 1828–51*, New York, 1936. Also, *Letters of John Pintard*, New York, 1941, Vol. III, p. 51.

6. "Report of the Select Committee Appointed to Examine into the Condition of Tenant-houses in New York and Brooklyn," New York State Assembly Document No. 205, 1857.

7. Drawn from Ken Wooden, *Weeping in the Playtime of Others*, McGraw-Hill, 1975.

8. By the late 1990s, there was at least one group home for teenage girls ages fifteen to nineteen at Hegeman and Schenck Avenues. It was poorly fund-

ed and poorly managed; many of the girls spent their time outside the house meeting men, using drugs, and having sex. Wendy Davis, *Nobody's Homes*, City Limits, November 1998.

9. *New York Times*, p. 36. Clip is undated, but from the Lindsay administration.

10. Unfortunately, the citation for this news story has been lost. It was not located before publication.

11. "No Lid on Racial Volcano in the East New York Slums," *The Guardian*, May 27, 1967.

12. Robert Conot, *Rivers of Blood, Years of Darkness*, Bantam Books, 1967.

13. Interview of an East Flatbush teenager by David Gurin, of my staff.

14. "The Youngest Ex-Cons: Facing a Difficult Road out of Crime," *New York Times*, November 17, 1996.

15. Ibid.

16. Greg Donaldson, *The Ville: Cops and Kids in Urban America*, Ticknor and Fields, 1993. Donaldson reports on conditions in Brownsville and East New York, on a teenager Sharron Corley, one of its residents, and on Gary Lemite, one of its cops.

17. Ibid.

18. Ibid.

19. Ibid.

20. Ibid.

21. Citizens Committee for Children, "Keeping Track of New York City's Children," 1999.

22. For a vivid account of the myriad pressures that drive youngsters into gangs, see Luis Rodriguez, *Always Running, La Vida Loca: Gang Days in L.A.*, Simon and Schuster, 1994.

23. Interview with Zachary Brown, June 27, 2000. In 1997, Zachary Brown was a public health educator with the New York City Health Department.

NOTES TO CHAPTER 7

1. My firm had been selected to do the work, not only because of our experience in working for local communities but as a political favor to David Stoloff, of my staff, for his work in helping to elect John Lindsay mayor.

2. Several others, including Herman Rollins and Gilberto Matos, also entered degree programs in urban planning as a result of their experience with the Vest Pocket Program.

3. Martin E. Eisenberg, "Being Left in East New York; Tensions between Race and Class in Community Organizing, 1954–1980," Ph.D. diss., City University of New York, February 1999.

4. This entire section is drawn from reports of meetings prepared by my staff.

5. Crane's hospital proposal was a minor part of his analysis of the Spring Creek area development potential.

6. *East New Yorker*, June 1974.

7. Citizens Committee for Children of New York City, Inc., "Keeping Track of New York City's Children," 1999.

8. Interview with Dr. Anthony Rajkumar, May 10, 2001.

NOTES TO CHAPTER 8

1. David Stoloff, of my staff, was in charge of this activity.

2. I believe that the CRF members had already learned that a large new construction project offered greater scope for profiteering than a small rehabilitation project.

3. Andrea Malester interview with Bob Brodsky, April 30, 1970.

4. Walter Thabit, Planning Consultant, "Report on Relocation, East New York Vest Pocket Housing Program," November 1968.

5. Betty Woody, "Nonprofit Sponsorship—General Problems," June 1970, staff report.

6. The agreement is spelled out in a February 2, 1981, letter to Alan Drezin, the attorney for Remeeder, from Colon's attorneys, Cullen and Dyckman.

7. Mentioned in an October 3, 1975, letter to John Williams, president of Remeeder, from Winsco Construction Corp., builder of the project. Winsco disputed the HUD findings and sat down together with HUD officials and resolved the issue. The fault continued, however (see discussion).

8. Letter signed by Bill Wright, vice president of Remeeder, dated December 18, 1989.

9. Detailed in a letter written to board secretary by Fred L. Wallace, Remeeder's legal counsel, dated July 29, 1992.

10. Noted in Bill Wright letter to HUD, May 24, 1996.

11. Fred L. Wallace letter to CRF board secretary, July 29, 1992.

NOTES TO CHAPTER 9

1. A small contract extension with some additional money was negotiated with Eugenia Flatow, but it too was insufficient.

2. Around August 1968.

3. Walter Thabit, Planning Consultant, "Report on Relocation, East New York Vest Pocket Housing Program," November 1968.

4. Details in chapter 10.

5. *New York Times*, August 24, 1970.

6. Walter Thabit, Planning Consultant, "Status of the ENY Model Cities Housing Program," November 1971.

NOTES TO CHAPTER 10

1. As part of our Model Cities contract, my firm was required to prepare a school facilities plan for the Model Cities area.

2. Walter Thabit, with Tunney Lee and Bernard Rothzeid, "A School Planning Concept for East New York," March 1969. Also, Jacqueline Leavitt, "Schools: The Need in East New York," April 1969.

3. Interview with Dolores Schaefer, September 23, 1998.

4. In more recent years, school construction funding was no better than it had been thirty years ago. In 1997, the Board of Education estimated that $21 billon would be needed over the next ten years to create sufficient space and to return the system to a "state of good repair." Under Mayor Rudy Giuliani, less than $1 billion a year was being spent. Overcrowding was a major problem in many districts.

5. Meeting, February 23, 1968.

6. Martin E. Eisenberg, "Being Left in East New York; Tensions between Race and Class in Community Organizing, 1954–1980," Ph.D. diss., City University of New York, February 1999.

7. One would expect the owners of good homes to organize swiftly, bitterly oppose the project, press for alternate sites, and probably win the day. In East New York, however, the atmosphere was so highly charged with the community's efforts to make any kind of progress with the bureaucracy, that individual needs and desires were readily sacrificed for the common good. The owners didn't like it but wouldn't fight the whole community on the issue.

8. Several charter high schools have opened in ghetto areas, but these are relatively small in size and attended almost exclusively by minority students.

9. Dr. Wolff was an active supporter of Milton Galamison's 1960s boycotts and of the Brownsville Demonstration District (see chapter 13).

10. Traditionally, architectural students who faced a presentation deadline in the morning and who stayed up all night to complete their work carried their voluminous plans to the presentation in a wagon, called a charrette. In the present context, "charrette" means an intense concentration of effort in a limited time to produce a desired product.

11. The idea could have been originated by the United Community Centers, which organized a coalition of groups into the Ad Hoc Committee for the Complex and was demanding an educational park from the Board of Education for East New York.

12. Eisenberg, "Being Left in East New York."

13. Ibid.

14. Ibid.

NOTES TO CHAPTER 11

1. Interviews with four brokers, two black and two white, August 1968.

2. The following information is reported in an interview with a Mr. Hayner, chief realty manager at FHA's Hempstead office by Andrea Malester of my staff on April 7, 1969.

3. Douglass J. Kramer, "Protecting the Urban Environment from the Federal Government," *Urban Affairs Quarterly*, March 1974.

4. Central Brooklyn Model Cities memo, August 27, 1968.

5. This was an important factor, even through the mid-1990s, according to Perry Winston, Pratt Planning, and Architectural Collaborative.

6. *New York Times*, February 3, 1976.

7. In addition to the 1,350 families relocated, 500 units in vacant buildings and 650 vacant units in occupied buildings were also removed from the stock. In the East Brooklyn High School site, there were 350 families living in a total of 500 units. Approximately 150 families were still on site when the survey was taken.

NOTES TO CHAPTER 12

1. Edith Evans Ashbury, "Dun & Bradstreet among 50 Named in Housing Fraud," *New York Times*, March 30, 1972.

2. New York *Post*, March 29, 1972.

3. New York Times, March 30, 1972.

4. Ibid.

5. Jerry Capeci and Mary Connelly, "Bare Huge Ghetto Home Loan Swindle," New York *Post*, March 29, 1972.

6. *New York Times*, May 8, 1972.

7. "$15 M Realty Frauds Hit FHA, Poor," New York *Post*, September 24, 1971.

8. *New York Times*, March 30, 1972.

9. Josh Friedman and George Capozzi Jr., "Figure in FHA Bribery on Babylon Town Board," New York *Post*, September 28, 1972.

10. Ibid.

11. New York *Post*, September 28, 1972.

12. Ibid.

13. *New York Times*, May 8, 1972.

14. Ibid.

15. Ibid.

16. *New York Times*, February 28, 1972.

17. Jerry M. Flint, "Rommey Says His Agency Can't Solve Housing Problem: Concedes Errors," *New York Times*, March 28, 1972.

18. Douglass J. Kramer, "Protecting the Urban Environment from the Federal Government," *Urban Affairs Quarterly*, March 1974.

19. *New York Times*, December 11, 1975.

20. Ibid.

21. "Indict Bank Officer in Housing Scheme," New York *Daily News*, November 14, 1975.

22. New York *Daily News*, July 22, 1998.

23. *New York Times*, April 2, 1972.

24. Kramer, "Protecting the Urban Environment from the Federal Government."

25. *East New Yorker*, June, 1974.

26. Polly Kline, "Tenants Sue U.S. to Bar Eviction in Housing Fraud," New York *Daily News*, July 5, 1972.

27. *New York Times*, July 24, 1972

28. Ibid.

29. *New York Times*, December 11, 1975.

30. *New York Times*, February 3, 1976.

31. New York *Post*, November 20, 1975.

NOTES TO CHAPTER 13

1. Marilyn Gittell, "Participants and Participation: A Study of School Policy in the City of New York," circa 1965.

2. The second demonstration district was I.S. 201 in Harlem. The third, chosen as a control, was in the Two Bridges section of Manhattan.

3. Marilyn Gittell, "Local Control in Education—Three Demonstration School Districts in New York City," Praeger, 1972.

4. Ibid.

5. "Reconnection for Learning, A community School System for New York City," Mayor's Advisory Panel on Decentralization of the New York City Schools, McGeorge Bundy, Chairman, November 8, 1967.

6. *Mid-Brooklyn Times*, September 18, 1968.

7. Recollection of Mary Nelson, a teacher at P.S. 63 at the time.

8. *New York Times*, May 3, 1968.

9. Much of what follows is drawn from Marilyn Gittell, "School Boards and School Policy," Praeger, 1973.

10. Ibid.

11. Martin E. Eisenberg, "Being Left in East New York; Tensions between

Race and Class in Community Organizing, 1954–1980." Ph.D. diss., City University of New York, February 1999.

12. Ibid.

13. Ibid.

14. Election to CSBs were decided using the proportional representation method.

15. Sister Vergie Rasheeda Muhammad, "Black Leaders' and Black Administrators' Opinions and Perceptions about the Decentralization of New York City Schools, 1969–1978." Ph.D. diss., Teachers College, May 1988.

16. Anthony Creswell and Paul Irvin, "State Politics and Federal Aid to Education in New York State," unpublished paper, p. 20.

17. This and the following examples of UFT powers are taken from Gittell, "School Boards and School Policy."

18. Ibid.

19. Ibid.

20. Ibid.

21. Ibid.

22. Finally, in 1989, a law was passed prohibiting school employees or elected officials from serving on CSBs.

23. Nancy M. Lederman, Jeanne S. Frankl, and Judith Baum, "Governing the New York City Schools: Roles and Relationships in the Decentralized System," Public Education Association, 1987; "Improving the Odds, Making Decentralization Work for Children, for Schools, for Communities," First Report of Manhattan Borough President's Task Force on Education and Decentralization, November 1987; "People Change Schools: A practical Agenda to Turn Our Children's Schools Around," Second Report of the

Manhattan Borough President's Task Force on Education and Decentralization, 1989; "Findings and Recommendations of the Joint Commission on Integrity in the Public Schools," (the Gill report), April 1990; "Governing for Results: Decentralization with Accountability," New York State Temporary Commission on New York City School Governance (the Marchi Commission), April 1991.

24. The Board of Examiners was finally abolished in the 1990–1991 school year. New licensing procedure requires that teachers now have only to pass an interview in addition to meeting the educational requirements.

25. New York *Daily News*, May 13, 2001.

26. Ibid.

27. Freedman, *Upon This Rock.*

28. Susan Breslin, "Promoting Poverty: The Shift of Resources Away from Low-Income New York City School Districts," Community Service Society, 1987.

29. Public Education Association, "Parents' Guide to Mathematics, Science, and Technology Education in New York City Public Schools," 1997.

30. On the Lower East Side, while conservative Jewish Defense League members were able to fire the old superintendent, they could not handpick a new one. Parents outvoted them on the selection committee and picked their own.

31. In fact, Mayor Michael Bloomberg, having gained control of the schools from the state legislature, has announced his intention of doing away with local school boards altogether.

32. The actual test scores were better than first reported. McGraw-Hill, the creator of the test, finally admitted to an error in marking them.

33. "Levy, Board to Mull Dis of Protégé," New York *Daily News*, May 11, 2001.

34. New York State Temporary Commission on New York City School Governance, *"Governing for Results: Decentralization with Accountability."*

35. Edward N. Costikyan and Maxwell Lehman, "Re-structuring the Government of New York City," Task Force on Jurisdiction and Structure, State Study Commission for New York City, March 15, 1972.

NOTES TO CHAPTER 14

1. Tour and conversation with Marshall Stukes, May 9, 1996.

2. Interview with Priscilla Wooten, May 6, 1998.

3. Until his death in 1972, Saul Alinsky swaggered through public life as an American original, educated in sociology at the University of Chicago, tutored in street life by a Capone mob enforcer, descended in spirit from such radical patriots as Tom Paine and John Brown. Alinsky's political manual, *Reveille for Radicals*, became a best seller. Through the Industrial Areas Foundation, which he established in 1940, Alinsky trained such protégés as Nicholas von Hoffman and Cesar Chavez who would ultimately lead the United Farm Workers.

4. *New York Times*, June 30, 1982.

5. Conversation with Mike Gecan, July 6, 2000.

6. Remarks at a meeting on empowering local communities, October 15, 1999.

7. Conversation with Mike Gecan, July 6, 2000.

8. *New York Times*, June 10, 2001.

9. *New York Times*, November 15, 2000.

10. *Newsday*, August 4, 1985.

11. Ibid.

12. *New York Times*, October 12, 1987.

13. Discussion with Walter Campbell, executive director of Community Board 5, September 9, 1999.

14. The tour was organized as part of the Planners for Equal Opportunity reunion on October 15, 1999.

15. Tom Robbins, "Hardball in Brooklyn," New York *Daily News,* February 8, 1998.

16. Freedman, *Upon This Rock.*

17. EBC undertook a similar campaign five or six years ago but has not felt the need to repeat it since.

18. "Special Report Small Business: East New York Sheds Bad Old Image —Low Rents Attract New Businesses," Cara S. Trager, *Crains New York Business,* June 12, 2000.

19. *1999 East Brooklyn Business to Business Directory,* a publication of the Local Development Corporation of East New York.

20. Interview with Bill Willkins, East New York zone coordinator and Ojeda Hall-Phillips, director, East New York Business Assistance Center, July 26, 2001.

21. "Issues and Opportunities in East New York: A Report on the Envisioning Forums and Recent Developments in East New York," First Year Report of the East New York Planning Group, July 1996.

22. This section is drawn from "Pitkin Avenue, Filling the Gaps," Pratt Institute Graduate Center for Planning and the Environment, Neighborhood Planning Studio, spring 1996.

23. WIC coupons are given to households that receive regular food stamps for use only at farmers' markets.

24. *The New York Times,* March 25, 2001.

NOTES TO CHAPTER 15

1. As of this writing, in March 2002, only part of the U.S. Census results has been released.

2. Freedman, *Upon This Rock.*

3. Citizens Committee for Children, "Keeping Track of New York City's Children," 1999.

4. *New York Times,* July 27, 1999.

5. Patrick Markee, "Housing a Growing City—New York's Bust in Boom Times," Coalition for the Homeless, New York, 1999.

6. *New York Times,* November 15, 2000.

7. Markee, "Housing a Growing City."

8. Ibid.

9. *New York Times,* November 15, 2000.

10. Ibid.

11. Greg Donaldson, *The Ville: Cops and Kids in Urban America*, Ticknor and Fields, 1993.

12. Freedman, *Upon This Rock*.

13. Ibid.

14. Ibid.

15. Tom Robbins, "Gore-Test: Candidate Challenged to Take on Issue of Affordable Housing," *Village Voice*, July 5–11, 2000.

16. Conversation with Mike Gecan, July 6, 2000.

17. Ibid.

18. Freedman, *Upon This Rock*.

19. Ibid.

20. Ibid.

21. Ibid.

22. Ibid.

23. Glenn Thrush, "Anatomy of a Machine," *City Limits*, February 1996.

24. Ibid.

25. Ibid.

26. *Village Voice*, February 9, 1999.

27. Thrush, "Anatomy of a Machine."

28. Ibid.

29. Ibid.

30. *City Limits*, October, 1996.

31. Tom Robbins, *Hardball in Brooklyn*, New York *Daily News*, February 8, 1998.

32. A tarpaulin put over an open roof but not securely held in place was ripped off during a rainstorm, ruining weeks if not months of work.

33. Started during the Dinkins administration, community-based organizations (CBOs) were funded to operate Beacon programs. They kept schools open in the evenings, offering a variety of educational and recreational activities.

34. Thrush, "Anatomy of a Machine."

35. Ibid.

36. Freedman, *Upon This Rock*.

37. Charles Barron, *"Spark the Fire,"* *City Limits*, date unknown.

38. Ibid.

NOTES TO CHAPTER 16

1. As reported in Greg Donaldson, *The Ville: Cops and Kids in Urban America*, Ticknor and Fields, 1993. In Eli B. Silverman, *NYPD Battles Crime*, Northeastern University Press, 1999, a book more favorable to the police, Dowd is referred to as Officer Dowd of the 94th Precinct.

2. *The Ville*, published in 1993, appeared before the merger of the housing police and the NYPD in 1995.

3. This and the following quotes are from Donaldson, *The Ville*.

4. The NYPD would allow none of these officers to be interviewed by the author.

5. Interview with Mike Gecan, EBC lead organizer, July 6, 2000.

6. Ibid.

7. Silverman, *NYPD Battles Crime*.

8. Ibid.

9. The NYPD claims to have confiscated more than 50,000 guns citywide since 1993 and now takes in more than 2,500 weapons a year.

10. Christian Parenti, *Lockdown America*, Verso, 1999.

11. Wayne Barrett, *Rudy! An Investigative Biography of Rudolph Giuliani*, Basic Books, 2000. The apologist Silverman, in *NYPD Battles Crime*, cites John Jay College Professor Andrew Karmen's claim that New York City homicides committed out-of-doors with guns fell more abruptly than those committed indoors or with knives or other weapons, but he fails to provide the documentation to back up his claim.

12. Malcolm Gladwell, "The Tipping Point," *New Yorker*, June 3, 1996.

13. Parenti, *Lockdown America*.

14. German-made machine guns.

15. "Patrol Guide," New York Police Department, January 1, 2000.

16. New York City Department of Correction. Internet report of its Gang Intelligence Unit, October 19, 2000.

17. New York *Daily News*, November 26, 2000.

18. New York City Department of Correction. Internet report of its Gang Intelligence Unit, October 19, 2000.

19. New York *Daily News*, November 26, 2000.

20. New York *Post*, April 5, 2001.

21. Interview with Marilyn Bayona, Catholic Charities field worker.

22. Of course, if the police were visibly present, people wouldn't try to jump the turnstiles in the first place.

23. New York City Police Department Compstat reports.

24. Ibid.

25. John Mollenkopf and Ken Emerson, eds., *Rethinking the Urban Agenda*, Century Foundation, 2001. See esp. Michael Jacobson, "From the Back to the Front: the Changing Character of Punishment in New York City."

26. Parenti, *Lockdown America*.

27. Richard Perez, speaking on David Seers's talk show on WBAI, January 15, 1999, was commenting on the six counts brought against King Tone, leader of the Latin Kings, a major Puerto Rican gang in Manhattan. Tone accepted a plea bargain through which he would get a minimum ten-year sen-

tence in a maximum-security prison, though his alleged offenses were non-violent.

28. Ibid.

29. New York *Daily News*, May 10, 2000.

30. New York *Daily News*, May or June 2000.

31. Joel Dyer, *The Perpetual Prisoner Machine*, Westview Press, 2000.

32. Parenti, *Lockdown America*.

33. Ibid.

34. Dyer, *The Perpetual Prisoner Machine*.

35. Ibid.

36. Prison expansion has also given rise to a major jail-expansion industry and a highly political projail lobby.

37. *New York Times*, September 2, 2001.

38. In 1998, there were approximately 1,800 probationers in the Seventy-fifth Precinct.

39. Conversation with Jack Ryan, director of Public Information, DOP.

40. Ibid.

41. "An Analysis of Brooklyn Homicides at Mid-Year 2000—Strategies for Saving Lives," Charles J. Hynes, District Attorney, Kings County, 2000.

42. The struggle to maintain the Stanley Avenue retail business center is described in Freedman, *Upon This Rock*.

43. Ibid.

44. Silverman, *NYPD Battles Crime*.

45. Alison Mitchell, "On a Frontier of Hope, Building Homes for the Poor Proves Perilous," *New York Times*, October 4, 1992.

46. In fact, the only group to successfully reject the attempted shakedown was the East Brooklyn Congregations, as described in chapter 14.

47. Instead of ten-year terms, how about ten-month terms that included treatment and rehabilitation initiatives?

48. The actual number may be somewhat lower, since some males may have been arrested more than once.

49. NYPD Crime Comparison Report, 1999.

50. Patrick Markee, "Housing a Growing City—New York's Bust in Boom Times," Coalition for the Homeless, 1999.

51. Visit by the author, November 13, 2000.

52. Interview with Dennis Taylor, ENYUYC, November 13, 2000.

Index

About the Author

For the past thirty-five years, in various planning positions and as head of his own planning consulting firm, Walter Thabit has had a wide range of experience in serving local communities, cities, and nonprofit housing developers. As a principal founder and 8-year President of Planners for Equal Opportunity, a national civil rights organization of 600 members, Walter Thabit led the fight to empower poor and minority communities in their struggle for equal treatment as well as stimulating social responsibility in the planning profession. He was consultant to the East New York community from 1967 through the mid-1970s.